SIMPLICITY—

THE FORMULA FOR SUCCESSFUL COMMUNICATION

Have you ever felt the frustration
of not being able to say exactly what you mean?

Do you become bogged down
in jargon that makes your writing stale, heavy,
cliché-ridden—instead of direct and forceful?

Would you like to be persuasive,
to catch and hold the attention of your audience?

In this exciting book, Dr. Rudolf Flesch
outlines a systematic program for self-expression.
Following a step-by-step sequence of lessons,
using specific examples and definite rules,
he helps you to build a set of mental processes
that will result in the habit of clear thinking
and effective communication.

DR. RUDOLF FLESCH is a renowned authority on
writing improvement, a teacher, a consultant, and the
author of many books and articles. His books, among them
The Art of Plain Talk and *Why Johnny Can't Read &
What You Can Do About It*, are nationwide bestsellers
and recognized classics in the field of communication.

SIGNET and MENTOR Books for Your Reference Shelf

How to
WRITE,
SPEAK,
and *THINK*
more effectively

BY Rudolf Flesch

A SIGNET BOOK
NEW AMERICAN LIBRARY
TIMES MIRROR

SIGNET TRADEMARK REG. U.S. PAT. OFF. AND FOREIGN COUNTRIES
REGISTERED TRADEMARK—MARCA REGISTRADA
HECHO EN CHICAGO, U.S.A.

SIGNET, SIGNET CLASSICS, MENTOR, PLUME, MERIDIAN AND NAL
BOOKS *are published by The New American Library, Inc.,
1633 Broadway, New York, New York 10019*

12 13 14 15 16 17 18 19 20

PRINTED IN THE UNITED STATES OF AMERICA

Contents

v

PART 2: HINTS AND DEVICES

Introduction

This book will do for you exactly what its title promises: it will help you write better, speak better, and think better.

As you'll see, it is different from other self-help books in these fields. Books on writing usually concentrate on spelling, grammar, usage, vocabulary, and composition; books on speaking usually stress self-confidence in front of an audience; and books on thinking usually tell you to read the classics fifteen minutes a day.

You'll find none of these things here. Instead, this book gives you a scientifically tested system designed to improve your three main mental activities—your writing, your speaking, and your thinking. Writing, after all, is nothing but speaking on paper, speaking is nothing but thinking out loud, and thinking is nothing but silent speech. You cannot help thinking in words; you write—or should write—the way you talk; and you talk according to the way ideas come to your mind and spring to your lips.

I admit I didn't quite realize this simple truth when I started my work in this field almost twenty years ago. At that time—back in 1940—all I was looking for was a scientific way of measuring the "readability" of a given piece of writing. I did find such a formula and after a few years I published my first book, "The Art of Plain Talk."

That was in 1946. Since then, my readability formulas have penetrated into schools of journalism, advertising agencies, textbooks on business writing, and many other places. Grad-

ually, they contributed to a tremendous change in news writing, business writing, and practical writing in general, so that today's average newspaper or business letter is measurably different from what it was fourteen years ago. What was a novel approach in 1946 has become the accepted practice among professional writers.

But in all those years I was mainly interested in something else. I had hoped that my scientific writing formula would become known among the general public rather than remain a specialty of the professionals. So I kept on simplifying the formula and wrote books and articles trying to show the application of my technique to everyday problems.

Eventually my publishers came up with the idea of extracting the gist of my books and articles and putting it all together in one volume. As soon as I drew up the outline for this book, I realized that I had done at last what I should have done years ago—I had compiled, in one book, a systematic way of improving the mind. As you read Part 1 from the opening words of Chapter 1 to the last words of Chapter 30, you go through a step-by-step sequence of lessons designed to give you a different set of mental habits.

What exactly is it that you'll learn? The quick self-test formula at the end of Part 2 spells it out. It tests two elements of writing, and two elements only—the punctuation devices that show the extent of your contact with your audience, and the names, dates, places, numbers, etc., that show whether your thinking is based on facts and events. Why? Because good thinking never loses touch with the people and the world around you. It is like the thinking of a scientist, who is trained to publish all he finds out and to document every idea with factual evidence. In the same way, this book teaches you to think as if you had to explain all your ideas in public and illustrate each one of them by a concrete example.

This is the thread that runs through the whole book. Part 1 begins with chapters from my older books on writing, then switches to chapters from a later book on English, and winds up with a series of chapters from a book on thinking. As you go along, you'll see that what applies to writing also applies to speaking, and that the principles of good thinking are only applications of the rules for expressing your thoughts. You'll learn to write better by training yourself in talking to your readers on paper; you'll learn to speak better by consistently reminding yourself of the principles of readability; and you'll learn to think better by carrying your new mental habits over into your silent conversations with yourself.

Naturally, the arts of writing, speaking, and thinking can only be learned by constant practice. You'll find exercises at the end of several chapters, and you'll profit from the book more if you do all those exercises conscientiously—particularly the continuing exercise on page 137. Beyond that, study carefully the many examples that are analyzed for their readability, especially those on pages 314-338.

Finally, keep on applying the quick self-test formula on pages 339-353. Set up a continuing training program for yourself so that eventually effective thinking and writing will become second nature to you.

You'll know that you have achieved your goal when you unconsciously do all your writing, speaking, and thinking in simple, conversational English, and feel an irrepressible urge to spell out each idea in concrete, practical terms.

Don't stop practicing until you've reached that point.

R. F.

The 25 rules of

1. Write about people, things, and facts

2. Write as you talk

3. Use contractions

4. Use the first person

5. Quote what was said

6. Quote what was written

7. Put yourself in the reader's place

8. Don't hurt the reader's feelings

9. Forestall misunderstandings

10. Don't be too brief

11. Plan a beginning, middle, and end

12. Go from the rule to the exception, from the familiar to the new

effective writing

13. Use short names and abbreviations

14. Use pronouns rather than repeating nouns

15. Use verbs rather than nouns

16. Use the active voice and a personal subject

17. Use small, round figures

18. Specify. Use illustrations, cases, examples

19. Start a new sentence for each new idea

20. Keep your sentences short

21. Keep your paragraphs short

22. Use direct questions

23. Underline for emphasis

24. Use parentheses for casual mention

25. Make your writing interesting *to look at*

Lessons

Chapter One

LET'S START WITH CHINESE

If you had a smattering of Chinese, you could teach yourself simple English in no time. You could apply the Chinese way of talking to your own language, and without much effort you would form the habit of terse, clear, picturesque talk.

But all you know about Chinese, I take it, is chow mein and chop suey, and you probably don't care much about adding to your Chinese vocabulary. Therefore—and because I don't know any Chinese either—we shall do the next best thing: we shall study Chinese from the outside, so to speak, just to get a rough idea of how it is put together. Even that will bring us a long way nearer plain English.

That may sound odd to you. Chinese, to you, is an exotic language, written in quaint Oriental characters and spoken in a sort of singsong. Besides, the Chinese can't pronounce *r* and say things like "velly ploud" instead of "very proud."

True, some of them do; it so happens that their language does not have the *r* sound. It's also true that the meaning of spoken Chinese words depends on musical "tones," which makes it hard for us to learn spoken Chinese. What's more, their writing is based not on the alphabet but on graphic symbols that stand for whole words, which again makes it hard for us to learn written Chinese. In other words, Chinese is hard to approach; it has a sort of Chinese Wall around it.

But if you look behind that wall, you find that Chinese is really simple. Think of other languages, and what makes them difficult: conjugations, declensions, irregular verbs, ablatives, subjunctives, aorists—nightmares that plague every student who sets out to learn French, German, Latin, Greek, not to speak of Russian or Sanskrit. I don't have to tell you that what makes a language difficult is grammar.

Chinese, however, is known as a "grammarless" tongue. The list of the things it does *not* have is amazing: it has no inflections, no cases, no persons, no genders, no numbers, no degrees, no tenses, no voices, no moods, no infinitives, no participles, no gerunds, no irregular verbs, and no articles. There are no words of more than one syllable, every word has only one form, and all you have to learn is how to put these one-syllable words in their proper order. To make it still easier for you, this proper order is the same as the usual order in English: subject, predicate, object.

You may wonder how it is possible to talk in such a language so that other people understand you; and maybe you think this must be the most primitive, uncivilized language of the world. It would be a common error: up to about fifty years ago all language experts agreed that Chinese is the "baby talk of mankind." They were wrong: it is the most grown-up talk in the world. It is the way people speak who started to simplify their language thousands of years ago and have kept at it ever since.

For, thanks to research, we know now that thousands of years ago the Chinese language had case endings, verb forms, and a whole arsenal of unpleasant grammar. It was a cumbersome, irregular, complicated mess, like most other languages. But the Chinese people, generation after generation, changed it into a streamlined, smooth-running machine for expressing ideas. This isn't just a figure of speech: the main principle of modern Chinese is exactly the same as that of modern machinery. It consists of standardized, prefabricated, functionally designed parts.

In other words, Chinese is an assembly-line language. All the words are stripped to their essential meaning and purpose, and put together in a fixed order. Word order is as all-important as the order of operations on the assembly line: if you line it up in any other way it doesn't work. For instance, take the famous sentence "Dog bites man" that is not news but becomes news when it is turned around to "Man bites dog." Here, word order is as important in English as it is in Chinese: it makes all the difference. In classical Latin, however, if you want to tell about the dog biting a man, you have to say something like "He-the-dog bites him-the-man." Now try to turn it around: "Him-the-man bites he-the-dog." No difference whatsoever: still no news. You see, the ancient

Romans hadn't found out yet about the assembly-line principle.

Let's look closer at this example. In Latin you have to talk about "he-the-dog" and "him-the-man." Why? Because the word and the case ending are fused together and you can't say "man" or "dog" without also saying "he" or "him," whatever the case may be. The reason is that Latin, like other difficult languages, expresses almost all grammatical relationships by endings (suffixes), or sometimes by prefixes at the beginning of a word. The significant thing about these prefixes and suffixes—the grammarians call both of them affixes—is the syllable "fix." They are fixed, firmly attached, stuck. If you try to use word order—the word-assembly-line—they get in the way. What you get in the end is not the striking headline you were after but "Him-the-man bites he-the-dog."

So what did the Chinese do after they had got hold of the assembly-line idea? Simple: they threw out all the affixes. It was the logical thing to do. Soon—that means in Chinese after many thousands of years—they got rid of everything that fills our grammar textbooks and were left with a few thousand little syllables and rules for putting them in order. Now, if they wanted to say "A man bites a dog" they said "Man bite dog"; for "Two men bite two dogs" they said "Two man bite two dog"; for "Two men bit two dogs," "Two man finish bite two dog"; and so on all through the language.

That was long before the time of Confucius, 500 B.C. Ever since, no Chinese school child has been plagued by grammar. In fact, the Chinese never knew that there was such a thing as grammar until they heard about it from us. All their language teachers ever did was to sort out full and empty words and let it go at that.

Now you will ask, What are full and empty words? If you look at words closely, the answer is easy. Full words say something, empty words do not. They are just there to tie the full words together—language tissue that is necessary but doesn't convey any meaning. If somebody started talking to you and said: "Besides, however, nevertheless, as it is, with regard to, inasmuch, hence, indeed, but . . ." you would look at him in amazement and think, When will he start saying something? Up to now, he used only empty words.

Possibly this one-and-only feature of Chinese grammar may seem pointless to you. But the Chinese knew how to use it. After they had successfully stripped their language of all the unnecessary affix underbrush, they naturally wanted to go further in the process of streamlining. So they discovered that they could do without many of the empty words, and out they went. Why should anyone say "A dog is an animal," if the same idea can be expressed by "Dog: animal"? Articles have no place in an assembly-line language. Neither has the verb *to be* wherever it is just filling the space between subject and predicate.

But all this was just the first step in simplification. You have to think this thing through to really understand what it means. You have to imagine a language where there is a difference between full and empty words *but no other distinction between words.* The Chinese never heard about nouns, verbs, and adjectives. To them, a word is just a word, and you use it where it fits in and makes sense. If a Chinese says "Sun shine," he may mean "sunshine," or "The sun is shining," or "The sun is bright and shiny." Or, to be more exact, he doesn't mean any of these things, because his language doesn't work that way; he means that the *sun* (subject) has something to do with *shine* (predicate), and that's all. You may understand me better if I give two examples in English where a word has a meaning regardless of its grammatical function. If you say: "Got your hair cut?" you don't think or care whether the word *cut* is a noun, a verb, or an adjective. Neither does the fellow who had, or had not, his hair cut. Still, both of you know what you are talking about. In the same way, if you read a headline THE AXIS SPLIT, you don't care about the grammatical function of *split,* but you are not in doubt what it means. Now imagine, if you can, a language that consists only of words like *cut* or *split* in these examples, and you will get some notion about Chinese.

If you started to talk and write in such a language, you would soon notice that it forces you into plain talk by various means. Try, for instance, to use complex sentences, or qualifying clauses and phrases. You will find that Chinese makes it hard to be hard. Can you start a sentence like this: "Biting a dog, a man . . ."? You can't. You have to stick to the good old assembly-line word order and say: "A man bit a dog. Then he . . ." Or how about the passive voice: "A dog, bitten by a man . . ."? Not in Chinese. Back to the assembly line: "A man bit a dog. The dog . . ." So you see, fancy language doesn't work in Chinese. Suppose you give that famous news story the works and write a headline like this:

TRAMP'S DENTAL ATTACK ON
WESTCHESTER PEKINGESE REPORTED

In Chinese you could use neither affixes nor the passive voice and you couldn't tack on *reported* at the end. You would have to start out with something like

> THEY SAY TRAMP-MAN TOOTH-HIT
> PEKING-TYPE DOG IN WESTCHESTER

and in no time you would be back at the old

> MAN BITES DOG

But even that is not all. Chinese does more to you than just simplify your constructions. It simplifies your ideas. In other languages, the affixes are a splendid means of getting away from reality into vague generalities and abstractions. For instance, in English you have the simple word *sign,* meaning "a mark." Now you add an affix to that word and you get *signify,* "to make a mark." Next you add another affix, and you arrive at *significant,* "making a mark." Now you add a prefix for a change, and you have *insignificant,* "making no mark." Finally you add another suffix, and you come out with *insignificance,* "the making of no mark." What did you do? You took a simple noun, and made it successively into a verb, an adjective, another adjective, and again a noun. You have added no meaning but just four empty syllables. Now you can be serious and philosophic and talk about the "insignificance of man." A Chinese would say something about "Man no mark." So, while you give in to the temptations of English affixes and fill your talk with masses of empty syllables and words, he keeps his feet on the ground and says everything in the most concrete, specific words. He has to; there are no other words in Chinese.

Not only that, Chinese never loses the human touch. Remember that in Chinese you always have to express subject and predicate, otherwise the words make no sense. Also, there is no passive voice. Therefore, in Chinese, you have to say clearly Who did What. You cannot say things like "It is reported by reliable authorities . . ." You have to say "People I rely on say . . ."

If you think, however, that Chinese has no way of expressing abstract ideas, you are wrong. Remember, the Chinese were talking and writing about religion and philosophy long before our own civilization started. If they had no exact word for an abstraction, they used the concrete word, or words, that came nearest to the idea. So, naturally, instead of using words like *institutionalization* or *antiprogressivism,* as our thinkers do, they formed the habit of expressing ideas by metaphors, similes, and allegories, in short, by every known device for making a thing plain by comparing it with something else. This is the feature of Chinese that is almost impossible to explain without going into the language itself; it's the flavor, the overtones, that are usually lost in translation. However, you may get the idea if I tell you that Chinese is full of things like

> He who raises himself on tiptoe cannot stand firm; he who stretches his legs wide apart cannot walk.

or

> Do not wish to be rare like jade, or common like stone.

And maybe you will understand why I have gone into all this and started a book on plain English with a chapter on Chinese, if you look at two passages I found on the same newspaper page. They are from two war communiqués. One is the United Nations communiqué: cold, abstract, impersonal, official. The other is the Chinese communiqué (translated from a broadcast in the Mandarin language): it is concrete, human, grimly touching. Somehow you get the feeling that the two communiqués are about different wars, ours about World War II and the Chinese about some other distant, medieval, heroic war. Yet it's the same war, all right; the same bombs, the same tanks. The difference is not between Tommies or doughboys and Chinese soldiers; it is between the English language and Mandarin Chinese.

Here are the two reports:

UNITED NATIONS

Enemy resistance in certain sectors of the Fifth Army front was strong, but further progress was made by our troops. The important road center of Teano was captured, and elsewhere on the front more ground offering good observation was taken.

The recent heavy rains are

CHINESE

On October 25 our forces engaged the enemy in a fierce battle in the vicinity of Chiuchiwu. The enemy troops were driven off and the area of Chiuchiwu was taken by our troops.

With encouragement from the excellent results in killing the enemy, our forces bravely making movement very difficult in the coastal sector.

launched several more thrusts, and more of the enemy troops were killed. During that engagement, the enemy commanding officer of Siaofeng was killed by our forces.

The total number of the enemy soldiers and officers killed amounted to more than 1,300. That was only the number of corpses found in the field. The enemy remnants fled to Siaofeng in a chaotic manner. Our troops followed the victory and continued to attack.

You will feel the difference even better if you try to imagine what the Chinese communiqué was like in the original. It must have sounded somewhat like this:

October 25. Our force meet enemy. Fierce battle near Chiuchiwu. Our force drive off enemy troop; take Chiuchiwu country.

Kill enemy good work: courage to our force. Launch some more brave thrust. Kill more enemy troop . . .

And so on; you can figure out the rest for yourself.

I am sure you will admit at this point that Chinese is a simple language. But, you will say, what has all that to do with plain English? You are already wondering whether I am going to make you write sentences like "Kill enemy good work"; and you don't particularly care for being quaint.

Don't worry: this book is about plain talk, and I mean plain talk. All we are going to do with our new nodding acquaintance with Chinese is to keep its two main principles firmly in mind: first, get rid of empty words and syllables and, second, stick to the subject-predicate-object order. That's how the Chinese simplified their language, and that's how we can simplify ours. All the rest follows: simple sentences, concreteness, the human touch.

And now you can already start with your first

EXERCISE

Translate the following passage into English that sounds like Chinese:

An indigenous American faith in the desirability and necessity of applying the democratic principle to the intellectual life continued to bulk large among the forces back of all the emphasis on popularizing knowledge. The lyrical faith in education as the best means of promoting equality of opportunity was a main cause for the increasing public responsibility for schools and for the vast expansion of other agencies for popularizing knowledge. The traditional argument that mass education was necessary for intelligent participation in political democracy and that it must extend beyond the common school was heard in discussions regarding high schools, libraries, and Chautauquas. The growing complexity of American life and the recognition that this imposed new burdens on democratic political machinery were additional arguments for spreading knowledge through every possible channel.

In this exercise you have to throw out affixes and empty words and rewrite the sentences in subject-predicate-object order. Then take the basic word meanings, stripped of all affixes, and line them up in order. Finally, build simple English sentences from these elements: you will get a free translation of the original paragraph into Chinese-flavored English.

Here is the first sentence as a sample. First, the word roots listed in order:

Born—America—believe—wish—want—people—mind
—life—stay—big—force—drive—people—know

Now let's make this into a sentence:

Born Americans believe they wish and want mind-life for the people; this belief stayed: a big force in the drive to make people know.

Do the rest of the paragraph in the same fashion.

(If you would rather skip this exercise to read on, turn to the next chapter. But don't forget to go back to it if you want to get out of this book everything that's in it.)

Chapter Two

LISTEN TO PLAIN TALK

After reading so much about Chinese, you may think that simplified language is a Chinese specialty. Of course, that isn't so. All peoples simplify their languages. Whenever scientists had a chance of comparing an old language with its modern offspring, they found that inflections and irregularities had been dropped in the course of the centuries. No wonder: nobody uses a lot of difficult grammar if he can help it. I am sure you know plenty of people who keep on speaking broken English all their lives simply because they have found out they can get along; in the same manner nations use broken languages because it's easier to talk that way. Chinese is simpler than most other languages only because the Chinese people happened to be earlier in the game; the difference is really in time.

Among the world's great languages, the runner-up to Chinese is English. It's simpler, more flexible, more practical than any other Western language because it has gone furthest in losing inflections and straightening out irregularities. We say today *named* for what was in Old English *genemnode;* and we say *had* for what was in Gothic *habaidedeima.* We have almost no inflections or irregularities left now; in other words, we are approaching the point Chinese reached some time before 500 B.C. You would think we might catch up with them in a few thousand years.

But this will never happen. We lost our chance in the race when we became a literate people. For languages change only in the mouths of illiterates; if you start to teach children the three R's you stop them from simplifying their parents' language. If all Gothic boys and girls had learned how to spell *habaidedeima* generation after generation, they would never have got it down to *had;* billions of written and printed

22

habaidedeimas would have been in the way. You have to take a language with an alphabet and a written literature as is; if you want to change *theatre* into *theater* it takes decades of crusading. (The Chinese, of course, had the added advantage of never having used an alphabet but a system of word symbols; so they could streamline their words without changes in spelling. Chinese just doesn't spell.)

That does not mean, however, that a literary language does not change at all. It does; but the changes are not in grammar and spelling but in style and expression. English settled down to its present spelling and grammar around 1600; but the prose style of that time was very different from ours. It was elaborate and slow; ours is informal and fast. Read, for instance, this sentence from Milton's *Areopagitica*, written in 1644:

> For if we be sure we are in the right, and do not hold the truth guiltily, which becomes not, if we ourselves condemn not our own weak and frivolous teaching, and the people for an untaught and irreligious gadding rout, what can be more fair, than when a man judicious, learned, and of a conscience, for aught we know, as good as theirs that taught us what we know, shall not privily from house to house, which is more dangerous, but openly by writing publish to the world what his opinion is, what his reasons, and wherefore that which is now taught can not be sound.

This is beautiful; but the point here is that nowadays nobody writes like that. If one of our own literary people had written that passage, it would read somewhat like this:

> Supposedly we know and don't purposely suppress the truth, our education is neither inefficient nor irresponsible, and there is no rampant ignorance and irreligion. Consequently, whoever is intelligent, educated and presumably honest should in all fairness be allowed to publish his arguments against current doctrine.

The main difference between the two versions is that a modern writer feels unable to take a long breath like Milton. He thinks he must condense everything important into few words and short sentences, and leave out everything else; no modern reader would stand for Miltonian periods.

That is true. But our modern authors have jumped out of

the frying pan into the fire; their sentences are faster than those of the Elizabethans but less readable. Milton, in all his stateliness, is simpler reading than most modern literary prose. Instead of simplifying our written language, we have made it more complex.

So, if we look for a recipe for modern plain English, we find ourselves in a peculiar spot: we could try to imitate seventeenth-century English, but that would sound impossibly old-fashioned; or we could try to approach some future "Chinese" English, but that would sound impossibly modernistic. We have to take our language as it is today and find some compromise solution.

But where is the problem? you say. Doesn't everybody know the trouble with difficult English is those big five-dollar words? Can't we just use plain one-syllable or two-syllable words instead and there we are? Can't we find the vocabulary range of our audience and then use only the words they know?

Unfortunately, we can't. There is no way of saying, This man has a vocabulary of 10,000 words, that one has a vocabulary of 10,001 words and so on. And even if we could say that, we couldn't go on and say, The one word Man No. 2 knows but Man No. 1 *doesn't* know is *hirsute;* therefore we can use *hirsute* with Man No. 2 but not with Man No. 1. That's all very ridiculous; but it's the logical conclusion to what most people think about plain language. To them, it's simply a vocabulary problem.

It's no vocabulary problem at all. In the first place, everybody recognizes words he never uses in talking. That's why you can safely talk about *irreligion* to people who would never say *irreligion* in their lives. In the second place, everybody is able to understand an unfamiliar word if only the circumstances make clear what it means. If I said to you, out of a clear sky, "Barberiana," you wouldn't understand. It may mean a Latin-American dance, or anecdotes about the late Professor Roderick W. Barber, or whatever. But if you had passed the barbershop in Rockefeller Center, and had seen in the window an exhibit of shaving mugs, barber's basins, and paintings of people who are having their hair cut, with a big sign underneath: barberiana, you wouldn't need an explanation. And now your vocabulary has 27,394 words instead of 27,393.

Anyway, if you ever tried to write within a limited vocabulary, you would know that it can't be done. There are always words you specially want to use, and other words you *have* to use. For instance, in the first chapter of this book I used the word *aorist*. Possibly you don't know what an aorist is; or maybe you have just a vague idea that it is something in Greek grammar you are glad you forgot. Splendid: that's exactly what I wanted you to know or guess about the word. I didn't use it for its precise meaning; I used it for the unpleasantness it stands for. If it had been fully familiar to you, it wouldn't have been as frightening as I meant it to be.

Or, to take another example, I used the word *affix* in Chapter 1, and I am going to keep on using it in this book. In fact, I couldn't write this book without using the word *affix* because that's what much of it is about. You may not have heard it before; so I have tried to give you a good explanation, and I hope that by now *affix* is part of your vocabulary.

In other words, to limit one's speaking and writing vocabulary is unnecessary, on the one hand, and impossible, on the other. True, the big five-dollar words are stumbling blocks for your audience; but now, in the middle of the twentieth century, there is almost nothing you can intelligently speak or write about without using those key words. For instance, there wouldn't be much point in talking about our form of government without using the word *democracy*.

Well, then, you will say, if simplified grammar is out, and slow-paced sentences are out, and limited vocabulary is out, how *can* we simplify our prose style? How does anyone achieve plain talk anyhow?

For, strange as it may seem to you at this point, people talk plainly as long as they don't think about it. In conversation, without rehearsal or preparation, they somehow manage to express themselves so clearly that nobody asks for an explanation. How do they do it?

The solution to this puzzle is easy: they use big words, and a fast pace, and the ordinary rules of grammar, *but they give the other fellow time to understand*. They pause between sentences; they repeat themselves; they use filler words between the big important ones; they space their ideas. The secret of plain talk is in-between space.

That sounds simple; in fact, it *is* simple. Everyone does it every day. But when it comes to writing, or to formal speaking, we forget about the in-between space. It doesn't seem right to fill pages with filler words or repetition, and that sort of thing doesn't go with oratory. So we compress and condense; we make one word out of three, and leave out ten more that seem irrelevant. They *are* irrelevant; but without them, your reader or listener has no time to understand the relevant words. You have to use small talk in between if you want your big talk to go over. What you say may be clear for anybody with average intelligence; but don't forget that you force that average-intelligent man to make an effort to follow you. Maybe he has other things on his mind; maybe he is tired; or maybe he simply is not interested enough to make that effort. If you fill in space, you won't add anything to what you say; but you will put your audience at ease.

To give you an exact idea of colloquial prose, I reprint here two rather long pieces that are as accurate reproductions of conversation as can be found. They are not perfect; but I hope they will give you the right idea.

The first excerpt is from a story by Dorothy Parker, entitled "Too Bad." Two gossiping women serve as a sort of Greek chorus, interpreting the story to the reader; and Dorothy Parker is remarkably successful in making gossip sound like gossip:

"My dear," Mrs. Ames said to Mrs. Marshall, "don't you really think that there must have been some other woman?"

"Oh, I simply couldn't think it was anything like that," said Mrs. Marshall. "Not Ernest Weldon. So devoted—home every night at half-past six, and such good company, and so jolly, and all. I don't see how there *could* have been."

"Sometimes," observed Mrs. Ames, "those awfully jolly men at home are just the kind."

"Yes, I know," Mrs. Marshall said. "But not Ernest Weldon. Why, I used to say to Jim, 'I never saw such a devoted husband in my life,' I said. Oh, not Ernest Weldon."

"I don't suppose," began Mrs. Ames, and hesitated. "I don't suppose," she went on, intently pressing the bit of sodden lemon in her cup with her teaspoon, "that Grace—that there was ever anyone—or anything like that?"

"Oh, Heavens, no," cried Mrs. Marshall. "Grace Weldon just gave her whole life to that man. It was Ernest this and Ernest that every minute. I simply can't understand it. If there was one earthly reason—if they ever fought, or if Ernest drank, or anything like that. But they got along so beautifully together—why, it just seems as if they must have been crazy to go and do a thing like this. Well I can't begin to tell you how blue it's made me. It seems so awful!"

"Yes," said Mrs. Ames, "it certainly is too bad."

The other bit of conversation is not gossip but talk about current affairs between men; and it is not fictional but real. It is from a transcript of *The People's Platform,* a radio discussion program in the form of an overheard dinner-table conversation. These broadcasts were unrehearsed and spontaneous. I think the transcripts are the nearest thing to actual-conversation shorthand notes that can be found. Of course, the broadcast dinner guests knew they were on the air; but they talked to each other and not to their audience.

This particular program was about Russia. The chairman was Lyman Bryson; the guests, Walter Duranty, Louis Fischer, and Max Lerner. Listen:

FISCHER: . . . Of course, when Churchill and Roosevelt meet . . . they inevitably discuss the Pacific which is such an important phase of the whole war, but . . .

BRYSON: And to Russia also?

FISCHER: And to Russia, of course! But the Russians have been invited to previous conferences where the Pacific was also discussed, but they were *not* invited to this conference and I think they were not invited to this conference because Russia is being discussed in terms of Russian demands and the Russians want to know the answers.

LERNER: I don't know, Bryson, whether Fischer or Duranty, which of them is correct about this, but there's one observation I'd like to make about the whole thing and that is this seems to indicate what is to me the most serious problem in the relations of the Allies, and that is America and Britain are always meeting about something and Russia isn't meeting with them. There seems to have been developing a rift within the United Nations . . . we're becoming almost a house divided against itself. At least there is a danger that we may become a house divided or . . .

FISCHER: Well, isn't it true, Lerner, that Stalin has been invited several times and has not seen fit or not been able to come?

LERNER: I don't know, Fischer. I have been told that.

FISCHER: Well, we have been told that officially and

Roosevelt said only the other day at his press conference that he would have been glad to meet Stalin. . . .

LERNER: Well, may I just say this and that is that just this morning we had reports of an editorial published in a Russian semiofficial magazine asking for a meeting of the three powers. Now, it's very difficult to reconcile that with the statement that Stalin had repeatedly been invited to such a meeting and had not taken part.

FISCHER: Oh, he might have refused it in the past and sees the wisdom of it now.

LERNER: That's possible.

DURANTY: Yes. Well, you speak, Lerner, of a rift between Russia and the Western powers . . . has it grown up recently? Isn't it really more true that there has been concealed distrust and misunderstanding between Russia and the Western democracies ever since the foundation of the Soviet Republic and that actually today we are merely witnessing a progression of that and a continuation of it, and what's more . . .

LERNER: It's getting worse!

DURANTY: I say it's not getting much better because in many ways the situation is acute. For instance, this very question of the second front and other questions. I think on the whole it is probably getting better, but in a sense sharper at this time. And that, after all, many people in Germany and outside Germany have an interest in extending this squabble, or pretending it is a quarrel where it is not, perhaps even somewhat unconsciously.

LERNER: Yes, because I agree, Duranty, that this distrust is an old thing and one of the interesting things is that this distrust has not been destroyed by Russian bravery and Russian military accomplishment and by our co-operating with the Russians, our Lease-Lend. Distrust is rarely destroyed between nations and it seems to be really rechanneled . . . it's now seeking underground, subterranean methods of showing itself . . . in an enormous amount of rumormongering on both sides and the suspicions that the Russians have of us, in our tendency, as I say, to act with the British but not to act with the Russians so that I would suggest that one of the things for us as Americans . . . us Americans to think about is what can we do to . . . well, shall we say . . . destroy this distrust on our side?

FISCHER: Well, I think we can. . . . The first thing we

can do is to try to understand why it is sharper today, as Duranty says, than it has been throughout Soviet history, and I think that the reason is . . . lies in the nature of this war. . .

Now if you read these two conversation pieces carefully, you will notice how the speakers make themselves understood. They repeat phrases ("I don't suppose . . . I don't suppose"— ". . . they were not invited to this conference and I think they were not invited to this conference because . . ."); they correct themselves (". . . that Grace—that there was ever anyone . . ."—". . . whether Fischer or Duranty, which of them is correct . . ."—". . . the reason is . . . lies in the nature of this war . . ."); they repeat ideas in different words (". . . a progression of that and a continuation of it . . ."—". . . our co-operating with the Russians, our Lease-Lend"); they even contradict their own statements ("I say it's not getting much better . . . I think on the whole it is probably getting better . . .").

Sometimes the speakers use sentences of Chinese simplicity ("It was Ernest this and Ernest that every minute."—"America and Britain are always meeting about something and Russia isn't meeting with them"). At other times they use old-fashioned slow-moving sentences—but with the difference that they don't say them in one breath but break them into pieces ("If there was one earthly reason—if they ever fought, or if Ernest drank, or anything like that. But they got along so beautifully together—"—". . . just this morning we had reports of an editorial published in a Russian semiofficial magazine asking for a meeting of the three powers. Now it's very difficult to reconcile that with the statement that Stalin had repeatedly been invited to such a meeting and had not taken part").

Important key words are being used where they seem necessary, but always with some illustration or rephrasing to drive the point home ("So devoted—home every night at half-past six, and such good company, and so jolly, and all." —". . . a rift within the United Nations . . . we're becoming almost a house divided against itself."—". . . it seems to be really re-channeled . . . it's now seeking underground, subterranean methods of showing itself . . .").

Everything is put in personal terms ("Why, I used to say to Jim . . ."—"I can't begin to tell you how blue it's made me."—". . . what is to me the most serious problem . . ."— ". . . we have been told that . . ."—". . . I would suggest that one of the things for us as Americans . . . us Americans to think about . . .").

Filler words are freely strewn about ("Oh"—"yes"—"why" —"Heavens, no"—"well"—"of course"—"that is"—"well"— "now"—"oh"—"yes"—"I say"—"I think"—"well, shall we say"—"well").

And finally there is one element you can't see on the printed page: between the words and with them there are gestures and looks and intonations and pauses and silences.

So here we have the secret of plain conversational talk: it is not difficult ideas expressed in easy language, it is rather abstractions embedded in small talk. It is heavy stuff packed with excelsior. If you want to be better understood you don't have to leave out or change your important ideas; you just use more excelsior. It's as simple as that.

EXERCISE

Translate the following passage into conversational talk, as if it were spoken across a dinner table. Be sure to use all the ideas that are there, but provide space between them. Do not add any new ideas of your own.

> Perhaps the toughest job of thinking we have to do in this matter of European reconstruction is to realize that it can be achieved through nonpolitical instrumentalities. Reconstruction will not be politics; it will be engineering.
>
> It will be possible to operate Europe's primary economic plant directly, not through political controls. It is possible to make bargains with cartels and trusts, with trade unions and co-operatives, with farm unions and professional societies, without sending a single *démarche* through a foreign ministry or memorandum through a Department of the Interior. For a year or more after the First World War many cities and districts in central and eastern Europe provided for their immediate needs while their paper governments issued decrees and proclamations that meant exactly nothing. So long as food can be procured, politicians are expendable. And so long as the Commission can provide the minimum supplies needed to sustain local life it can make trains run, and ships sail, and oil wells spout, and factory chimneys smoke.
>
> Why it will often have to deal directly with non-

political bodies should be fairly clear. Unless a totalitarian police power is to administer everything (and it is unthinkable that our armies should provide and subsidize such forces) there can be in the more chaotic parts of Europe no responsible and effective national political authority for a long time.

As a sample, here is my own conversational version of the first paragraph:

Well, there is quite a tough job ahead . . . the toughest of them all, I think, as far as this matter of Europe—of European reconstruction is concerned. . . . Yes, the toughest job we have to do in this whole matter, and it's a job of thinking—of realizing how it can be done—how it will be done, I should say. . . . It will be done somehow, but not by politics. No, reconstruction in Europe won't be politics at all. . . . What I mean is this: it will all be nonpolitical. Nonpolitical bodies and agencies and bureaus—nonpolitical instrumentalities of all kinds. You see, it will be an engineering job. Like building a bridge, that's the way I look at it. . . . No politics whatsoever, mind you, just plain nonpolitical engineering. . . . Yes, that's the way you have to realize —to visualize this reconstruction job.

Now do the rest of the passage in the same manner.

Chapter Three

SENTENCES COME FIRST

Perhaps by now you have a general idea of what simplified language looks like and how people go about making themselves understood in conversation. Plain talk is mainly a question of language structure and of spacing your ideas. Now let's get down to work and learn how to do this.

We shall start with sentences, for the simple reason that language consists of sentences. Most people would say offhand that language consists of words rather than sentences; but that's looking at it the wrong way. We do not speak by forming one sentence after another from words we have stocked somewhere back in our brains: we try to say what we have in mind and tell it in sentences. This obvious fact is confirmed by what we know about the language of primitive peoples, where the issue is not confused by grammar and dictionary knowledge. Here is, for instance, what Frank C. Laubach, the famous teacher of illiterates, had to say about the Maranaw language: "When we tried to write the words we heard, nobody could tell us where one word began and another ended! If I asked Pambaya, 'What is the Maranaw word for *go?*' he did not know. But if I asked how to say 'Where are you going?' he answered at once, 'Andakasoong.' By many trials and errors we discovered that *anda* was *where,* *ka* was *you,* and *soong* was *go*—'Where you go?' "

Of course, English has advanced far beyond Maranaw; but the principle still holds that words are discovered by taking sentences apart, and that the units by which we express ideas are sentences rather than words. So, to learn how to say things simply, we have to start by studying sentences.

Now, what is a sentence? Let's take our definition from Fowler's *Dictionary of Modern English Usage.* (This is the most famous elbow book for English writers. Incidentally, it's fun to read.) "A sentence means a set of words complete in itself, having either expressed or understood in it a subject and a predicate, and conveying a statement or question or command or exclamation." Fowler adds, and this is important: "Two sentences (not one): *You commanded and I obeyed.*" Naturally, it would also be two sentences if you wrote: "*You commanded; I obeyed.*"

So you see that ordinarily a sentence expresses one thought and you need two sentences to express two thoughts. You can, however, work one sentence into another in place of a noun or adjective or adverb: it then becomes a clause and the other sentence a complex sentence. You can also work more ideas into a sentence by putting in more phrases or words.

Every word you set into the framework of a sentence has to be fitted into its pattern; it has to be tied in with invisible strings. In a simple sentence like *Man bites dog* there is one such string between *man* and *bites* and another between *bites* and *dog*, and that's all there is to the sentence pattern. But if a sentence goes beyond the subject-predicate-object type, it is liable to become a net of crisscrossing strings that have to be unraveled before we can understand what it says.

Take for instance this sentence from a recent book on Russia:

> Here is Edmund Burke, the eminent British Liberal, than whom no European statesman was more horrified by the outrages of the French Revolution.

As you see, the clause is tied to the main sentence by the word *whom,* from which an invisible string leads to *Burke,* five words back. To reach *whom,* however, we have to jump over *than* which in turn is tied to *more horrified,* five words ahead. In short, the sentence is a tangle and should have been revised to read:

> No other European statesman was more horrified by the outrages of the French Revolution than Edmund Burke, the eminent British Liberal.

Old-fashioned grammarians would point out that the main idea should never have been expressed in the subordinate clause; but that rule of thumb is pure superstition. The important thing is that the ties within the sentence should not run in different directions but straightforward so that the reader can read along. Here is a good example of what I mean (from the theater section of *The New Yorker*):

> In an otherwise empty week, we might as well give the play our attention, if only as an almost perfect example of how a script of no conceivable merit manages to get cast, rehearsed and finally produced at some expense without anybody connected with it being aware that the whole enterprise is a violent and batty flight in the face of providence. In this case, of course, Mr. Paley has put on his own work, but it still seems incredible that nobody once took him aside and explained that even in these queer times there is no reliable metropolitan audience for amateur theatricals.

These sentences are not hard to read in spite of their complexity. The trouble is, you have to be a skillful writer to turn this trick. Ordinarily, a sentence will get tangled up as soon as you start filling it up with ideas. If you remember what I said in the last chapter about spacing ideas, you will understand that the best plan is to write short sentences so that the reader, or listener, gets enough chances for breathing spells and doesn't get caught in invisible strings between words.

That sounds elementary; and you may wonder why you find so many long sentences in books, magazines, and newspapers. The explanation, to the best of my knowledge, is simply that those sentences are written, not to make it easy for the reader, but to ensnare him, catch him like a fly on flypaper, or buttonhole him to attention. There are reasons for doing this; sometimes even good reasons. The most commonplace is the let-me-finish-my-sentence feeling of the raconteur, the storyteller who doesn't want to let go of his audience. Here is a simple example of the raconteur-sentence from a story by Damon Runyon:

> Well, Charley takes the dice and turns to a little guy in a derby hat who is standing next to him scrooching back so Charley will not notice him, and Charley lifts the derby hat off the little guy's head, and rattles the dice in his hand and chucks them into the hat and goes "Hah!" like crapshooters always do when they are rolling the dice.

Such a sentence is very loosely tied together; besides, it is really two sentences joined by *and*. If we want to disentangle it, we can rewrite it easily:

> Well, Charley takes the dice. He turns to a little guy in a derby hat who is standing next to him scrooching back so Charley will not notice him. Charley lifts the derby hat off the little guy's head, rattles the dice in his hand, chucks them into the hat and goes "Hah!" Crapshooters always do that when they are rolling the dice.

Now listen to a charming literary raconteur, Alexander Woollcott:

> If this report were to be published in its own England, I would have to cross my fingers in a little foreword explaining that all the characters were fictitious—which stern requirement of the British libel law would embarrass me slightly because none of the characters is fictitious, and the story—told to Katharine Cornell by Clemence Dane and by Katharine Cornell to me—chronicles what, to the best of my knowledge and belief, actually befell a young English physician whom I shall call Alvan Barach, because that does not happen to be his name.

This is already more difficult to unravel, but here we go:

> If this report were to be published in its own England, I would have to cross my fingers in a little foreword explaining that all the characters were fictitious; and that stern requirement of the British libel law would embarrass me slightly because none of the characters *is* fictitious. The story was told by Clemence Dane to Katharine Cornell and by Katharine Cornell to me: it chronicles what, to the best of my knowledge and belief, actually befell a young English physician. I shall call him Alvan Barach because that does *not* happen to be his name.

Similar in purpose to the raconteur-sentence is the newspaper lead-sentence. The reporter, following a hoary rule of journalism, tries to get everything important into the first sentence so that the reader whose eyes happen to get caught by the headline starts reading and cannot stop until he knows the gist of the story. This system gets the news down the reader's throat whether he wants it or not, but it makes newspaper reading a very unpleasant job. This is what you are likely to get with your breakfast:

> The Germans have completed a mine belt three miles wide along the west coast of Jutland in Denmark as part of their invasion defenses, and preparations to meet the Anglo-American onslaught from the west have been reviewed in Berlin where Adolf Hitler and Field Marshal Gen. Wilhelm Keitel, chief of staff of the Supreme Command, met Field Marshal Gen. Karl von Rundstedt, commander of the Wehrmacht in France.

Or, translated from tapeworm English into plain language:

> The Germans have completed a mine belt three miles wide along the west coast of Jutland in Denmark. This is part of their invasion defenses. Adolf Hitler, Field Marshal Gen. Wilhelm Keitel (chief of staff to the Supreme Command), and Field Marshal Gen. Karl von Rundstedt (commander of the Wehrmacht in France) met in Berlin. They reviewed preparations to meet the Anglo-American onslaught from the west.

Scientists, eager to win their argument, also often buttonhole their readers with long sentences. For instance:

> Learning a language need not be dull, if we fortify our efforts by scientific curiosity about the relative defects and merits of the language we are studying, about its relation to other languages which people speak, and about the social agencies which have affected its growth or about circumstances which have molded its character in the course of history.

Maybe the argument would sound even more convincing like this:

> Learning a language need not be dull. We can fortify our efforts by scientific curiosity about the language we are studying: What are its relative defects and merits? How is it related to other languages people speak? What social agencies have affected its growth? What circumstances have molded its character in the course of history?

The most notorious long-sentence writers are the lawyers. The reason is again similar: they won't let the reader escape. Behind each interminable legal sentence seems to be the idea that all citizens will turn into criminals as soon as they find a loophole in the law; if a sentence ends before everything is said, they will stop reading right there and jump to the chance of breaking the rule that follows after the period.

Well, that's questionable psychological doctrine; what is certain is that legal language is hard even on lawyers. Here is a mild example:

> Sick leave shall be granted to employees when they are incapacitated for the performance of their duties by sickness, injury, or pregnancy and confinement, or for medical, dental or optical examination or treatment, or when a member of the immediate family of the employee is affected with a contagious disease and requires the care and attendance of the employee, or when, through exposure to contagious disease, the presence of the employee at his post of duty would jeopardize the health of others.

Now I cannot believe that sick leaves would generally increase or decrease if this were formulated as follows:

> Employees shall be granted sick leaves for these four reasons:
>
> (1) They cannot work because of sickness, injury, or pregnancy and confinement;
>
> (2) They need medical, dental or optical treatment;
>
> (3) A member of their immediate family is affected with a contagious disease and needs their care and attendance;
>
> (4) Their presence at their post of duty would jeopardize the health of others through exposure to contagious disease.

Finally, long sentences can be used for artistic reasons. Marcel Proust, the great French writer, built his novels from never-ending sentences—with the effect that the reader feels magically transposed into a world of dreamy memories and intense feelings. This is hard to describe; but you may want to taste just one sentence:

But now, like a confirmed invalid whom, all of a
sudden, a change of air and surroundings, or a new
course of treatment, or, as sometimes happens, an organic change in himself, spontaneous and unaccountable,
seems to have so far recovered from his malady that he
begins to envisage the possibility, hitherto beyond all
hope, of starting to lead—and better late than never—
a wholly different life, Swann found in himself, in the
memory of the phrase that he had heard, in certain
other sonatas that he had made people play over to him,
to see whether he might not, perhaps, discover his phrase
among them, the presence of one of those invisible
realities in which he had ceased to believe, but to which,
as though the music had had upon the moral barrenness
from which he was suffering a sort of recreative influence, he was conscious once again of a desire, almost,
indeed, of the power to consecrate his life.

I am not going to translate this sentence into simple prose,
first, because, in cold print, this would look like an insult to
Proust's memory and, second, because this will be an excellent exercise for you after you finish this chapter. I am
afraid it will keep you busy for a while.

Meanwhile you may ask, what is the moral of all this?
Shall we write nothing but short, simple sentences? Shall we
dissect every long sentence we find? Is there any rule?

No, there is no rule. But there are scientific facts. Sentence
length has been measured and tested. We know today what
average Americans read with ease, and what sentence length
will fit an audience with a given reading skill. So you get not
a rule but a set of standards.

To understand the table that follows, remember two
things:

First, sentence length is measured in words because they
are the easiest units to count: you just count everything that
is separated by white space on the page. But don't forget that
you might just as well count syllables, which would give you
a more exact idea of sentence length: a sentence of twenty
one-syllable words would then appear shorter than a sentence
of ten one-syllable words and six two-syllable words. Keep
that in mind while counting words.

Second, remember Fowler's definition of a sentence. Count
two sentences where there are two, even if there is no period
between them but only a semicolon or colon. But don't

bother about sorting out sentences with conjunctions between them: the difference is not worth the added effort.

Now look at the table:

Average sentence length in words

VERY EASY	8 or less
EASY	11
FAIRLY EASY	14
STANDARD	17
FAIRLY DIFFICULT	21
DIFFICULT	25
VERY DIFFICULT	29 or more

Just what EASY and DIFFICULT mean on this table I shall explain in detail later (see p. 302). For the moment, notice that an average reader will have no trouble with an average sentence of 17 words. (In a book or article, shorter sentences will, of course, cancel out the longer ones.) Easy prose is often written in 8-word sentences or so. Such writing consists mostly of dialogue and, as everybody knows, a book with a lot of dialogue is easy to read. On the upper half of the scale, literary English runs to about 20 words a sentence, and scientific English to about 30 words.

So, if you want to rewrite or edit something for people who are just about average, measure it against the 17-word standard. If the sentences are longer, look for the joints in their construction and break them into smaller pieces until they are of the right average length.

As an

EXERCISE

as I said before, you may try your hand at the Proust passage. If this seems too forbidding, here is another newspaper lead-sentence for you to dissect:

Because Allied postwar planning groups like the United Nations Relief and Rehabilitation Administration realize the chaotic conditions with which they will be confronted by legally unidentifiable persons following the German collapse, leading British and American archivists are here on a tour that will probably lead to redefinition within the framework of military necessity of a system of handling damaged or newly occupied properties, it was learned today.

Rewrite this in easy 11-word sentences.

Chapter Four

GADGETS OF LANGUAGE

Now that we know what to do about sentences, the next question is, of course, what kind of words to put in them. This is the main topic of all books on how to write and I cannot start this chapter better than by quoting the beginning of the best of the lot, Fowler's *The King's English* (where you can study systematically what is arranged by the alphabet in his *Dictionary of Modern English Usage*): "Any one who wishes to become a good writer should endeavour, before he allows himself to be tempted by the more showy qualities, to be direct, simple, brief, vigorous, and lucid. This general principle may be translated into practical rules in the domain of vocabulary as follows:—

Prefer the familiar word to the far-fetched.
Prefer the concrete word to the abstract.
Prefer the single word to the circumlocution.
Prefer the short word to the long.
Prefer the Saxon word to the Romance.

These rules are given roughly in order of merit; the last is also the least."

Sir Arthur Quiller-Couch, in his Cambridge lectures *On the Art of Writing,* adds one more rule: "Generally use transitive verbs, that strike their object; and use them in the active voice, eschewing the stationary passive, with its little auxiliary *is's* and *was's*, and its participles getting into the light of your adjectives, which should be few. For, as a rough law, by his use of the straight verb and by his economy of adjectives you can tell a man's style, if it be masculine or neuter, writing or 'composition'."

This is, in a nutshell, the best advice you can get anywhere. If you look at these rules closely, you will find that those about short and Saxon words are admittedly not worth much, and that Quiller-Couch's rule starts with an arbitrary preference for transitive verbs—as if *lay* were a better word than *lie*. You will also see that the first rule about familiar words depends not on your own familiarity with words but on your reader's, which is hard to guess. And you will realize that the excellent rule about the single word being better than the circumlocution is unnecessary as long as you stick to what you learned from the last chapter and use as few words as possible in your sentences.

This leaves us with Fowler's second rule: "Prefer the concrete word to the abstract." Very good. Plain talk, as we all know, consists of concrete words; that's practically a definition of it. But which words are concrete and which abstract? You think you know? Well, is *apple* a concrete word? Of course, you say: you can look at apples, smell them, touch them, eat them. But how about the concept *apple?* Isn't it true that the word *apple* also stands for what all the apples in the world have in common, for their "appleness"? Isn't that abstract? How can you tell about any word whether it is abstract or concrete?

Actually, it is a question of meaning and of degree. Some words, like *democracy,* can safely be called abstract since they are used chiefly with abstract meaning; others, like *apple,* are felt to be concrete because they usually apply to concrete objects. It is possible—I have done it once—to draw up a long list of the most common abstract words and then check the abstractness of writing by the proportion of those words. But this is a cumbersome thing to do. You can get the same result in a far quicker and easier way if you count the language gadgets.

For language consists of two parts: the things we say and the machinery by which we say them. To express our thoughts, as we have seen, we use sentences; and we cannot express a thought by any single word unless it is able to do the work of a sentence if necessary. So we can tell the meaningful words apart from the mere language machinery by the sentence test: if a word can form a sentence, it refers to something outside language; if it cannot, it is just a language gadget. This has nothing to do with abstractness and concreteness; it is a linguistic difference. For instance, the abstract word *sin* can be used as a sentence, as in the famous answer to the question "What was the sermon about?" But the next question, "What did the preacher say?" had to be answered by a whole sentence: "He was against it." *Against* by itself wouldn't do as an answer; neither would *dis-* for "He disapproved of it." That's because *against* and *dis-* are examples of language gadgets; they have no meaning except combined with meaningful words in a sentence.

Now, the point of all this is that difficult, complex, abstract language is cluttered up with gadgets. If we stick to this purely linguistic test, we can measure difficulty by counting gadgets, and we can simplify our speech and writing by throwing them out.

Language gadgets, as you have seen, are of two kinds: words by themselves, like *against,* and parts of words (affixes), like *dis-*. The more harmful of the two for plain talk are the affixes, since the reader or hearer cannot understand what the gadget does to the sentence before he has disentangled it from the word it is attached to. Each affix burdens his mind with two jobs: first, he has to split up the word into its parts and, second, he has to rebuild the sentence from these parts. To do this does not even take a split second, of course; but it adds up.

If you want to measure word difficulty, therefore, you have to count affixes. Here is what you do: You count every affix you find in your text, every prefix, suffix, or inflectional ending, with the exception of -s at the end of a word, -en in *children, oxen* etc., and -d or -t in *could, did, had, might, ought, should, stood, went, would.* Some words have two affixes, like *dis-ap-prove,* some have three, like *dis-ap-prov-ing.* Some seem to have nothing but affixes like *philo-soph-y;* discount one in such words. When you have finished counting, figure out how many affixes there are per 100 words; or, of course, you can take a 100-word sample to begin with. Then you can check the result against this table:

Number of affixes per 100 words

VERY EASY	22 or less
EASY	26
FAIRLY EASY	31
STANDARD	37
FAIRLY DIFFICULT	42
DIFFICULT	46
VERY DIFFICULT	54 or more

Again, for the time being, the average-reader standard of 37 is most important for you to know. The best example of VERY EASY prose (about 20 affixes per 100 words) is the King James Version of the Bible; literary writing tends to be FAIRLY DIFFICULT; scientific prose is VERY DIFFICULT.

To simplify a given passage, count first the number of affixes; then replace affix words systematically by root words, or at least by words with fewer affixes, until you arrive at the level you want to reach. The translating job is sometimes difficult and a dictionary with simple definitions will help. (A good dictionary of this type is the *Thorndike-Barnhart High School Dictionary,* published by Doubleday & Company.)

Let me show you how it is done on a passage from *Reflections on the Revolution of Our Time* by Harold J. Laski. Laski, a leading British Socialist, wrote well, and his topic was exciting; but unfortunately, he was a professor by trade and his language was pure academic jargon. Here is a key passage that seems worth translating into plain English:

What is the essence of fascism? It is the outcome of capitalism in decay. It is the retort of the propertied interests to a democracy which seeks to transcend the relations of production implied in a capitalist society. But it is not merely the annihilation of democracy. It is also the use of nationalist feeling to justify a policy of foreign adventure in the hope, thereby, of redressing the grievances which are the index to capitalist decay. Wherever fascism has been successful, it has been built upon a protest by the business interests against the increased demands of the workers. To make that protest effective, the business interests have, in effect, concluded an alliance with some outstanding *condottiere* and his mercenaries who have agreed to suppress the workers' power in exchange for the possession of the state. But as soon as the condottiere has seized the state, he has invariably discovered that he cannot merely restore the classic outlines of capitalism and leave it there. Not only has his own army expectations. Having identified himself with the state he has to use it to solve the problems through the existence of which he has been able to arrive at power. He has no real doctrine except his passionate desire to remain in authority. His test of good is the purely pragmatic test of success. And he finds invariably that success means using the state-power over the nation partly to coerce and partly to cajole it into acquiescence in his rule. That acquiescence is the sole purpose of, and the sole justification for, the methods that he uses. The only values he considers are those which seem likely to contribute to his success.

Now this has 56 affixes per 100 words and rates VERY DIFFI-CULT. The following translation has 32 and should read fairly easily:

What makes fascism? It comes from capitalism in decay. It is the rich people's answer when democracy tries to go beyond the capitalist way of running production. But it does not stop at wiping out democracy. It also plays on the people's love for their country to put over dangerous plans against other countries and so, they hope, to set right the wrongs capitalism in decay brings about. Wherever fascism has been successful, it has been helped at the start by businessmen trying to keep the workers from getting more. To do this, the businessmen have, in fact, joined up with some outstanding gang leader and his hired soldiers who have made a bargain to put down the workers' power and become owners of the state in return. But as soon as the gang leader has seized the state, he has always found that he cannot just bring back the standard forms of capitalism and leave it there. Not only does his own army wait for rewards. Now that he and the state are the same, he has to use it to solve the problems that made the businessmen put him in power. He has no beliefs except his strong wish to stay in power. His test of good is the test of success. And he always finds that success means using state-power to force or coax the people to yield to his rule. This is the sole purpose or reason for his methods. He has no use for anything that doesn't seem likely to add to his success.

You will notice that some of the key words have been left untouched, like *fascism, capitalism, democracy, production.* Other affix words, like *decay, problem, success, methods,* did not seem worth translating since they are easy to understand for every reader and would be hard to replace in this passage. Remember that whenever you try to limit your vocabulary rigidly, you become artificial and maybe un-English. If you want to achieve plain talk, you have to avoid that mistake.

Another feature of the translation is that it is much shorter, not only in syllables but also in words. Ordinarily, if you replace affix words by root words, you will have to use more words. But it so happens that there is a lot of deadwood in this type of academic jargon that naturally falls by the wayside once you start rewriting. *He has no real doctrine* becomes *He has no beliefs,* and *the methods that he uses, his methods.*

I admit that it is not easy to write about economics or political science in easy language. Gifted writers are rare in this field; and a truly readable book like Bernard Shaw's *Intelligent Woman's Guide to Socialism and Capitalism* is a great exception. Let me quote to you, as contrast, how Shaw begins his "Appendix instead of a bibliography":

> This book is so long that I can hardly think that any woman will want to read much more about Socialism and Capitalism for some time. Besides, a bibliography is supposed to be an acknowledgment by the author of the books from which his own book was compiled. Now this book is not a compilation: it is all out of my own head. It was started by a lady asking me to write her a letter explaining Socialism. I thought of referring her to the hundreds of books which have been written on the subject; but the difficulty was that they were nearly all written in an academic jargon which, though easy and agreeable to students of economics, politics, philosophy, and sociology generally, is unbearably dry, meaning unreadable, to women not so specialized. And then, all these books are addressed to men. You might read a score of them without ever discovering that such a creature as a woman had ever existed. In fairness let me add that you might read a good many of them without discovering that such a thing as a man ever existed. So I had to do it all over again in my own way and yours. And though there were piles of books about Socialism, and an enormous book about Capitalism by Karl Marx, not one of them answered the simple question, "What is Socialism?" The other simple question, "What is Capital?" was smothered in a mass of hopelessly wrong answers, the right one having been hit on (as far as my reading goes) only once, and that was by the British economist Stanley Jevons when he remarked casually that capital is spare money. I made a note of that.

This is splendid writing, excellently readable for people like you and me. (It has 38 affixes per 100 words.) It just so happens that Shaw seems unable to write like this:

> The extensiveness of the present volume is such that it

appears almost inconceivable that female readers should desire to prolong the study of Socialism and Capitalism for an additional period of time. This circumstance apart, a bibliography traditionally is supposed to serve as an acknowledgment offered by the author of the original sources that contributed to the genesis of his compilation. In contrast, however, to this usually followed procedure, the present volume differs radically from a compilation inasmuch as it was solely and entirely conceived and executed by the author himself. . . .

And so on. Translating normal English into affix English s easy; with the help of Roget's *Thesaurus* it's no work at all. Moral: if you want to write plain English, don't use your Roget.

EXERCISE

Translate into FAIRLY EASY English (30 affixes per 100 words) the following passage from Laski:

All government arises because men move in opposed ways to their objectives; no one but an anarchist would deny that its existence is, under any circumstances we can foresee, a necessary condition of peaceful social relations. But the argument that, especially in the economic sphere, we are overgoverned, is not one with which it is easy to have patience. Less government only means more liberty in a society about the foundations of which men are agreed and in which adequate economic security is general; in a society where there is grave divergence of view about those foundations, and where there is the economic insecurity exemplified by mass-unemployment, it means liberty only for those who control the sources of economic power.

Chapter Five

THE GRAMMAR OF GOSSIP

Time magazine prides itself that "our subscribers can under stand the event in terms of the personality who caused it (Joe Stalin drinks his vodka straight. Admiral Turner of the Central Pacific delights in growing roses. Air Marshal Harris' men love him because he is 'so bloody inhuman.')"

I wonder whether personalities really cause events and whether *Time* readers understand the event better be cause they are told about Stalin's vodka and Turner's roses. But there is no doubt about one thing: human interest makes for easier reading. Scientific tests have shown that people are better at reading about other people than about anything else.

Why is this so? Probably because man knows nothing so well as man. His thinking and his language started out as simple talk about what he and people around him were doing, and primitive man did not doubt that there was a person be hind every event and behind every tree and mountain. Our modern languages, of course, have gone a long way toward abstraction; but most of them still keep male and female genders for names of things, and in German, for instance, the answer to the question "Where is my coat?" is "He hangs in the closet."

So it seems to be naturally easier to read and understand *Stalin drinks vodka* than *Vodka contains alcohol*. To use once more my comparison between language and a machine shop where thoughts are prepared for the trade: think of your entering such an empty shop and being baffled by it, and of your relief when you at last find somebody to guide you. This is what the name of a person in a sentence does to the reader.

Therefore, after you have shortened your sentences and thrown out bothersome affixes, you have to do one more thing to make yourself well understood: you have to keep talking about people.

How can you do this, you ask. Many of the things you have to talk and write about just don't have any human interest; you cannot properly discuss the situation on the stock market by telling stories about two Irishmen. The human touch in plain talk is not a question of language, you say, but of subject matter.

If you look closely at the way the human element is used in speech and writing, you will find that this is not so. People come up in our sentences and paragraphs not only when we are gossiping but in discussions of everything under the sun. *Time* magazine, whose journalistic formula is built upon human interest, is of course full of good examples. Here is how various techniques are used for various subjects in a random issue:

The classic newspaper device, the eyewitness report, is used for a war story:

It was three days after the major part of the battle had ended and we were out a few miles from the island patrolling our little sector of the ocean, swinging back and forth in huge figures of eight. The noise and colors of battle were gone. The bombing had ceased and the big guns on the ships were silent.

Now there was only a little smoke on the island and though we could see occasional puffs from the guns of the one destroyer which was still firing, the sound didn't carry to us. . . . A few of us were standing by the rail thinking our own thoughts when someone called attention to some objects in the water. . . . There were three of them, a hundred yards or more apart, and as we came closer we could see that they were men and that they were dead. . . .

The interview technique is used for a bit of foreign news:

Everyone in Helsinki tells me that the Finnish food situation is now substantially better than it was twelve months ago. . . . As far as most ordinary Finns can see both on the front and in the rear, Finland is a defeated country in which wartime life is difficult but by no means intolerable.

The impression of most observers in Helsinki whom I have talked to is—in any case the Government should not close the doors for further negotiations with the Russians, but should try to get better terms than those which are now being discussed. Most Finns want peace under conditions which would assure Finland liberty and independence, but many doubt whether the present Russian proposals guarantee these to Finland.

A local story from New York is presented in the thriller-fiction manner:

At 4:50 A.M. the elevator signal buzzed in International House, the massive 13-story lodging place built by John D. Rockefeller for foreign students. The elevator man had a blind right eye, but as he stopped the car he turned to look at his lone passenger. She was Valsa Anna Matthai, 21, a pretty Indian girl from Bombay, a Columbia University student. She was not wearing the Indian sari pulled over her hair, but a bright kerchief; and as she walked out of the empty, lighted lobby, the operator noticed she wore a tan polo coat, dark slacks, and sport shoes. She had no bag. The street lights along Riverside Drive made pale yellow pools on the drifted snow, but beyond, Grant's Tomb and the park sloping down to the Hudson River were lost in gloom. That was the morning of March 20.

A speech is reported so that the reader never forgets the person who is talking:

The U.S. heard some plain talk last week on reconversion. It came from War Mobilization Director James F. Byrnes in a speech before the Academy of Political Science in Manhattan. His most significant point: the harsh realities are at hand; big war plants are going to close down; in the next 20 months war production will be cut back some $16,750,000,000 at least; another $1,402,000,000 will be slashed from the spare parts program of the Army & Navy by the end of this year. Then Assistant President Byrnes warned:

"The Government must take a firm stand and close plants no longer needed in the war effort. From civic groups and from men in public office, there will come the cry: 'Woodman, spare the plant!' But we must realize that Santa Claus has gone."

Then Jimmy Byrnes came to grips with the question of dismissal pay for war workers. . . .

A dramatic story like a Congressional committee hearing is written up as stage drama:

At committee hearings the people's representatives can give the admirals some uneasy moments.

One of these moments came when Vermont's Representative Charles A. Plumley found an item of $7,000,000 to build a stadium at Annapolis. That did not seem to Mr. Plumley to be essential to the war. Ernie King's deputy, Vice Admiral Frederick J. Horne (not the least of whose qualifications is his ability to get along with Congress), quickly admitted that the item should not have been put in the bill. "The bureau chiefs are here, and I think you are going to give them a bad quarter of an hour," said wry Admiral Horne.

For Mississippi's Jamie Whitten that dodge was not enough to excuse plushy requests for appropriations. Said he: "We just had Admiral King in here, and Admiral King says: 'I have to pass it right back to Admiral Horne'; now we have Admiral Horne here and he says 'I have to depend on the bureau chiefs,' and then the bureau chief says 'I have to depend on the men under me,' and it goes right down to the fellow who is at the Academy and wanted the stadium." Out went the stadium. Declared Jamie Whitten: "It takes a mighty small item to make you suspicious of the big items."

And, of course, no issue of *Time* is without its biographical profile, skillfully woven together out of little anecdotes:

All his life Jack Curtin, 59, had never felt the need to see the non-Australian world. Years ago, Vance Marshall, an Australian laborite now living in London, visited Jack in Perth. "I'm on my way to England," Marshall said. . . . "Australia's in the backwash. It's back of beyond of even the fringe of things that matter. I want to be where history is written."

Jack reached for his well-worn hat, suggested a "walkabout." They walked all afternoon, coming to the Esplanade beside the leisurely, looping Swan River at sunset. Said thoughtful Jack Curtin: "Vance, you should have said where past history is written. This is where history is going to be written. Why don't you stay and help write it? Australia's big, Vance, not England. There's room to breathe here, to grow, to live."

Straight biography is also part of the profile:

Jack Curtin was an Aussie who had to do things—and to have a cause for doing them. His cause was Socialism.

He started out in staid and proper Melbourne—in the Melbourne Club, smoking in the dining room is still prohibited—but he started as a lowly printer's devil. In no time at all he was holding office in a union. Soon he was haunting Socialist Hall (smoking permitted) in Exhibition Street, watching the great orators sway their audiences, learning their tricks. . . .

And here is a close-up portrait:

In the Prime Minister's office, a cool room with blue leather and a blue rug, a couple of etchings and a map, Jack Curtin affects a huge uncluttered desk. A reserved man, shunning formal gatherings, he nevertheless likes to cock one foot on the desk and talk at length. He smokes incessantly—through a bamboo holder—and drinks tea without pause. . . .

Time's human-interest devices are, of course, not all there are. Argument, for instance, lends itself very well to the discussion form—invented two thousand years ago by Plato. Scientific research is often made exciting as a sort of indoors adventure story. Educational material is best written by directly addressing the reader. (A handy example is the book you are reading now.) And there are many other ways of bringing in people.

But all these tricks do not help much if you want to make a given piece of impersonal prose humanly interesting without doing a complete rewrite job. What then? Is there any easy way out?

The thing to do in such a situation is to go through the text sentence by sentence and to look for the logical—not the grammatical—subject. After a while you will discover that the logical subject is always a person and that every sentence can be written so that this person is mentioned. Let's try this with another item from the same issue of *Time* which has, on the surface, almost no human interest:

> Du Pont this week announced a new product as highly potential as its nylon. It is wood impregnated with chemicals which transform it into a hard, polished material. Engineers call it "compreg."
>
> The treatment makes pine as hard as oak, oak as hard as ebony. Wood so treated does not warp, split, swell or shrink appreciably. It resists fire, rotting and termites, can be made as strong as many metals. It can be dyed any color so that it never needs painting or refinishing. If the surface is scratched, its glossy finish can be restored by sandpapering and buffing. Impregnated wood makes possible among other things, doors, windows, and drawers that do not stick or get loose.

Look at these sentences one by one. "Du Pont this week announced a new product as highly potential as its nylon." Du Pont? The corporation? Certainly not: the announcing was done by Mr. So-and-so, their public relations man. How about "The Du Pont *people* announced . . ."?

Next: "It is wood impregnated with chemicals which transform it into a hard, polished material." Who impregnated the wood? The Du Pont people. Therefore: *"They* have impregnated wood with chemicals . . ." "Engineers call it 'compreg.'" That is: *"Their* engineers call it 'compreg.'"

"The treatment makes pine as hard as oak, oak as hard as ebony." Treatment by whom? Why not "With this treatment they can make pine as hard as oak, oak as hard as ebony"?

"Wood so treated does not warp, split, swell or shrink appreciably." To find the logical subject in such a sentence, you have to ask, How do you know? Well, how does anyone know a scientific fact? By testing. Every such statement can be reduced to a test somebody made at some time. (This is what philosophers call operationism.) So let's rewrite: "Their tests show that wood so treated does not warp," etc.

"It resists fire, rotting and termites, can be made as strong as many metals." The first half of this sentence refers again to tests; and the passive "can be made" translates easily into *"They* can make it . . ." Next: "It can be dyed any color so that it never needs painting or refinishing." Who would have to do the painting and refinishing? This is where the reader comes in: ". . . so that *you* never need to paint or refinish it." And again: "If the surface is scratched, its glossy finish can be restored by sandpapering and buffing." This refers to anyone who is interested in the practical use of "compreg," and certainly also to the reader. Therefore: "If *you* scratch the surface, *you* can restore its glossy finish . . ."

And now the last sentence: "Impregnated wood makes possible among other things, doors, windows and drawers that do not stick or get loose." Possible for whom? For the public, the reader, you. "Among other things, impregnated wood will make it possible for *you* to have doors, windows, and drawers that do not stick or get loose."

Here is the whole passage with all personal references in their proper places:

> The Du Pont people announced this week a new product as highly potential as their nylon. They have impregnated wood with chemicals and transformed it into a hard, polished material. Their engineers call it "compreg."
>
> With this treatment, they can make pine as hard as oak, oak as hard as ebony. Their tests show that wood so treated does not warp, split, swell or shrink appreciably; it resists fire, rotting and termites. They can make it as strong as many metals and dye it any color so that you never need to paint or refinish it. If you scratch the surface, you can restore its glossy finish by sandpapering and buffing. Among other things, impregnated wood will make it possible for you to have doors, windows, and drawers that do not stick or get loose.

Naturally, this version is not as readable as if the story of "compreg" had been told by a dramatic description of its discovery; but even the few *theirs* and *yous* serve to point up the human interest that was buried in the original story.

The difference, as you see, is linguistic; and it can be measured by simply counting the proportion of *theirs* and *yous* and other references to people in the text. A practical method to do this is the following:

First, count all names of people. If the name consists of several words, count it as one, e.g., "Vice Admiral Frederick J. Horne." Next, count all personal pronouns except those that refer to things and not to people. Then count the human-interest words on this list:

Man, woman, child; boy, girl, baby; gentleman, lady; sir, mister, madam (e), miss; guy, dame, lad, lass, kid.

Father, mother, son, daughter, brother, sister, husband, wife, uncle, aunt, cousin, nephew, niece; family; parent; sweetheart; dad, daddy, papa, mamma.
People (not peoples), folks, fellow, friend.

Count also combinations of these words with each other and with grand-, great-grand-, step- and -in-law, and familiar forms of them like *grandpa*.

When you have found the number of these names, pronouns and human-interest words per 100 words of your text, you can check the degree of human interest against this table:

Number of personal references per 100 words

VERY EASY	19 or more
EASY	14
FAIRLY EASY	10
STANDARD	6
FAIRLY DIFFICULT	4
DIFFICULT	3
VERY DIFFICULT	2 or less

The standard of 6 personal references per 100 words is found, for instance, in feature articles in popular magazines. Very easy prose, for instance love stories in pulp magazines, runs to about 20 such words in 100: that means, every fifth word in such fiction refers to a person. Very difficult scientific material, of course, may be written without mentioning any persons at all.

EXERCISE

Rewrite the rest of the article on impregnated wood to the human-interest standard of *Time* (about 8 personal references per 100 words):

The product developed from research begun by the U.S. Forest Products Laboratory. The impregnating material, called methylolurea, is made principally from two cheap, plentiful chemicals—urea and formaldehyde—which are synthesized from coal, air and water. In the impregnating process, wood is pressed and soaked in methylolurea solution, which is converted by the wood's acids into hard, insoluble resins. The wood becomes brittle, but this disadvantage can be partly offset by impregnating only the outer part of the wood, leaving a resilient core.

Impregnated wood is so cheap and versatile that Du Pont claims it will compete with the much more expensive plastics and light metals. Moreover, the process will make usable vast resources of little-used soft woods —maples, poplars, gums, etc. The impregnation process simplifies the making of veneers and plywoods, because pressed and impregnated layers of wood need no glue.

Chapter Six

LIVE WORDS

You now know the recipe for simplicity: talk about people in short sentences with many root words. Here is an easy trick for killing these three birds with one stone: Use verbs. Let me repeat that: *Use verbs*.

Nothing is as simple as a brief three-word sentence that follows the pattern: somebody *does* something. It is the verb that gives life to any sentence; it literally makes the sentence go.

But we have seen that in Chinese, the simplest of all languages, there is no such thing as a verb (or noun or adjective, for that matter). How, then, do the Chinese make their sentences go? Well, the explanation is simple: one word in each sentence serves, so to speak, as its motor; for this particular sentence, it works as a verb. If a Chinese says "Man bite dog," the word *bite,* otherwise unclassified, serves as a verb; that's why it has been put after *man* and before *dog*.

In modern English, which gets more and more "Chinese," we do that all the time and "appoint" a word to do verb service by putting it in a certain place in a sentence. We can say "Raise your face" or "Face your raise"; "Ship a book" or "Book a ship"; "Spot the cover" or "Cover the spot." There is no question that each of these sentences has a verb in it, and no question which is the verb.

The point of all this is, of course, that I am talking here only of those words that are used as verbs in a sentence. They are what the grammarians call the "finite active verb forms" and they are the only ones that have life in them. Hearing of verbs, you probably think of passive participles and infinitives and gerunds and all the other fancy varieties that have plagued your grammar-school days. Well, forget about them: for all practical purposes they are not verbs, but nouns or adjectives—lifeless words that won't make your sentences move. The verbs you want to use are those that are in active business doing verb work; if you use a verb in the passive voice or make a participle or noun out of it, you have lost the most valuable part in the process: it's like cooking vegetables and throwing away the water with all the vitamins in it.

If you go through any newspaper or magazine and look for active, kicking verbs in the sentences, you will realize that this lack of well-used verbs is the main trouble with modern English writing. Almost all nonfiction nowadays is written in a sort of pale, colorless sauce of passives and infinitives, motionless and flat as paper. Listen to this, for instance (from an essay by Paul Schrecker in the *Saturday Review*):

> Maybe the gradual actualization of this solidarity was the result of scientific and hence technological progress which caused distances to shrink and required ever-expanding markets. But it is a preconceived and entirely unwarranted idea to believe this technological unification to have been a primary cause, and hence to overlook the fact that its triumphant appearance on the world scene would not have been possible without the prior existence of a potential world-civilization. The ever-expanding sphere of influence of literature, science, and works of art, which rarely respects any national or regional boundaries, cannot be accounted for by the introduction of faster and easier means of communication or by the improved technological methods of mass reproduction. The phenomenon reveals mankind's preparedness to respond promptly to incentives emerging from the fields of knowledge and the arts, irrespective of their national and regional origin.

Or how about this (from "Mary Haworth's Mail"):

> Morbid preoccupation with thoughts of sex gratification, after one has attained the age of reason, is not a sign of emotional precocity, as some may suppose; but just the opposite, namely: evidence of a definitely infantile type of emotional egocentricity; what the psychologists call a state of arrested development. The uncomprehending inarticulate infant's sense of well-being is wholly related to bodily feelings,—of being well fed, comfortably clothed and bedded, fondly caressed, etc. His sole concern, insistently registered, is with physical

gratification, because instinct tells him that pleasurable sensations, at his helpless level of development, are synonymous with a reassuring sufficiency of creature care and healthy survival.

Now, if you look closely, you will notice that the only active, finite verbs in the first passage are *caused, required, respects,* and *reveals:* four mildly active verbs matched by 27 passive forms, infinitives, participles, verbs made into nouns, and forms of the auxiliary verb *to be.* In the second passage, we have *suppose, call,* and *tells,* against 32 inactive verb forms of various types.

And now let us look at the language of Shakespeare or the Bible, for contrast. Here is a speech by Brutus:

> No, not an oath; if not the face of men,
> The sufferance of our souls, the time's abuse—
> If these be motives weak, break off betimes,
> And every man hence to his idle bed;
> So let high-sighted tyranny range on,
> Till each man drop by lottery. But if these,
> As I am sure they do, bear fire enough
> To kindle cowards, and to steel with valour
> The melting spirits of women; then, countrymen,
> What need we any spur, but our own cause,
> To prick us to redress? what other bond,
> Than secret Romans, that have spoke the word,
> And will not palter? and what other oath,
> Than honesty to honesty engag'd,
> That this shall be, or we will fall for it?
> Swear priests, and cowards, and men cautelous,
> Old feeble carrions and such suffering souls
> That welcome wrongs; unto bad causes swear
> Such creatures as men doubt; but do not stain
> The even virtue of our enterprise,
> Nor the insuppressive mettle of our spirits,
> To think that or our cause or our performance
> Did need an oath; when every drop of blood
> That every Roman bears, and nobly bears,
> Is guilty of a several bastardy,
> If he do break the smallest particle
> Of any promise that hath pass'd from him.

And these are words of Job:

Wherefore do the wicked live, become old, yea, are mighty in power?

Their seed is established in their sight with them, and their offspring before their eyes.

Their houses are safe from fear, neither is the rod of God upon them.

Their bull gendereth, and faileth not; their cow calveth, and casteth not her calf.

They send forth their little ones like a flock, and their children dance.

They take the timbrel and harp, and rejoice at the sound of the organ.

They spend their days in wealth, and in a moment go down to the grave.

Therefore they say unto God, Depart from us; for we desire not the knowledge of thy ways.

What is the Almighty, that we should serve him? and what profit should we have, if we pray unto him?

Lo, their good is not in their hand: the counsel of the wicked is far from me.

How oft is the candle of the wicked put out! and how oft cometh their destruction upon them! God distributeth sorrows in his anger.

They are as stubble before the wind, and as chaff that the storm carrieth away.

Clearly, most of the power, movement, and beauty of these passages comes from the succession of active verbs: Shakespeare makes tyranny *range,* men *drop,* and a cause *prick us to redress;* the Bible makes a bull *gender,* a cow *calve,* and children *dance.* There are 19 live verbs in the Shakespeare passage against 11 passive verb forms, verbal nouns, etc.; in the Bible passage the ratio is 20 to 11.

Maybe you will say that I am unfair in using the Bible and Shakespeare as examples. After all, newspapers and magazine articles are written to meet a deadline, by writers who don't dream of being literary geniuses; so why compare their style with all-time masterpieces? I admit I am a little biased here; but anybody can try to use active, working verbs wherever possible. It won't make him a Shakespeare but it will make him write good, plain English. Here is, for instance, one modern example from Ernie Pyle:

The company I was with got its orders to rest about 5 one afternoon. They dug foxholes along the hedgerows, or commandeered German ones already dug. Regardless of how tired you may be, you always dig in the first thing.

Then they sent some men with cans looking for water. They got more K rations up by jeep, and sat on the ground eating them.

They hoped they would stay there all night, but they weren't counting on it too much. Shortly after supper a lieutenant came out of a farmhouse and told the sergeants to pass the word to be ready to move in 10 minutes. They bundled on their packs and started just before dark.

Within half an hour they had run into a new fight that lasted all night. They had had less than four hours' rest in three solid days of fighting. That's the way life is in the infantry.

There are 16 working verbs there and not a single verb form or noun that could, or should, be turned into an active, finite verb. And now compare it with this sentence from a popular article on economics:

In somewhat over-simplified technical terms, inflation is caused by the existence, at any given time in an economic system, of an aggregate of *effective* purchasing power greater than the aggregate of the goods and services for sale.

What a definition! "Inflation" is caused by the *existence* of an *aggregate* that is *greater* than another *aggregate*. This shows clearly how impossible it is to describe a process—something happening—without using a single active verb. Obviously the writer realized that himself, because the next sentence reads like this:

. . . When we add up the amounts of cash and credit of all kinds at the disposal of everybody who is ready to buy something, and find that the sum is larger than the sum of all the things to be bought at existing prices, then prices are likely to go up.

Now the verbs are in their proper places, and everything becomes crystal-clear: First we *add* something, then we *find* that it is larger than something else, and then prices will *go up*. This is the classic type of scientific explanation: If you do X and Y, what happens is Z. (Or, in the De Kruif manner: The great scientist did X and Y, and what happened was Z.)

And now, let's get down to work and try to rewrite a "verbless" passage ourselves. Here is another bit from the literary essay I quoted on page 58:

> Integrated into the circulation of national life much more completely than any other modern literature, American belles-lettres also give a much more faithful and adequate picture of the entire civilization to which they belong than literature abroad, whose very compliance with—or willful opposition to—traditions that have long lost their anchorage in the depths of their respective national civilizations, renders them unable to keep abreast of the rejuvenated spirit of their epoch.

Here is the same sentence with the nouns made into verbs:

> American belles-lettres circulate in the national life much more than other modern literatures do; they picture the entire civilization to which they belong more faithfully and adequately. The spirit of the times has become young again, and literatures abroad cannot keep abreast with it because of certain traditions they comply with or willfully oppose. These traditions were once anchored in the depths of their national civilizations, but have lost that anchorage long ago.

And now I expect you to go ahead and pepper your speech and writing with active verbs. But before you start using this rule of thumb, let me warn you. There is one place where it does not work: in written dialogue. You know the sort of thing I mean:

> "She is, I think, a lady not known to Monsieur," murmured the valet . . .
> "Show her out here, Hippolyte," the Comte commanded . . .
> "My descent upon you is unceremonious," she began . . .
> "But seat yourself, I beg of you, Mademoiselle," cried the Comte . . .
> "But yes," she insisted . . .
> "Certainly people are wrong," agreed the Comte . . .

"Perhaps," he murmured . . .
"The jewels!" she breathed . . .

Fowler, in his *Dictionary of Modern English Usage,* says that this mannerism was started by George Meredith; wherever it comes from, it is nowadays an excellent means to tell a bad novel from a good one. Apparently all bad writers do it and all good writers don't. Look at the fearless way in which John Hersey repeats the word *said* in *A Bell for Adano:*

Zito said: "What is this Liberty Bell?"

Major Joppolo said: "It is the bell the Americans rang when they declared themselves free from the English."

Zito said: "The idea is good. But would America be willing to part with this bell for Adano?"

Major Joppolo said: "We would have to get a replica, Zito."

Zito said: "Describe this bell."

Major Joppolo said: "Well, it hangs in a tower in Philadelphia, I think . . ."

Imagine this with *Zito ventured* and *Major Joppolo reminisced* . . .

And now for your

EXERCISE

Translate the two passages on page 58 into plain English by making as many words as possible into active working verbs. Or try your hand at this second quote from "Mary Haworth's Mail":

As nearly as I can make out, this is a case of deferred adolescence. Mentally you are abreast of your years or maybe a bit beyond. But emotionally or psychologically, you are still the fledgling 14 which you assiduously exemplify in your chosen garb. The conundrum is whether your unseasonable green-gourd personality is directly related to organic or glandular subnormality,—which is staying your physical development more or less at child level,—or whether it is, rather, the outpicturing of subconscious stubborn reluctance to grow up and thus take lasting leave of the special prerogatives and adulation you may have enjoyed as a charming child prodigy.

Chapter Seven

CROWDED WORDS

Voltaire once said: "The adjective is the enemy of the noun." This sentence is one of the most famous epigrams about language; many young journalists have been started off with it and taught to hunt adjectives in their copy.

It's a good rule, but a little confusing. The fact is, grammarians still can't agree on what an adjective is. If you say, for instance, "A ravishing math teacher," some of them will tell you that *ravishing* and *math* are adjectives; some will say that *ravishing* is a verb form; some others will insist that *math* is a noun (if they admit it is a word at all). The best thing for us is to leave grammatical labels behind and see what the words do in and to a sentence. Then, at once, we see that *math* defines *teacher*, and that *ravishing* is a comment on the math teacher. In other words, there are two kinds of so-called adjectives: commenting and defining. Now we can see what Voltaire meant: obviously he didn't mean that a defining adjective is the enemy of the noun, because it really belongs to the noun (What is she teaching?—Math) in fact it is a part of the noun and you could just as well write *math-teacher*, with a hyphen. On the other hand, the commenting adjective is hostile to and literally kills the following noun: what we remember is that she is ravishing, not that she teaches math. If we want to "save" the noun from the commenting adjective, we have to write this description in two sentences: "She is ravishing. She is teaching math."

As you see, the trouble with comment—whether adjective, adverb, or anything else—is that it raises havoc with a sentence where it doesn't belong. In really simple language all sentences are just subject-predicate sentences: "Man bite dog." "Man short." "Dog tall." If you make one sentence out of three and stick two comments into the first simple sentence

("Short man bite tall dog"), you are already on your way toward difficulty and sophistication. You force the reader, or listener, to take in three ideas in one sentence and you make understanding just so much harder. (James Joyce went even further and packed several ideas into one word, like "brooder-in-low" or "I was just thinking upon that.")

So our rule for plain talk is: Don't try to save a sentence by sticking a comment into another. Reason: Two short sentences are easier to understand than one long one, with extra stuff in it.

I said in the beginning that newspapermen are now being taught that adjectives are Bad. The trouble is, they are also being taught to save words and so, after a while, they forget all about adjective hunting and become sentence stuffers. Here is a mild case:

> Married, he lives with his wife and three sons in New Jersey.

What he means is: "He is married and . . ."
Sometimes the two ideas don't match:

> The 53-year-old commentator left high school to carry copy on the Brooklyn *Times*.

Or:

> Kyser, bespectacled, was born thirty-eight years ago in Rocky Mount, N.C.

Some writers habitually fill their sentences up to the brim. Here is an extract from a book review by Harrison Smith in the *Saturday Review* (I have put all the comments in italics):

> The two sisters, *island aristocrats, whose lifelong fate was sealed when they saw one morning in Saint Pierre a handsome boy of thirteen, whose father, an untidy but a heart-of-gold physician, had just returned a widower to his native town*. Marguerite, *the younger of the sisters, a happy, blue-eyed, blonde child*, wins his love; Marianne, *dark, passionate, self-willed, determinedly* molds his life until he leaves the island, *a lieutenant in the Royal British Navy, bound for the China coast*. The young ladies sit behind and wait *frigidly* for over ten years for word from him. William, in the meantime, had been lured by

a *half-caste* girl in a Chinese port into losing his ship and one morning, *penniless, half-naked, and drugged,* finds himself aboard a *clipper* ship, *bound for New Zealand, an exile.*

Sorted out, this reads:

> Marguerite and Marianne were sisters. They were island aristocrats. Marguerite was the younger; she was a happy, blue-eyed, blonde child. Marianne was dark, passionate and self-willed.
>
> One morning, in Saint Pierre, they saw a handsome boy of thirteen. His name was William and he was the son of an untidy physician with a heart of gold. His father had just become a widower and returned to his native town.
>
> That moment sealed the lifelong fate of the sisters: Marguerite won the boy's love, Marianne molded his life.
>
> Then, one day, William left the island. He had joined the Royal British Navy and become a lieutenant. Now he was bound for the China coast . . . etc. etc.

Or let's have a look at our friend from the last chapter, Mary Haworth:

> Is it *fine philosophic* restraint or is it *craven* expediency to *tacitly* assent, as you have done so far, to your wife's *outre* performance, when you are confident it is part of a pattern of infidelity? If it were in truth the *large* reaction of a *nobly magnanimous* mind, would it be accompanied on the other hand by the *primitive male-egoist* emotional attitude that the marriage is wrecked for you, if she is indulging in a *passing* fancy, as you believe?
>
> Have you feared *subconsciously* to force and face a showdown lest the *resultant* dissection of the marital relationship and her *possible* counter-charges confront you with a *shrewd and merciless* delineation of yourself as one *pallidly* devoid of *salient traits* of *thorough* masculinity?

Nearly all the key ideas have been put into commenting adjectives and adverbs. Here is another, more sophisticated example (from a film review by James Agee in *The Nation*):

> Very belatedly I want to say that "The Watch on the

Rhine" seemed much better on the screen than it did, *almost identically,* on the stage—*though I still wished Henry James might have written it;* and that *I join with anyone whose opinion of* Paul Lukas' performance is superlative. Also that *a simple-hearted* friendliness *generated between audience and screen* at "This Is the Army" made that film happy *to see even when it was otherwise boring; though* I am among an *apparent* minority which feels that Warner Brothers' *cuddly-reverential* treatment of President Roosevelt—in "Mission to Moscow," "This Is the Army," and *the forthcoming* "Princess O'Rourke"—is subject to charges *certainly* of indecent exposure and, *quite possibly,* of alienation of affection.

If you read this without the italicized words, you will see that it still makes sense; but the real point of the whole passage is expressed in those casually tucked-in adjectives like "simple-hearted" or "cuddly-reverential." Mind you, I don't say that this is bad writing; but it isn't plain talk either, by a long shot.

But how about descriptions, you say: How can you describe anything—a city, a landscape—without using descriptive, commenting adjectives? How can you get away from the pattern of "the flowery summer meadows, the lush cow-pastures, the quiet lakes and the singing streams, the friendly accessible mountains"? Simple: put your description in verbs, in predicates, in defining adjectives; don't comment but describe what happens; report, don't analyze.

Here is a description of America (from a *New York Times* editorial):

It is small things remembered, the little corners of the land, the houses, the people that each one loves. We love our country because there was a little tree on a hill, and grass thereon, and a sweet valley below; because the hurdy-gurdy man came along on a sunny morning in a city street; because a beach or a farm or a lane or a house that might not seem much to others was once, for each of us, made magic. It is voices that are remembered only, no longer heard. It is parents, friends, the lazy chat of street and store and office, and the ease of mind that makes life tranquil. . . .

It is stories told. It is the Pilgrims dying in their first dreadful winter. It is the Minute Man standing his ground at Concord Bridge, and dying there. It is the army in rags, sick, freezing, starving at Valley Forge. It is the wagons and the men on foot going westward over Cumberland Gap, floating down the great rivers, rolling over the great plains. It is the settler hacking fiercely at the primeval forest on his new, his own lands. It is Thoreau at Walden Pond, Lincoln at Cooper Union, and Lee riding home from Appomattox. . . .

In short, if you want to give descriptive detail in plain language, describe what you see, even using adjectives if you must; but don't stuff your descriptions down the reader's throat, whether he wants them or not, by filling all the odd corners and empty spots in your sentences with little dabs of observation.

Which brings us, of course, to *Time* magazine. As you know, the little descriptive adjectives—"beady-eyed, thin-lipped"—are the hallmark of *Time;* its editors say that they help the reader get a better picture of what's going on in the world. Well, let's have a look:

Bevin v. Bevan

Ernest Bevin, *the bull elephant* of British labor, last week sat *bulkily silent, beadily watchful,* in the back row at a caucus of Parliament's Laborite members. The proposal: to expel from the Party *his homonym—pink, grizzled Welshman* Aneurin Bevan. The crime: Laborite Bevan's revolt against Labor Minister Bevin in the House of Commons.

At the *tense and troubled* meeting, Aneurin Bevan refused to recant. He argued that if he were bounced, 15 other Laborites who sided with him would also have to go. All over Britain, he warned, labor unions were rising against *tough, truculent* Ernie Bevin's Defense Regulation 1-AA (five years in prison for strike fomenters).

As Aneurin Bevan talked, Ernie Bevin *restlessly* shifted *his weight, impatiently* flung his *farm-hardened* hands about *in gestures he had long used to brush aside opponents, soundlessly* worked his *pudgy* lips. . . .

This is the first part of a story about a British antistrike regulation. But, because of the *Time* formula, the reader is allowed only a quick glimpse at the topic in a brief parenthesis. What he really learns from this first third of the story is that Bevin and Bevan have similar names (this is made the heading) and that Bevin, in contrast to Bevan, is a heavy man (this he gets from four comments, with slight variations upon the theme, plus two photographs of Bevin and Bevan to show what they look like). What the trouble is about, or what the arguments are on each side, he cannot even guess at this point.

Now, psychologists have found that one of the main troubles in reading is the "overpotency" of certain words. Since we always read a few words at a time, those that are specially effective or colorful tend to blot out the others. The result is often that we get a wrong impression or, at least, read an emphasis into the text that isn't there. So it's quite obvious that *Time* readers are apt to learn a lot about the faces, figures, hands, lips and eyes of world leaders, but are liable to misread or skip what these people do.

So, for plain talk, here is a special rule about *Time*style adjectives: Don't use any. People will get you better without them.

And now, as your

EXERCISE

Rewrite, without commenting words, the rest of the passage on page 65 and the passages on pages 65 and 66.

Chapter Eight

THE GLAMOUR OF PUNCTUATION

Some time ago, Sylvia F. Porter, the financial reporter, wrote a *Reader's Digest* article on the income-tax nightmare. Among other things, she said, "there's an improvement upon which all agree. And that is exiling from Washington forever the writers of the incredible thing called income tax prose and making it mandatory for the new authors of tax instruction sheets to use (1) short words, (2) short sentences, (3) no semicolons and (4) no parentheses."

The first two of these points are fine, of course; but the last two just go to show that the average writer considers punctuation marks an invention of the devil that makes everything more complex and harder to understand.

That's an odd idea. After all, when people started writing, they just put one word after the other; as for punctuation, the reader was on his own. Only later writers marked their copy with little dots and dashes and started to give the reader a break. And now people complain that punctuation makes reading harder!

I think the reason must be that punctuation, to most people, is a set of arbitrary and rather silly rules you find in printers' style books and in the back pages of school grammars. Few people realize that it is the most important single device for making things easier to read.

When we are talking, of course, we don't use any punctuation marks. We use a system of shorter or longer pauses between words to join or separate our ideas, and we raise or lower our voices to make things sound emphatic or casual. In other words, we make ourselves understood not only by words but also by pauses and by stress or pitch.

Punctuation gets pauses and stress (but not pitch) down on paper. The system is simple to get the hang of:

	Between Words	*Between Sentences*
Normal pause	White space	Period
Shorter pause	Hyphen	Semicolon (or colon)
Longer pause	Dash	Paragraph
Normal stress	Normal type (or writing)	
Unstressed	Parentheses (or two dashes)	
Stressed	Italics (or underlining)	

Let me explain this little table: As long as you use normal pauses and normal stress in talking, don't use anything but periods and commas in writing. When you run two or more words together with almost no pause between them (because you use them in that sentence as one word), hyphenate them. When you use a longer pause—Watch out for the next word! —make a dash. Same with sentences: When you run two or more sentences together (because you use a string of sentences as one), use a semicolon or, if the first sentence introduces the second, a colon. When you use a longer pause— Now comes something else!—make a paragraph. And don't forget to use italics or parentheses for emphasis or casual mention.

When you put plain talk in writing, two punctuation marks are particularly important for you: hyphens and semicolons. The reason is this: The fewer empty words you use and the more you rely on word order, the more important it is for you to show which words belong closely together; this you do by using hyphens. On the other hand, in plain talk you often use two or more short sentences instead of one long one and show the connection by semicolons.

Here is for instance a collection of hyphenated expressions from a colloquial piece on Wendell Willkie:

. . . this now-you-see-it-now-you-don't impression . . . no Landon-like also-ran obscurity . . . the big-shaggy-bear manner . . . the verbal give-and-take of a lawyer . . . passion for face-to-face debate . . . the halcyon, high-wide-and-handsome days of Wall Street . . . a financial-district Democrat . . . a Willkie-packed audience . . . Steve Hannagan of bathing-beauty fame . . . tailoring his words to his on-the-spot listeners . . . it was a heads-I-win-tails-you-lose proposition . . . his forty-nine-day junket around the globe . . . slow, unglamorous, personal-contact stuff . . . a twentieth-century Henry Clay . . .

As you see, hyphens come in handy when you want just to hint at a general idea or quickly describe an impression. Here is a good example from Westbrook Pegler:

> . . . one of those continued-among-the-leather-belting-ads analyses in *Fortune* . . .

Another from a *Harper's* article on de Gaulle:

> Churchill apparently succeeded in explaining away the no-longer-a-great-power clause in the Smuts speech and at the same time persuading de Gaulle that it was to his interest to support the bloc-of-Western-Europe policy it announced.

And, of course, this just-to-give-you-the-idea device is a boon for reviewers. Here are two examples from David Lardner's film reviews:

> . . . the old invisible-man setup . . . one of those lost-patrol affairs . . .

And three from Wolcott Gibbs's theater reviews:

> Mr. Hammerstein is dealing in basic humor, an extension of the snowball-and-silk-hat principle . . .
> . . . Mr. Hart put heroism on a theirs-but-to-do-or-die basis . . .
> . . . there is some conversation of a gallant, rueful, and won't-you-sit-down nature . . .

The semicolon also has its special uses. Since it wields several facts into a single event, it is one of the favorite tools of the news digester. Here is John Lardner writing about General Montgomery in *Newsweek:*

> I saw him in Reggio the first day I spent in Italy; saw him 100 miles up the road talking to troops in a wood the next day; and the day after that his car suddenly pulled up 100 yards from my truck at a point 30 miles to the east.

And this is a typical bit from *Time:*

No V-day?

Untie those whistles; take those boards off the shop-windows; disband those parades; put that bottle of bourbon back on the shelf—there may be no V-day.

So said the War & Navy Departments last week in an OWI statement: V-day may be spread gradually over days and weeks. No general surrender of the German Armies is expected; they may gradually disintegrate and surrender piece-meal. And the Allies' policy is not to accept surrender from any hastily contrived substitute German Government; the Allies are not looking for any Nazi Badoglio; the war with Germany will be finally over only when all Germany has been occupied, town by town.

Also, semicolons, the short-sentence mortar, are the trademark of a good popularizer. For instance, *Microbe Hunters* by Paul de Kruif literally teems with semicolons. This is the pattern:

Pasteur started hunting microbes of disease and punched into a boil on the back of the neck of one of his assistants and grew a germ from it and was sure it was the cause of boils; he hurried from these experiments to the hospital to find his chain microbes in the bodies of women dying with child-bed fever; from here he rushed out into the country to discover—but not to prove it precisely—that earthworms carry anthrax bacilli from the deep buried carcasses of cattle to the surface of the fields. . . .

. . . The time for the fatal final test drew near; the very air of the little laboratory became finicky; the taut workers snapped at each other across the Bunsen flames . . .

. . . One dead child after another Loeffler examined; he poked into every part of each pitiful body; he stained a hundred different slices of every organ; he tried—and quickly succeeded in—growing those queer barred bacilli pure . . .

. . . They went at it frantic to save lives; they groped at it among bizarre butcherings of countless guinea-pigs; in the evenings their laboratories were shambles like the battlefields of old days when soldiers were mangled by spears and pierced by arrows . . .

. . . He shot his mixture into new guinea-pigs; in three

days they grew cold; when he laid them on their backs and poked them with his finger they did not budge.

However, not all popularizers agree on this point. One of them, Walter B. Pitkin, the author of *Life Begins at Forty,* always wrote extremely short sentences, from six to ten words. Since he despised semicolons, his style read like this:

> In 1919 I began to work with shell-shocked Army officers who were having a tough time returning to the world of business. Here was one who had broken almost every bone in his body and had lived to resume his old job with hardly any mental upset. Here was another whose injuries were trivial. If he carried a cane he could get around easily. But he loathed the cane. He seemed to regard it as a public confession of weakness. He was forever trying to do without it. Worse yet, he strove to walk without a limp. The strain was terrible. He insisted that life was empty for a cripple. Within two years he killed himself.
>
> I reached two conclusions. Many people are better off with grave handicaps than with trifling ones. The grave handicap releases copious energies. The trifling handicap seems to stir the person too feebly to open up the big valves of nervous and mental power. Then, too, people often try to mask the petty handicap, which leads to further complication of the personality.

Now let's put in semicolons, colons, dashes, and paragraphs:

> In 1919 I began to work with shell-shocked Army officers who were having a tough time returning to the world of business. Here was one who had broken almost every bone in his body and had lived to resume his old job with hardly any mental upset. Here was another whose injuries were trivial: if he carried a cane he could get around easily. But he loathed the cane—he seemed to regard it as a public confession of weakness. He was forever trying to do without it; worse yet, he strove to walk without a limp. The strain was terrible; he insisted that life was empty for a cripple; within two years he killed himself.
>
> I reached two conclusions:
>
> Many people are better off with grave handicaps than with trifling ones: the grave handicap releases copious

energies, the trifling handicap seems to stir the person too feebly to open up the big valves of nervous and mental power.

Then, too, people often try to mask the petty handicap, which leads to further complication of the personality.

See the difference?

In fact, without colons and semicolons no one could imitate spoken language in print. As an example, listen to a little eye-witness account from a detective story by the British poet Cecil Day Lewis (Nicholas Blake):

"I knows my way about here in the dark like a mole. I'd a torch, of course; but I didn't want to use it in case it should give away my position to the enemy. A proper night attack—that's what I wanted to spring on the blighter. See? Well, I came upstairs quiet, and just as I rounded the corner at the other end of this passage I saw some one outside the door of Mr. Bunnett's room. There's a bit of light comes in through the skylight just above; not what you'd call light but not as dark as the stairs: just enough for me to see a sort of figure. So I clicks on my torch: only, me standing close against the wall, the movement hit the torch against it about a second before the light went on: the button's a bit stiff, you see. The blighter heard the sound and it gave him time to nip round the corner and be off; moved like a bleeding streak of lightning, he did. If you'll pardon the expression, just saw his tail light whisking off, as you might say. I goes after him, thinking he'd be bound to run out by the front entrance, but seems like he didn't."

So, punctuation marks are handy gadgets in writing plain language. If you want to, you can even go further and explore the frontiers of punctuation, so to speak: new punctuation marks are always cropping up. Here is one that seems to have a future: figures for enumeration. Of course, figures have always been used in outlines and so on; but nowadays you can watch them becoming a punctuation mark proper. *Time* is an inveterate numberer:

Britain's adherence to unconditional surrender is based on: 1) the determination to reform and re-educate Germany; 2) the equal determination to avoid any truck whatever with Hitler and his gang; 3) the acceptance of the argument that a war between ideas means a European civil war rather than one between nations . . .

. . . But the Nazis did have the sense to install as their No. 1 puppet a Slovak who commands a real following: a canny, bullet-headed nationalist and priest named Joseph Tiso. With political craft and German aid, Tiso has: 1) fed his countrymen relatively well; 2) provided state jobs; 3) promoted Slovaks in government service; 4) suppressed pro-Czechs, by deporting them or threatening to . . .

. . . Costa Rica's Presidential campaign, so bitter that it threatened civil war, ended last week in a comparatively peaceful election (two were killed in an interior village). The winners: 1) Teodoro Picado, candidate of incumbent President Rafael Calderon Gardia's Republicans and of the Leftist *Vanguardia Popular;* 2) Costa Rica, which kept its status as the only democracy in dictator-ridden Central America . . .

EXERCISE

Here is, without punctuation, a piece from Leo M. Cherne's *The Rest of Your Life:*

The United States will not suffer a serious postwar inflation because slowness of reconversion unemployment both business and public uncertainty will work against the dissavings that economists fear so much we wont have inflation because everything that will happen to you will compel you to hold on to your money rather than spend it here is a preview of the kind of deflationary developments that will occur first of all there will be termination unemployment secondly theres the absolute certainty that take home pay will fall youll hold on to your savings much tighter when your weekly pay envelope is thinner and thinner it will be because of the reduction in hours and overtime third youre going to wait for prices to come down wartime conditions forced prices up youll be saying to yourself and youve waited so long you can wait a little longer fourth youll be waiting for the new products that you read about and havent seen in the shop windows why rush out and get a radio when that swell FM television standard short wave combination may be just a few months away fifth and most important theres the basic fact of what the war economy didnt do to you it didnt tighten your belt too uncomfortably and there will be no real pressure for you to slip the strap out of the buckle immediately you havent been starved enough so that youll want to rush out madly and buy if you had been going without shoes in patched up pants in a cotton overcoat as our allies have been doing then certainly youd let loose in the greatest buying spree of your life but no matter how long the war lasts you wont be brought to desperation furthermore however insufficient our future production you will go into the stores and shops certain that you will be able to get all you need for your bodys comfort even if you cant get all you want for your hearts desire no we will not be exclaiming after the war good grief how the money rolls out people will not be letting go instead of a flight from the dollar we will have a desperate clinging to the dollar until employment begins to pick up again and job tenure begins to look more real

Looks like a page from a stream-of-consciousness novel this way, doesn't it? Now translate it into a sane economic argument by punctuating it up to the hilt. Here are the first few lines as a starter:

The United States *will not suffer* a serious postwar *inflation* because:
(1) slowness of reconversion;
(2) unemployment;
(3) both business and public uncertainty—
will work against the "dis-savings" that economists fear so much.

We won't have inflation because everything that will happen to you will compel you to hold on to your money rather than spend it.

Here is a preview of the kind of "*de*-flationary" developments that will occur:

First of all, there will be *termination unemployment . . .*

Chapter Nine

CAN SCIENCE BE EXPLAINED?

When people talk about something that's difficult to read, they are apt to say it's "too technical." The ordinary person, when he gets bogged down in a book or article, wouldn't think of saying, "The author of this can't write"; he will say, "A layman like me will never understand this" and let it go at that. In other words, most people think that some subjects are easy and some difficult and it hardly matters what language is used in explaining them.

I don't agree with those people. The principles of simple language are just as important, or maybe more so, in explaining, say, biochemistry, than they are for a news broadcast. The only difference is this: When you use simple language for anything that is *not* scientific or technical, you can explain it to anybody; but when you simplify science, you will find that only part of it will be understandable to the layman, and another part, however simply stated, will be clear only to people who have some training in that branch of science. There is no scientific discovery or theory that cannot be popularized—up to a point; the important thing is to know just what can be explained to the ordinary person and what can't.

Let me show you an example of what I mean: Some time ago International Business Machines Corporation working with Dr. Howard S. Aiken of Harvard University developed a so-called mathematical robot, that is, an automatic calculator that can solve tremendous, otherwise insoluble mathematical problems. Now how can anybody explain this incredible machine to a layman? At first sight, you would think it's impossible; but that isn't so. In fact, the machine is being operated by laymen; they get a code book prepared by a mathematician and all they have to do is to follow the code and punch holes in a tape. So the *operations* of the machine can be explained very simply; the book probably says something like "First punch hole A6; then punch hole C31" and so on.

But you can also go one step further and explain to a layman what IBM and Dr. Aiken were about when they were building that machine: you can tell what the problem was, for what purpose the machine was going to be used, what theory they had in mind and how they put it into practice, and finally what tests they used to be sure the monster-gadget worked. All this can be told in simple, ordinary language, and if it's properly dramatized and made interesting, it will go a long way toward explaining the *meaning* of this scientific development: not exactly what was done, but why and how it was done. It will give the layman an explanation he can understand, and usually that will be all he wants.

There is, of course, a third kind of explanation, a mathematical explanation of the machine for mathematicians. This, too, can be put in simple language, that is, short sentences, simple words and so on, and that will save mathematicians time and effort in reading their professional journals. But— let's face it—the layman will never understand the formulas and graphs. To understand exactly what IBM and Dr. Aiken have done, you have to have so-and-so many years of higher mathematics, and that's that.

Or let's take another example that happens to be handy. How can the scientific yardstick formula of this book be explained? The answer is exactly the same. Again, there are three levels of explanation, two for laymen, one for scientists only. First, there is the *operation* of the formula: that can be explained by the simple set of directions which you will find in the back of the book. Second, there is the *meaning* of the formula: to explain that properly, I would have to go into the history of language simplifying, the relationship between language and understanding, the readability formulas that were developed by other researchers, the differences between those formulas and this one, and so on. Then I could dramatize the whole story and that would probably give most people all the explanation they want. However, there is still the third level, that of the *scientific* explanation; and here I would have to get into statistical regression formulas and multiple correlation and whatnot, and nobody who hasn't had a course in statistics would know what I am talking about.

Now let's see how the principles of language simplifying apply to these three types of scientific explanation. First, let's take a look at the language of operation sheets, directions, shop manuals, popular mechanics, the literature that tells how to do a technical job. Here is an example I picked at random from a book on papermaking:

> In the event of there being more than one screen serving the machine (as is usually the case) it is necessary to watch carefully the operation of the screens with reference to the stock supplied them, and each valve should be opened or closed in proportion to the capacity of the screen it is feeding. If there is any difference in the capacities of the screens, it is probably due to the cams or toe-blocks being worn, or some other thing affecting the oscillation of the diaphragm.

Now obviously this is not very readable. But what are the obstacles the reader has to face? Certainly *not* the technical terms; in fact, any reader interested in papermaking machines is apt to know what a cam or a toe-block is, and if not, will have no trouble finding out. But that technical knowledge won't make it any easier for him to work his way through "in the event of there being" or "with reference to the stock supplied them" or "in proportion to the capacity." The simple fact is that people who know something about certain technical operations are usually those least equipped for writing about them or explaining what they know to somebody else.

Not so long ago a *New York Times* story described the excellent instruction manuals put out by Bell Telephone Laboratories for the Army and Navy. Let me quote one sentence: "The company has discovered that it is easier to hire a qualified editor and teach him what he needs to know about the technical terms involved than it would be to take a qualified engineer and teach him what he would need to know about the art of editing . . ."

If those papermakers had followed the same principle, our passage would probably read somewhat like this:

> Usually the machine is served by more than one screen. If so, watch carefully how much stock goes through each. To keep the flow even, just open or close the valves. (If you want to make the screens work evenly, look first for worn cams or toe-blocks. Most often that's what makes the difference.)

In other words, all writing of the operation-sheet type should address the reader directly, and should tell him step by step what to do. It's as simple as that. Anybody who writes how-to-do prose should start off by reading a good cookbook; here, for instance, is a model paragraph from Fannie Farmer:

Apple Pie

Line pie plate with pastry. Pare, core, and cut apples in eighths, put row around plate ½ inch from edge, and work towards center until plate is covered; then pile on remainder. Mix sugar, nutmeg, salt, lemon juice, and grated rind, and sprinkle over apples. Dot over with butter. Wet edges of undercrust, cover with upper crust, and press edges together. Prick several places with fork. Bake.

Anybody can understand that, and anybody can understand any kind of technical directions that are written in the same style.

When we come to the second level of scientific explanation, we find, oddly enough, that there is also one single standard formula. The reason is simple: Since the meaning of any modern scientific fact can only be explained by the method of its discovery, and since the scientific method is the same in all branches of science, any such explanation will be the story of a scientist, or several scientists, going through the classic four stages of modern scientific method: observation, hypothesis, deduction, and experimental verification. So this type of popularization will show how a scientist got curious about certain facts, thought up a theory to explain them, devised experiments to prove the theory, and finally tested it and found that it worked. If two scientists working on the same problem can be shown, so much the better: this will make the reader appreciate not only the scientific method, but also the fact that modern science is never a one-man affair.

Popular science written by this standard formula is probably the most educational type of writing there is: it's the only way of making laymen appreciate scientific method. But let's not get into this; let me rather show you a classic example. This is from a *Reader's Digest* article on penicillin by J. D. Ratcliff:

The story of penicillin begins in 1929, when Dr. Alexander Fleming . . . was examining a glass culture plate milky with millions of bacteria. His sharp eye detected something. There was a fleck of green mold on the plate, and around this fleck was a halo of clear fluid. *Something was destroying the bacteria!* A mold that had dropped in from the air was causing their sudden death on an unprecedented scale . . .

Dr. Fleming fished out the mold but research on it stood still for ten years. . . . Then the sulfa drugs came along to reawaken interest in this field.

The sulfa drugs were amazing performers against some bacterial diseases; sorry failures against others. Something better was needed. . . . Dr. Howard Florey of Oxford remembered Fleming's work. That green mold was poison to bacteria on culture plates. Might it not also work in the bodies of men?

Florey and his colleagues . . . decided to investigate . . . They set to work at the tedious task of growing the green mold in earthen-ware flasks. When the mold had grown into a hard, rubbery mat the chemists took over. Hidden somewhere in the mold was a bacteria killer.

By a slow process of elimination, the chemists discarded chemical components of the mold that had no antibacterial effect. In the end they turned up with the minutest pinch of a yellow-brown powdery stuff. This *might* be the bacteria murderer.

The first trials of the yellow powder were run in test tubes. It appeared that as little as one part in 160 million would slow the growth of bacteria! . . . This looked splendid. But there was still a big hurdle to overcome. The stuff somehow poisoned microbes. Might it not also poison men?

Florey and his helpers . . . shot huge doses of sure streptococcus death into 50 mice. Then the mice were divided into two groups of 25 each. One group would get no further attention; the other would get penicillin.

Within 17 hours all the unprotected mice were dead. . . . Hundreds of other mice trials followed, with similarly favorable results.

At last Florey was ready to carry his work from mice to men. . . .

And so on. This is science for laymen at its best, and it's written in typical *Reader's Digest* manner, so that an average person can understand it. But I hope you realize that it is a piece of what might be called science appreciation, not of scientific explanation. It does not even have the chemical formula for penicillin in it. In short, from a scientist's point of view, it offers no explanation at all.

To explain science fully, as I said before, you will have to use a third level of explanation, and this is where the layman will never be able to keep up with you. Suppose, for instance, you are asked for an explanation of what retene is, and the *Encyclopaedia Britannica* gives you the following clue:

> RETENE, an aromatic hydrocarbon occurring in wood tars and obtained by distilling resinous woods. It crystallises in colourless plates melting at 98.5° C and boiling at 394° C. Chromic acid oxidises the hydrocarbon to retene quinone (an *ortho*diketone) and permanganate oxidises the quinone to 3-hydroxy-*iso*propyldiphenyl—1:1′:2′—tricarboxylic acid. These reactions show that retene is methyl-*iso*propylphenanthrene, $C_{18}H_{18}$, with the adjacent structural formula.

Plainly, there is no way of really telling a layman what retene is. To understand it, with or without simple language, you have to be a chemist, and that's that.

There is only one bit of advice I can offer in this business of giving laymen an exact scientific explanation: don't try. It is far better to be as frank as Bertrand Russell in his popular explanation of the relativity theory, who says at one point:

> . . . this part can be expressed by the method of "tensors." The importance of this method can hardly be exaggerated; it is, however, quite impossible to explain it in non-mathematical terms.

Or, if you are unfortunate enough to be assigned to such an impossible job, you might add some sort of apology, the way Gove Hambidge did in the 1941 *Yearbook of Agriculture:*

> . . . The editor would like to point out that to visualize even the more elementary aspects of atmospheric circulation over the earth is not easy, since you have to imagine that you are a mile or two up in the air, on your stomach with your head toward the North Pole, a clock nearby lying on its back so you can readily tell which is clockwise and which counter-clockwise rotation—also a mirror so you can see how everything would be reversed if you

were in the Southern instead of the Northern Hemisphere, and you have to remember constantly that a south wind is a northward-moving wind, an east wind a westward-moving wind, and vice versa.

Chapter Ten

℞ FOR READABILITY

And now let's get down to brass tacks.

Suppose you are facing some bread-and-butter writing job —like the Employee Manual of the Wondrous Widget Company—and you want to apply what I've told you so far in this book.

Here is what you do:

First, make sure you know for whom you are writing. Have a look at your prospective readers. Talk to them. Find out what they know, what they don't know, and what they *want* to know. Take your own private opinion poll on the questions and answers they have in their minds. Use the results: write for your readers and nobody else.

Now collect your material. Get all the information you need; pay special attention to little things that will add color and human interest. Look out for human touches like the fact that old Christopher Crusty, the founder of the firm, was laid up with poison ivy when the millionth Wondrous Widget rolled off the assembly line.

Then, when you have all the stuff you need, stop for a while and do something else. Catch up with your correspondence or work on another assignment for a couple of days. Give your unconscious a chance.

When you are ready to start writing, you will probably have at least one idea for an "angle" or a "plot." Maybe you can build your manual around the life of Matthew Mumble, who has just finished his fiftieth year as assistant bookkeeper; or you can describe the first day at work of Betty Brandnew who has just been hired as a typist. Or maybe that sort of thing doesn't suit your purpose; but *some* kind of basic structure will. There must be a way for you to write something people are going to read—not just a heap of facts.

Once you have gotten that far, it will be easy to figure out what should come first and what last. Don't make that old mistake and start your Employee Manual with four pages on how the company got off to a slow start in 1853. Start with something interesting and promising; wind up with something the reader will remember.

As you write, make sure there's plenty of narrative and a good deal of dialogue. There should be live people in your booklet. When you talk about the company, say *we;* when you talk about the employee, say *you.* There's no excuse for the It-is-expected-that-Employees-of-the-Company-shall school of manual writing.

And now do something about your sentences and words. Short sentences are easy to write. Remember that *compound* sentences—those with *ands* and *buts*—are not so bad; go after the *complex* sentences. Look for the joints where the conjunctions are—*if, because, as,* and so on—and split your sentences up. If you feel this makes your style too choppy, change the punctuation. There's a lot that can be done with semicolons, for instance. "I have raised the semicolon to its zenith," Alexander Woolcott once wrote. Can you say the same?

Short words are harder to manage. Again, it's not the long word that's the trouble, but the *complex* word. Look out for prefixes and suffixes—syllables like *pre, re,* or *de,* and *ality, ousness,* or *ization.* Words with these syllables are those to split or replace. Do it consistently and you'll be surprised at the results.

Probably it won't be easy for you to express yourself in short, simple words. You *say* them every day, but they don't come to you when you sit down to write. This is where you need help—devices, tricks, rules. Here are a few:

First of all, get yourself a dictionary of simple synonyms. I don't mean an ordinary book of synonyms, and I certainly don't mean Roget's *Thesaurus.* (If you pick synonyms out of Roget, you will poison your style in no time.) What I mean is a dictionary where words are explained by the simplest possible definitions. Ordinary dictionaries don't do that; the one I recommend to you is the *Thorndike-Barnhart High School Dictionary.*

Let's say you want to use Thorndike to improve this sentence in your manual: "The Company encourages the continued education of staff members of all ranks to supplement the practical training and experience acquired during office hours."

Look up the key words in this sentence in Thorndike. You will find:

encourage ....urge
continue ....keep up
supplement ....add to
acquire ....get *or* gain

Now use these simpler words with *we* and *you:* "We urge you to keep up your education and add to the practical training and experience you get during office hours."

This gives you a fair idea what Thorndike will do to improve your style.

But you don't even have to use Thorndike to find simple synonyms. I shall give you a sort of miniature Thorndike right here and now.

My simple-word-finder comes in three parts—three lists of words. If you use these three lists conscientiously and fully, your style will soon lose its heaviness and begin to look like the girl in a Success School advertisement *after.*

The first list consists of "empty words." These are particles —prepositions, conjunctions, adverbs, etc.—that belong to the structure of the language. When you remember that these words make up more than 50 per cent of all the words you use, you will understand that it makes a tremendous difference whether they are simple or elaborate. Follow the rule that in general one "empty" word is better than two or three, and a short one is better than a long one. If you can get rid of the "empty" word altogether, so much the better, of course. Here is my list:

Too heavy prepositions and conjunctions

along the lines of: like
as to: about (or leave out)
for the purpose of: for
for the reason that: since, because
from the point of view of: for
inasmuch as: since, because
in favor of: for, to
in order to: to
in accordance with: by, under
in the case of: if
in the event that: if
in the nature of: like
in the neighborhood of: about

in terms of: in, for (or leave out)
on the basis of: by
on the grounds that: since, because
prior to: before
with a view to: to
with reference to: about (or leave out)
with regard to: about (or leave out)
with the result that: so that

Too heavy connectives

accordingly: so
consequently: so
for this reason: so
furthermore: then
hence: so
in addition: besides, also
indeed: in fact
likewise: and, also
more specifically: for instance, for example
moreover: now, next
nevertheless: but, however
that is to say: in other words
thus: so
to be sure: of course

And here are three more words that are almost always superfluous:

concerned
involved
respectively

(Example: "The employees concerned should consult the supervisors involved, respectively.")

My second list consists of auxiliary verbs. This one works on the principle that the more natural and idiomatic English gets, the more it expresses ideas by auxiliary verbs. Take, for instance, this passage from an employee manual: "With a view to broadening the individual's training and increasing his knowledge of the Company's organization, operations and service, members of the staff are selected periodically for advanced training. These training programs are designed to give the individual an opportunity . . ." etc. What you would *say* is something like this: "We'd *like to help you add* to your training and *get to know* the company better . . . Our advanced training programs are *meant to* give you the opportunity . . ." etc. So you see that ordinarily you use a lot of such words as *like to, get to,* and *mean to.* Here is my list:

aim to	help ——ing
be apt to	keep ——ing
be bound to	like to
be known to	mean to
be supposed to	mind ——ing
care to	plan to
claim to	seem to
get to (got to)	stop ——ing
happen to	use(d) to
hate to	want to
have to	

My third list is the longest. Maybe it needs a little explanation. It's a list of simple verbs that describe movements of the human body, with a list of adverbs that can be combined with them. Verb-adverb combinations are a specialty of the English language; it's what the language naturally uses when it needs a new expression for a new idea. Think of the war and of *breakthroughs, blackouts* and *pinup girls.* Or think of sports and of *line-up, strike-out,* and *touchdown.* Or think of *tryout* and *standin, walk-on* and *close-up, checkoff* and *sit-down.*

Of course all kinds of verbs can be combined with all kinds of adverbs, but most important are a group of short Anglo-Saxon verbs that deal with movements of the human body. They are the most idiomatic words in the language; there is a theory that they are also the oldest—those all others stem from. Whether that's true or not, the fact remains that practically all abstract ideas can be expressed by one of these verbs, either by itself or combined with an adverb. Translating high-sounding abstractions into such words as *set up* or *fall through* is a fascinating game.

My list contains fifty verbs and twenty adverbs. Not every verb can be combined with every adverb, of course; but what with different meanings in different contexts, the list covers about a thousand abstract ideas. So it really *is* a miniature Thorndike dictionary.

Verbs			Adverbs	
bear	go	slip	about	forth
blow	hang	split	across	in
break	hold	stand	ahead	off
bring	keep	stay	along	on
call	lay	stick	apart	out
carry	let	strike	around	over
cast	look	take	aside	through
catch	make	talk	away	together
come	pick	tear	back	under
cut	pull	throw	down	up
do	push	tie		
draw	put	touch		
drive	run	turn		
drop	set	walk		
fall	shake	wear		
get	show	work		
give	skip			

This list will not only make your words simpler but will force you to streamline your sentences too. You'll learn to rely on verbs rather than nouns and adjectives. Psychologists have used the ratio between adjectives and verbs for years to measure the forcefulness of writing; writing teachers have been preaching the gospel of the active verb ever since anybody can remember.

The main trouble with most current writing is that it consists of nothing but nouns and adjectives, glued together with prepositions or with *is, was, are,* and *were.* Here are a few random examples:

A historian: "His [Charles A. Beard's] attack on the consequences of intervention is not accompanied by any demonstration of the feasibility of isolation."

An economist: "A problem which has deadlocked top corporate and union officials with no prospect of satisfactory solution is the determination of the appropriate subjects for collective bargaining and the definition of spheres of authority which are of sole concern to management. Rulings of the National Labor Relations Board have not been helpful in drawing a line of demarcation between those matters which are bargainable and those which remain the sole function of management."

An English teacher: "Marcel Proust's vivid description of

the long train of recollections invoked by the taste and smell of a little cake dipped in tea, in *Remembrance of Things Past,* is the ultimate expression of the tremendously important role played by associative processes arising from re-experiencing a sensory impression which was originally associated with a powerful emotion."

A biologist: "Modern taxonomy is the product of increasing awareness among biologists of the uniqueness of individuals, and the wide range of variation which may occur in any population of individuals. The taxonomist is, therefore, primarily concerned with the measurement of variation in series of individuals which stand as representatives of the species in which he is interested."

(This last example is taken from the Kinsey report *Sexual Behavior in the Human Male*—which seems to prove that it wasn't exactly readability that made it a best-seller.)

Now let me do a little translating with my verb-adverb list: "He *takes a stand* against intervention and what *it brings about,* but he doesn't *show* how we could have *got along with* isolation."—"Management and labor have been trying to *set down* rules for what should be *worked out* by collective bargaining and what should *stay under* the authority of management alone. But they are deadlocked and it doesn't *look* as if a real solution is going to *turn up* soon. . . ." etc.

It so happens that these four passages also contain excellent examples on two other points. One is the question of the preposition at the end of the sentence. Take "the species in which he is interested." People don't talk that way. They say "the species he's interested in." Putting prepositions at the end of sentences is one of the things that will unfailingly turn stiff prose into idiomatic English.

The preposition at the end is one of the glories of English prose. Originally it was attacked by grammarians for the silly reason that *prepositio,* in Latin, means something that "comes before"; and when people realized that Latin rules don't always work in English, they defended the old rule for the equally silly reason that a preposition gets too much emphasis at the end of a sentence. The truth is, of course, that the English language is capable of fusing a preposition and another word together whenever they are closely joined by the meaning of the sentence. The word *in,* in the sentence from the Kinsey report, may be grammatically part of the phrase *in which,* but for the speaker of the sentence it is part of the expression *interested-in.*

Which is why the President of the National Council of

Teachers of English recently called a preposition "a good word to end a sentence with" and why Winston Churchill, when such an "error" was pointed out to him, answered: "This is the type of arrant pedantry, up with which I shall not put."

And what would English prose be without sentences like *He was an executive who knew what he was talking about. He could thus be argued with, not muttered at* or *The average American has a fixed idea that liver and iron are substances he ought to be getting more of?*

The four passages on pages 90, 91, are also good examples for the difference between *that* and *which*. There are eight *whiches* in those sentences—all of them misused. In good, idiomatic English it should be *A problem that has deadlocked* and *spheres of authority that are* and *those matters that are* and *those that remain* and *a sensory impression that was* and *the wide range of variation that may* and *individuals that stand* and, of course, the *species he is interested in*. The rule is this: *Which* should be used in a "non-restrictive" clause that could, without damage, be left out or put between parentheses; whenever you can't do that, the clause is "restrictive" and you should use *that*.

Now you will say that after ridiculing other grammatical rules I suddenly turn into a stickler for the *that*-and-*which* rule. But wait a minute. That's exactly the mistake the "progressive" grammarians are making. They see that *which* is used instead of *that* all over the place and so they proclaim that the rule should be thrown into the ashcan with all the other outmoded rules.

But the situation here is quite different. This isn't a case of a grass roots movement against a strict grammatical rule. It's exactly the other way round. The natural idiom is to use *that* for "restrictive" clauses; it always has been and still is. The use of *which* instead of *that* has been dragged into the language by the writers, the literati, the clerks. Jespersen, in his *Essentials of English Grammar*, says: "Which . . . has been gaining ground at the expense of *that*, chiefly in the last few centuries and in the more pretentious kinds of literature. One of the reasons for this preference was probably that [*which*] reminded classical scholars of the corresponding Latin pronoun. When Addison in the *Spectator* complains of the injury done recently to . . . *which* by the 'Jacksprat' *that*, he turns all historical truth topsy-turvy, for *that* was really the favorite relative word in literature from the Middle Ages on; but in deference to his erroneous view of the historical development he corrected many a natural *that* into a less natural *which,* when he edited the *Spectator* in book-form."

When I read this, I naturally looked the matter up in Addison. Sure enough, Jespersen was right: the original versions sound more natural in every single case. Here is one example:

> A screech-owl at midnight has alarmed a family more than a band of robbers; nay, the voice of a cricket hath struck more terror than the roaring of a lion. There is nothing so inconsiderable *that* may not appear dreadful to an imagination *that* is filled with omens and prognostics.

That's the way it originally appeared in the *Spectator;* in the book·edition Addison left it *imagination that is filled* but changed it to *nothing so inconsiderable, which may not appear dreadful.* He shouldn't have; the sentence was perfect as it stood.

Addison, however, was an exception. Usually writers, like the authors of the four examples I quoted, pepper their sentences with unnatural *whiches* right from the start. When they do find out about the distinction, it is often a real revelation to them and they turn into determined *which*-hunters and *that*-fans. Wilson Follett, for instance, who once ran a column on "The State of the Language" in the *Atlantic,* wrote that he was a *which*-writer until late in life, when he was "converted" and "saw the light." And H. W. Fowler tells us that Lord Morley, when he prepared a revised edition of his works, "was particularly keen on having the word *which,* wherever there was the possibility, exchanged for *that . . .*"

After reading all this, you will start *which*-hunting yourself, I hope. You will find it a pleasant and rewarding indoor sport.

Chapter Eleven

DEGREES OF PLAIN TALK

Popularization is a mysterious business.

In November, 1941, the *Journal of the American Medical Association* printed a paper by Drs. Rovenstine and Wertheim, in which the authors reported on a new kind of anesthesia called "therapeutic nerve block." This was obviously of interest to doctors, but nobody bothered to tell the general public about it. The nerve block was not then considered news.

Six years later, the popular magazines broke out into a rash of nerve-block articles. On October 25, 1947, *The New Yorker* began a three-part profile of Dr. Rovenstine; two days later, *Life* published a four-page picture-story of his work. Other magazines followed. Suddenly, the nerve block had become something everybody ought to know about.

I came across this mystery when I was looking for a good example of what popularization does to language and style. The nerve-block articles are perfect specimens. On its way from the *A.M.A. Journal* to *Life* and *The New Yorker,* the new method of anesthesia underwent a complete change of coloring, tone, and style. A study of the three articles is a complete course in readability by itself.

On the following pages are excerpts from the three articles. Nothing has been changed; but to show clearly the differences in sentence length, I have put / between the sentences, and to show the differences in human interest, I have put the "personal words" (see page 303) in boldface and the "personal sentences" (see p. 304, 305) in italics. (You will notice the difference in word length without my pointing it up.)

This is the beginning of "Therapeutic Nerve Block" by E. A. Rovenstine, M.D., and H. M. Wertheim, M.D. (*Journal of the American Medical Association,* vol. 117, no. 19, Nov. 8, 1941):

"Therapeutic nerve block" is but one of the many ramifications of regional analgesia./ The history of the introduction and development of perineural injections of analgesic and neurolytic agents for therapy coincides with that of similar types of injections to control the pain associated with surgical procedures./ The use of surgical analgesic nerve blocks has eclipsed by far similar procedures employed to cure or alleviate pain or symptoms resulting from disease or injury . . ./

The paper ends as follows:

The most interesting and probably more promising and fruitful results from therapeutic nerve blocking are the technics for interrupting sympathetic pathways with analgesic or neurolytic solutions./ This recent practice has already gained wide application and produced many favorable reports./ A comparison of the value of the chemical destruction of sympathetic pathways or surgical section cannot be made accurately with present knowledge and experience, but there are indications that for many conditions the former are to be preferred./

Interruption of the sympathetic pathways at the stellate ganglion is used to cure hyperhidrosis of the upper extremity./ It is useful to relieve sympathalgia of the face and causalgia./ It has been employed successfully to treat post-traumatic spreading neuralgia, the pain of amputation stumps and vasomotor disturbances./ The treatment of angina pectoris after medical remedies have failed to relieve pain is now conceded to include alcohol injections of the upper thoracic sympathetic ganglions./ The same procedure has been effective in controlling or alleviating the distressing pain from an aneurysm of the arch or the descending aorta./

Interruption of the lumbar sympathetic pathways is indicated for conditions in the lower extremities similar to those enumerated for the upper extremities./ This therapeutic nerve block has been employed also to treat thrombophlebitis of the lower extremity./ The results from these injections have been dramatic and largely successful./ Not only is the pain relieved immediately but the whole process subsides promptly./ This remedy represents so much of an improvement over previous therapeutic efforts that it should be used whenever the condition develops./

In *Life* (October 27, 1947) the article about the nerve block carried the heading

PAIN-CONTROL CLINIC

*New York doctors ease suffering by
blocking off nerves with drugs.*

Eight pictures were accompanied by the following text:

Except in the field of surgery, control of pain is still very much in the primitive stages./ Countless thousands of patients suffer the tortures of cancer, angina pectoris and other distressing diseases while their physicians are helpless to relieve them./ A big step toward help for these sufferers is now being made with a treatment known as nerve-blocking./ This treatment, which consists of putting a "block" between the source of pain and the brain, is not a new therapy./ But its potentialities are just now being realized./ Using better drugs and a wider knowledge of the mechanics of pain gained during and since the war, Doctors E. A. Rovenstine and E. M. Papper of the New York University College of Medicine have been able to help two-thirds of the patients accepted for treatment in their "pain clinic" at Bellevue Hospital./

The nerve-block treatment is comparatively simple and does not have serious aftereffects./ It merely involves the injection of an anesthetic drug along the path of the nerve carrying pain impulses from the diseased or injured tissue to the brain./ Although its action is similar to that of spinal anesthesia used in surgery, nerve block generally lasts much longer and is only occasionally used for operations./ The N.Y.U. doctors have found it effective in a wide range of diseases, including angina pectoris, sciatica, shingles, neuralgia and some forms of cancer./ Relief is not always permanent, but usually the injection can be repeated./ Some angina pectoris patients have had relief for periods ranging from six months to two years./ While recognizing that nerve block is no panacea, the doctors feel that results obtained in cases like that of Mike Ostroich (*next page*) will mean a much wider application in the near future./

The New Yorker (October 25, 1947) in its profile of Dr. Rovenstine describes the nerve block like this:*

> . . . . Recently, he [Rovenstine] devoted a few minutes to relieving a free patient in Bellevue of a pain in an arm that had been cut off several years before./ The victim of this phantom pain said that the tendons ached and that his fingers were clenched so hard he could feel his nails digging into his palm./ Dr. Rovenstine's assistant, Dr. E. M. Papper, reminded Rovenstine that a hundred and fifty years ago the cure would have been to dig up the man's arm, if its burial place was known, and straighten out the hand./ Rovenstine smiled./ *"I tell you,"* he said./ *"We'll use a two-per-cent solution of procaine, and if it works, in a couple of weeks we'll go on with an alcohol solution./ Procaine, you know, lasts a couple of weeks, alcohol six months or longer./ In most cases of this sort, I use the nerve block originated by Labat around 1910 and improved on in New Orleans about ten years back, plus one or two improvisations of my own."*/ (Nerve blocking is a method of anesthetizing a nerve that is transmitting pain.) Rovenstine does little anesthetizing himself these days, except when he is demonstrating his methods at his lectures./ He carries only a small practice outside Bellevue./ If he is called in on routine cases, he asks extremely high fees./ He proceeds on the principle that a person who wants him to handle a routine operation ought to pay well for him./ If he is asked to apply his specialized knowledge to an unusual case, he doesn't care what the fee is./ Like a great many other doctors, he feels that only millionaires and indigents get decent medical care./ People of these two classes are the only ones who feel that they can call on the leading surgeons and Rovenstine.
>
> The man with the pain in the non-existent hand was an indigent, and Rovenstine was working before a large gallery of student anesthetists and visitors when he exorcised the ghosts that were paining him./ Some of the spectators, though they felt awed, also felt inclined to giggle./ Even trained anesthetists sometimes get into this state during nerve-block demonstrations because of the tenseness such feats of magic induce in them./ The pa-

---

* From an article by Mark Murphy in *The New Yorker*. Copyright 1947 The New Yorker Magazine Inc.

tient, thin, stark-naked, and an obvious product of poverty and cheap gin mills, was nervous and rather apologetic when he was brought into the operating theatre./ He lay face down on the operating table./ *Rovenstine has an easy manner with patients, and as his thick, stubby hands roamed over the man's back, he gently asked, "How you doing?"*/ *"My hand, it is all closed together, Doc,"* the man answered, startled and evidently a little proud of the attention he was getting./ *"You'll be O.K. soon,"* Rovenstine said, and turned to the audience./

"One of my greatest contributions to medical science has been the use of the eyebrow pencil," he said./ He took one from the pocket of his white smock and made a series of marks on the patient's back, near the shoulder of the amputated arm, so that the spectators could see exactly where he was going to work./ With a syringe and needle he raised four small weals on the man's back and then shoved long needles into the weals./ The man shuddered but said he felt no pain./ Rovenstine then attached a syringe to the first needle, injected the procaine solution, unfastened the syringe, attached it to the next needle, injected more of the solution, and so on./ The patient's face began to relax a little./ *"Lord, Doc,"* he said. *"My hand is loosening up a bit already."*/ *"You'll be all right by tonight, I think,"* Rovenstine said./ *He was.*

That the language of the three articles is different, everybody can see. But it's not so easy to tell *how* different. For that, let's look at a few figures (see the readability test formula on pp. 296-306):

	A.M.A. Journal	Life	New Yorker
Average sentence length in words	20.5	22	18
Average word length in syllables (per 100 words)	194	165	145
Per cent "personal words"	0	2	11
Per cent "personal sentences"	0	0	41

What has happened is this: *Life* magazine naturally had to

be more readable than the *A.M.A. Journal*. So it avoided words like *analgesic* and *thrombophlebitis* and otherwise presented the facts in more or less newspaper fashion. Effect: The words in *Life* are 15 per cent shorter than those in the *A.M.A. Journal*. (The sentences would be shorter too if Drs. Rovenstine and Wertheim hadn't written exceptionally short sentences to begin with—for two doctors, that is.) But *Life* didn't bother to dramatize the facts and make them humanly interesting. (Probably the magazine relied on its pictures for that; I'll get to that question in Chapter 13.) *The New Yorker* began *its* popularization of the nerve block where *Life* left off: its sentences are a good bit shorter than those in *Life* (19 per cent), and aside from that, there's a story, there's drama, there's something that's interesting to read. The nerve block has become an experience to the reader.

This gives us a good clue to the baffling question of what readability means. In most dictionaries, *readable* is defined as "easy *or* interesting to read." (It also has another meaning, *legible*, but we'll skip that here.) Actually, to most people, readability means ease of reading *plus* interest. They want to make as little effort as possible while they are reading, and they also want something "built in" that will automatically carry them forward like an escalator. Structure of words and sentences has to do with one side of readability, "personal words" and "personal sentences" with the other.

That's why, in this book, a piece of writing is given not one readability score but two: a "reading ease" score and a "human interest" score. Length of words and sentences are

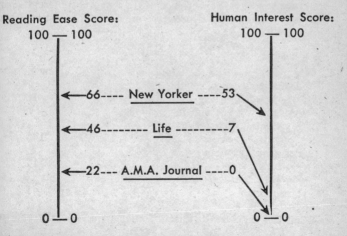

Reading Ease Score:
100 — 100

Human Interest Score:
100 — 100

←——66———— New Yorker ————53 ↘

←——46————————— Life ————————7 ↘

←——22———— A.M.A. Journal ————0 ↘

0 — 0   0 — 0

combined into one, "personal" words and sentences into the other. (If you want to learn how to figure a score, see pages 296-306.)

Working out the scores of our three articles on nerve blocking, we get this picture:

Life is much easier to read than the *A.M.A. Journal,* but gets hardly "off the ground" with human interest; *The New Yorker* is still easier than *Life,* and, in addition, is as interesting to read as fiction.

All this doesn't mean, of course, that the writers for *Life* and *The New Yorker consciously* did something about their sentences and words. Naturally not. But if we want to find out something about any art or skill, we must analyze the work of leading performers, and then laboriously imitate their seemingly effortless performance. There's no guarantee that we'll ever become champions this way, but at least we can try.

Chapter Twelve

THOSE UNPREDICTABLE READERS

Put this book down for a minute and think of what you do when you read. How does it work? Your eyes look at printed symbols on paper and your mind thinks the thoughts of the person who wrote the words. How does this miracle happen?

It is a miracle, all right. I won't go into the long history of the invention of writing and the alphabet; let's just look at you with the letters on a page in front of you. Scientists know pretty well what goes on in reading—up to a point; but when we have learned all about fixations, regressions, spans of recognition, and so on, the miracle is greater than ever.

If you think you just pick up the meanings of words one after the other, you are wrong. Language is not as simple as that. What you do is this: Your eyes move along the printed lines in rhythmic *jumps*. After each jump they rest for a short while, focus on a word or two, and move on. From time to time, when you unconsciously feel the need of checking back, your eyes move *back*. And that's the pattern: rhythmic movements, brief fixations on a word or two depending on your span of recognition, irregular regressions. All this at the rate of about 250 words a minute if you are an average person reading average writing—with your eyes taking about one-third of a second to do their work between movements. And in this third of a second, they take in, on the average, *more than one word*.

But that's not the whole story. Words don't mean anything by themselves or even in groups of two or three. Words get their meanings from the context—from the sentence they are in, or even the whole paragraph. So after your eyes have seen the words, your mind assigns to these words a *provisional* meaning, "good only until further notice." Then, when the end of the phrase, sentence, or paragraph is reached, your mind *rethinks* the words in the light of what came after. Reading is really a miracle: Your eyes pick up groups of words in split-second time and your mind keeps these words in delicate balance until it gets around to a point where they make sense.

Take the first sentence of this chapter, for instance. In slow motion, here is how you probably read it:

Put this
(No meaning yet)
   book down
(You didn't put the book down at this point, did you? You waited with your decision until you had read a little more.)
     for a minute
(You still didn't.)
       and think
(?)
         of what
(?)
           you do
(?)
             when you
(?)
               read.

(Now at last you were reasonably sure of what each word meant in this sentence. But you didn't put the book down at this point either. You waited until you knew how serious I was with my suggestion.)

And that's the way we read: we race along, making quick guesses at the meanings of little bunches of words, and quick corrections of these first guesses afterward. To anyone who knows the process, it's a wonder we ever read anything right.

What all this means to a writer is obvious. A writer must know how people read, what are the main sources of reading errors, and what can be done to possibly forestall them.

The commonest reading error, of course, is mistaking one word for another. As I said, our eyes take in a word or more in one-third of a second. That means that we don't have time to read words letter by letter; we look at the general shape of a group of letters and take them in *as a whole*. This is why good proofreaders are so rare: in ordinary reading we don't notice such things as typographical errors but take them in our stride.

For example, take the following passage from a story about prize fights by John O'Hara, which I read recently:

> "See what I mean, Arthur? He knows when the fix was in. And of course ring stragedy. Does he know ring stragedy! . . ."

It so happens that *stragedy* was the only word in that story that was deliberately misspelled to indicate the character's level of speech. When I read it the first time, I *thought* I was reading the correct spelling *strategy.* (Maybe you did too.) Only when I came to the second *stragedy* did I catch on to Mr. O'Hara's excellent transcription of spoken English.

Or take the following from a book review:

> Man has a brief memory for the gadgets he contrives to give him comfort and convenience in the world. He easily forgets, too, the means by which he labors to loose his spirit from the flesh . . .

When I had read up to this point, I realized that I had read first *to lose his spirit;* then, after having read *from the flesh,* I looked back and, for the first time, saw the second *o* in *loose.* At first sight, I had taken it for granted that the sentence dealt with the common kind of spirit that is being *lost* and not with the rare kind that is being *loosed.*

Or, to take a rather outrageous example, consider what happened to me once when I tried to read Toynbee's *Study of History* late at night after a tiring day. I held the book in my lap, vainly struggling against intense drowsiness, when suddenly I was pulled up wide awake by a word that simply didn't belong in Toynbee. The word was *horseradish.*

This couldn't be. I reread the passage and this is what I read:

> Perhaps we can discern this even in the reactions of the Christianized Celts of Britain under Roman rule. We know very little about them, but we know that they produced, in Pelagius, a heresiarch who made a stir throughout the Christian world of his day.

So that was it. My eyes had encountered *heresiarch,* a word I had never seen before, and had conveyed to my mind the only word I knew that could possibly produce a similar general impression: *horseradish.* My mind had been willing to put up with something ludicrous rather than believe the evidence before my eyes that such a word as *heresiarch* existed.

Moral of all this: Don't use unfamiliar spellings or strange words. People's eyes will refuse to read them.

Another source of trouble is little words. Since we usually read two or more words at one glance, it's the little words—like *of, in, if, that*—that we read out of the corners of our eyes, so to speak. In fact, we ordinarily don't read them at all but simply assume they are where they belong. This is the principle of much rapid-reading teaching—where people are trained to skip over particles—and it's also the basis of that money-saving language, *cablese*.

If you have never seen cablese, here is a nice example:

> OTTAWA MACKENZIEKING TUESDAY EQUALLED WALPOLE RECORD FOR LENGTH SERVICE AS PRIMINISTER BRITISH COMMONWEALTH COUNTRY
>
> RESOUNDING DESK THUMPING FROM ALL CORNERS CHAMBER GREETED PRIMINISTER AS HE TOOK SEAT SMILING BROADLY
>
> SINCE ELECTION 29/12 1921 MACKENZIEKING BEEN CANADAS NATIONAL LEADER 7629 DAYS
>
> SIR ROBERT WALPOLE PRIMINISTER BRITAIN SAME NUMBER FROM 3/4 1721 TO 11/2 1742
>
> MEMBERS ALL PARTIES JOINED SPEECHES TRIBUTE

The words left out here—*of, of a, of the, the, his, his, has, for, was, of, the, of, in, of*—are exactly those that we are apt to skip over in reading ordinary writing. We know we don't need to read them to get the meaning.

But that's where the trouble starts. Quite often the little words *are* important and by skipping them we are apt to misread the sentence. Here are a few trivial examples from my own reading:

> The fact that the more sensitive and subtle writing is, the more difficult it is to analyze, is significant of the intricacy of the art of the narrative.

(When I came to *is significant*, I had to start the sentence all over again. What I had first read was this: "In fact, the more sensitive and subtle writing is, the more difficult it is to analyze. . . .")

Another man told me that shortly after the United

States entered the war, he wanted a garbage can of a certain size, but because of priorities he was unable to locate what he wanted.

(I don't know at what point I realized here that I had skipped the fifth word, *that*.)

When that kind of talk got to Washington, it, of course, sounded like ridiculous—even dangerous—nonsense.

(The first time I read this, I simply didn't see the *it*.)
Or take the following excerpt from a bill of lading:

If this bill of lading is issued on the order of the shipper, or his agent, in exchange or in place of another bill of lading, the shipper's signature to the former bill of lading as to the statement of value or otherwise, or election of common law or bill of lading, shall be considered a part of this bill of lading as fully as if the same were written or made in or in connection with this bill of lading.

This excerpt was given to 250 college students as part of a psychological test in reading comprehension. To make sure they knew the vocabulary, two words were specially explained to them: *shipper* ("one who ships or sends goods") and *bill of lading* ("an account of goods shipped by any one, signed by the agent of the transportation line, thus forming a receipt for the goods"). Then they were asked the following question:

A bill of lading has been copied from a signed original because the shipper's copy is worn and torn and he wants a fresh copy. Must the shipper sign this new copy?

The right answer is "No." But one out of five students gave the wrong answer. Why? Part of the reason, it seems to me, is that you have to focus sharply on the little words if you want to get the right meaning out of all that legalistic jargon. Probably most students would have given the right answer had the little words been emphasized this way:

If *this* bill of lading is issued . . . in place of another . . ., the shipper's signature to the *former* bill of lading

... shall be considered a part of *this* bill of lading ...
as if ... written ... in ... *this* bill of lading.

There are two things you can do to avoid this kind of
reading mistake: Either make the particles less important by
rewriting your sentences or, if you feel you have to stick to
your sentence structure, underline (italicize) the particles.
(If you don't like underlining, make them long enough to
catch the eye: write *however* instead of *but,* and *but only if*
instead of *if*.)

The classic paper on mistakes in reading was written by
Professor Thorndike more than 40 years ago, in 1917. He
analyzed children's mistakes in reading and discovered an
important principle: Words and word groups may have so
much meaning for a reader that they blot out the meaning of
other words around them. Thorndike called this the "overpotency" of words. For example, one of his test passages
dealt with school attendance in the town of Franklin. But
some of the children couldn't resist the strong connotations
of the word *Franklin* and said the passage dealt with *Benjamin*
Franklin.

Another of the test passages read as follows:

> John had two brothers who were both tall. Their
> names were Will and Fred. John's sister, who was short,
> was named Mary. John liked Fred better than either of
> the others. All of these children except Will had red
> hair. He had brown hair.

When the children were asked "Who had red hair?" *one-
fifth* of those in grades 6, 7, and 8, and *two-fifths* of those in
grades 3, 4, and 5, gave the wrong answer. The word-combi-
nation *Will had red hair* was too strong for them.

I have no doubt that this important principle applies to
adult readers as well as to children. In fact, I have two pieces
of evidence from my own reading. Here they are, for what
they are worth:

In *Time's* Music Department I read this:

> To most U.S. music listeners, Milton Katims is not a
> familiar name, but it soon may be. No one else his age
> (38) has managed to link his career with the top names
> in two musical fields: Toscanini and the Budapest String
> Quartet. This week for the first time he conducted Tos-

canini's NBC Symphony Orchestra in the first of two Sunday broadcasts.

He has fashioned his career as carefully as Amati fashioned violins. As a violist, he bows to few besides William Primrose. His recording with the Budapest String Quartet of the Mozart *C Major Quintet* was chosen, by five U.S. music critics in the *Review of Recorded Music,* as the outstanding chamber-music album of 1946.

(Reading this, I first thought that Mr. Katims had been a *violinist.* The Amati violins had blotted out the comparatively rare word *violist.*)

In the *Saturday Review* I came upon this:

Dr. Barr resigned as president of St. John's College in December 1946 to start a new college in Stockbridge, Mass., but was forced to abandon the project because of construction costs. He originated the radio program "Invitation to Learning," and has been on CBS's adult educational board since 1928. Fired by Clarence Streit's "Union Now," he . . .

(At this point I had the impression that the *Union Now* organization had dismissed Dr. Barr. No wonder: The writer of the paragraph, with his over-potent words *resigned* and *abandoned,* had given me the impression of a record of failure. So, naturally, I gave the word *fired* the meaning that fitted in. But I was wrong!)

Fired by Clarence Streit's "Union Now," he became a director of the movement and served about a year as contributing editor to Freedom and Union.

There is no perfect remedy for this sort of thing, but it will help your writing if you watch out for pairs of "contagious" or "allergic" words—like *violins* and *violist,* or *resigned* and *fired.* Incidentally, there are two words in the English language that are constantly misused and misunderstood because of such a situation: *presently* (which is "allergic" to *present*) and *scan* (which is "allergic" to *skim*). *Presently* means *soon* (except in archaic English) and *to scan* means *to read carefully.* The dictionaries are beginning to yield to the universal mistake and to list *presently* (in current use) as *now,* and *to scan* as *to glance at.*

A very common source of misreading, as everybody knows,

is the use of the negative. This is so generally recognized that almost all languages provide for an emphatic double negative to make sure of understanding. In English, however, the double negative is frowned upon as illiterate, with the effect that practically every negative statement is open to error and misreading.

Part of the reason is that *not* is a short word—one of those we don't focus on or don't read at all. The Army and Navy had the sensible rule to use NOT REPEAT NOT in all telegrams. And a good idea it was, too.

Another reason is that the double negative comes naturally—sometimes even to educated people. Witness the following two sentences from the usually grammatical *New York Times:*

> This is only one of the pictures which *never* would have been made *unless* the enterprising, tireless and often audacious [Clarence S.] Jackson had *not* made them.

And:

> The house [the Duke and Duchess of Windsor rented on Long Island] is approached by way of a narrow, inconspicuous driveway that runs parallel with the rear entrance to the Cedar Creek Club and would *not* be noticed *only* by persons looking for it.

Or this from a court decision:

> In respect to the other quantity discounts, it does *not* appear that the differentials resulting from the discounts are *not* based upon or related to due cost allowances in the manufacture, sale and delivery of these products. *Neither* is there testimony to the contrary.

What people don't realize is that every negative word will turn a sentence upside down—not just *not, never* or *nothing,* but also *unless, neither, refuse, decline, lack, failure, unable, belie,* and hundreds of others. Read the following sentence from a recent dispatch and understand it without rereading if you can:

> NEW YORK, April 8 [1948]—A spokesman for Henry A. Wallace denied today that Wallace had messaged the Italian Foreign Ministry disavowing authorship of an

article front-paged in Rome last Friday by the Communist organ Unita.

If you want still more evidence, this little news item is to the point:

> COLUMBUS, Ga., April 15 [1948]—Embarrassed city attorneys today discovered one of their legal fences contained a *"not* hole."
>
> The city had haled a contractor into court on charges of failure to procure a license.
>
> The contractor pointed out the law which said no license was required if the construction job "exceeds a sum of $500."
>
> The city hastily dropped the charges and corrected the typographical error, making the law read that no license is required if the project "does not exceed a sum of $500."

My point is *not* that these illogical negatives don't make sense. On the contrary, the intended meanings were so clear that proofreaders and countless readers read them into the items without noticing what was actually there in black and white.

Which brings me back to the underlying theme of this chapter: Readers are apt to read words that aren't there. Sometimes, as I have shown, such mistakes can be predicted and avoided but often they cannot. There is nothing you can do about the kinds of mistakes Freud describes in his *Psychopathology of Everyday Life:*

> Both irritating and laughable is a lapse in reading to which I am frequently subject when I walk through the streets of a strange city during my vacation. I then read ANTIQUES on every shop sign that shows the slightest resemblance to the word; this displays the questing spirit of the collector.

Or:

> One woman who is very anxious to have children always reads *storks* instead of *stocks.*

Another case of misreading was reported by a psychologist who referred to Shakespeare's *Henry VIII* in one of his books.

What appeared in print was a reference to "Shakespeare's *Edward VIII*"—in spite of the fact that the author, his wife, his collaborator, and a proofreader had each seen the false reference in first galley proofs, second galley proofs, and page proofs. The explanation for this astonishing case of multiple misreading is simple: all this happened in the fall of 1936, when the front pages and people's minds were full of King Edward VIII.

Finally, here is a possibly Freudian case that concerns a negative. William Empson tells it in his book *Seven Types of Ambiguity:*

> Misreadings of poetry, as every reader must have found, often give examples of the plausibility of the opposite term. I had at one time a great admiration for that line of Rupert Brooke's about
>
> > The keen
> > Impassioned beauty of a great machine,
>
> a daring but successful image, it seemed to me, for that contrast between the appearance of effort and the appearance of certainty, between forces greater than human and control divine in its foreknowledge, which is what excites one about engines; they have the calm of *beauty* without its complacence, the strength of *passion* without its disorder. So it was a shock to me when I looked at one of the quotations of the line one is always seeing about, and found that the *beauty* was *unpassioned,* because *machines,* as all good nature-poets know, have no hearts. I still think that a prosaic and intellectually shoddy adjective, but it is no doubt more intelligible than my emendation, and sketches the same group of feelings.

It seems clear to me that in this case the reader, William Empson, was a better poet than the writer, Rupert Brooke. But the trouble is that you can't count on that kind of creative misreading: for every William Empson, who will read *unpassioned machines* into *impassioned machines,* there are thousands like you and me, who will read a *heresiarch* into *horseradish.*

Chapter Thirteen

ARE WORDS NECESSARY?

"Easy writing's vile hard reading," wrote Sheridan. The reverse is equally true: easy reading is difficult to write. In fact, it seems to be so difficult that most people would rather try anything else but write when they face a job of simple explanation. They escape from words into pictures, symbols, graphs, charts, diagrams—anything at all as long as it's "visual." They point to the movies, the comics, the picture magazines. Obviously, they say, the trend nowadays is away from reading. People would rather just look.

That may be so; but unfortunately the idea that you can explain things without explaining them *in words* is pure superstition. A favorite proverb of the picture-and-diagram lovers is "One picture is worth more than a thousand words." It simply isn't so. Try to teach people with a picture and you may find that you need a thousand words to tell them exactly what to look at and why.

If that surprises you, look at the evidence. There's the psychologist, for instance, who tried to find out whether children understood the charts and diagrams in the *Britannica Junior Encyclopedia*. It turned out that they did not. Most of the devices used blithely by the encyclopedia writers were way over the heads of the children. They had been taught how to read, but nobody had ever bothered to tell them anything about how to look at flow charts, statistical graphs, process diagrams, and the like. (Unfortunately, the experiment didn't show whether a normal child, reading an encyclopedia, will even stop and look at a diagram. I suspect he won't: the temptation to skip what is baffling is too great.)

Another psychologist tested grownups—soldiers and college students—on their understanding of graphs and charts. The results were even more startling. The vast majority were unable to see what the charts and graphs were supposed to show: they couldn't even grasp general facts or spot basic trends. Again, the reason is clear: people need training to learn from visual aids. Usually, they don't have that training. In fact, the less education they have, the less they are able to profit from these "helps to readers." Let me quote the experimenter's conclusions: "It is not often sufficiently recognized by those who advocate visual methods of presentation that the graph and the chart are no more immediately representational and no less symbolic of the information they are intended to convey than are verbal and mathematical statements. But whereas nearly everyone in the course of their upbringing acquires some facility in making verbal statements of ideas and meanings, only the specially educated learn to interpret general factual information from graphs and charts."

Naturally, that doesn't mean that you should never illustrate visually what you have to say. Not at all: anything pictorial or graphic does help *as long as there is enough text to back it up.* I don't mean captions; I mean that the running text has to tell the reader what the illustration means, how he should look at it, and why. Tell the reader what to see. Remember that graph-and-chart reading is not one of the three R's.

Let me give you an example. Some time ago *Time* magazine told its readers about a *Harper's* article by C. Hartley Grattan, entitled "Factories Can't Employ Everybody." *Time* summarized the article in three paragraphs plus the following chart:

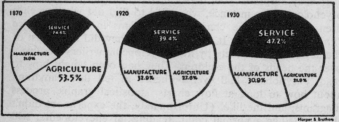

Harper & Brothers

The caption under this chart read: EXPANDING SERVICE INDUSTRIES NOW PROVIDE NEARLY HALF OF U.S. JOBS.

Now what did you get out of this chart? What do you think a *Time* reader got from it (*if* he bothered to look at it way down at the bottom of the page)? Certainly not more than what the caption says: almost half of the now employed work in service industries.

But Mr. Grattan in his original *Harper's* article meant to tell much more with his three pie charts. And he did, by tying them into his running text like this:

Look first at this statistical pie, which shows the proportions of Americans engaged in various main occupations in 1870:

You will see that more than half of all Americans who were classified as working in 1870 were in agriculture (with which we have included forestry and fishing); that a little over a fifth were in manufacturing (with which we have included mechanical occupations and mining); and that a little less than a quarter were in the service industries.

By 1920 a vast change had taken place. The agricultural slice of the 1920 pie had shriveled; both the manufacturing slice and the service slice had swollen. Here is the 1920 pie:

Now look at the 1930 pie, and you will note a curious fact. Not only has the agricultural part of the pie undergone further shrinkage; *the manufacturing part has also*

shrunk a little, relatively, while the service industries slice has grown still more:

Why this change? The best answer has been given by two British economists, Allan G. B. Fisher and Colin Clark. They have shown that a comparatively primitive economy has a large proportion of its people engaged in farming; that as it develops, more and more people move over into manufacturing; but that in a really advanced economy, the proportion of people engaged in the services gains at the expense of *both farming and manufacturing.*

You see? Mr. Grattan used his charts to make a special point but was wise enough to explain the explanatory chart with 227 words of text. He was obviously afraid that even the educated readers of *Harper's* magazine wouldn't get his point from the charts alone (although it's all there in black and white). There's hardly any doubt that he was right.

A second drawback in using visual aids is this. People not only don't know what to look for, their eyes also have a way of being caught by the wrong things. Take a dozen people and let them look at a picture in *Life.* Chances are that each one of them will focus on a different set of details.

It's an old story that pictures can be interpreted in different ways. Illustrations like this one

WHAT'S HAPPENING

TO WHERE YOU LIVE

In 1790

In 1840

In 1890

TODAY

BY RAY BETHERS

are old standbys in psychology texts. (You can "see" the cubes from above or from below.) There are even a number of widely used tests that are based on the fact that no two people will see the same things in inkblots or simple pictures. It's literally true that you can't tell what a given illustration will mean to a given reader.

Of course, even the most imaginative reader won't be able to do much with such simple charts as those used by Mr. Grattan. But as soon as you add a bit of decoration, you are apt to get into trouble. There is even some danger in the so-called pictorial statistics with their rows of little men or coins or bags or boats: chances are that your symbols for "one million unemployed" will remind at least one reader of his late uncle who was a millionaire.

Let me try to make my point by a little experiment. On page 115 you will find some census statistics as illustrated by Mr. Ray Bethers and printed in *This Week* magazine—except that I have left out the captions under the pictures and one line of explanatory text below.

Now look at this series of pictures and ask yourself what it suggests to you. Does it tell you what it is supposed to tell you—how the ratio between city and country population has changed? Does it tell you anything more? What else do the little pictures suggest?

When you have answered these questions, turn to page 118 and look at Mr. Bethers' little picture story the way it actually appeared. As you see, the point is that the country population has dropped from 95 per cent to 43 per cent, and the city population has risen from 5 per cent to 57 per cent. And there is that very important last line: "Cities and Towns are defined as having 2500 population or more." You couldn't possibly have guessed all that by just looking at the pictures; in fact, you probably were misled by the six-story apartment building under TODAY which made you think of a big metropolitan city rather than a small town. (At least that's what *I* thought at first.)

Mind you, I don't mean to disparage Mr. Bethers' pleasant and instructive piece of work. On the contrary, I think it shows well that the better and more imaginative the art work, the less it will be able to take the place of verbal explanation. If you want to give your reader something to look at, well and good; but if you have to tell him something, tell him.

In other words, nothing is self-explanatory—it's up to you to explain it. And you'll have to do it *in words*.

Chapter Fourteen

HOW TO OPERATE A BLUE PENCIL

I don't know whether efficiency experts ever made time and motion studies of the work done by copy editors in a publishing house. If they did, they must have found that editors spend 90 per cent of their time crossing out words in manuscripts and shifting around those that are left. Look over any editor's shoulder for a while and you'll see that I am right.

It's hard to remember this when you are your own editor, revising something you have written yourself. Let's face it: Those words you liked so well when you wrote them will probably have to be cut in half and completely rearranged.

Go to a library to get practical advice on writing and you'll find that nothing has been recommended so often and so warmly as cutting. Two thousand years ago Pliny the Younger wrote: "I apologize for this long letter; I didn't have enough time to shorten it." (This has also been attributed to a dozen other great writers.) Dr. Samuel Johnson's only rule for writing was: "Read over your compositions, and when you meet with a passage which you think is particularly fine, strike it out." This was echoed by the late Sir Arthur Quiller-Couch: "If you require a practical rule of me, I will present you with this: Whenever you feel an impulse to perpetrate a piece of exceptionally fine writing, obey it—whole-heartedly—and delete it before sending your manuscripts to press. *Murder your darlings.*"

In other words, whenever you write, you are tempted to use expressions of which you are fond and proud. Usually it will be just these words and phrases that will stop the reader or throw him off. While you are writing you can't spot them; you are too strongly attached to what has just sprung from your mind. But in the cold light of "the morning after" you are able to look at them with a detached reader's eye.

WHAT'S HAPPENING
TO WHERE YOU LIVE

In 1790

95% of the people lived in the Country—

while only **5%** lived in Cities and Towns

In 1840

90% of the people lived in the Country—

and only **10%** lived in Cities and Towns

In 1890

65% of the people lived in the Country—

and **35%** lived in Cities and Towns

TODAY

Only **43%** live in the Country—

while **57%** live in Cities and Towns

BY RAY BETHERS *Source: U. S. Bureau of the Census.*
Cities and Towns are defined as having 2500 population or more

The need for transposing may be harder to see. Somehow, at first writing, we don't always hit on the best arrangement of words for emphasis. The rule is simple enough: The place for emphasis is at the end. But while we write, we have a tendency to overlook the reader's need for sentence rhythm and buildup.

Newspaper lead sentences, with their perverse deliberate anticlimax, are fine material for anyone who wants to learn transposing. For example:

> VANCOUVER, Wash., March 24, 1948—Death instead of help came to all but two survivors of an Army plane crash in the snowcapped mountains north of here despite their frantic attempts to signal search planes.

Did you feel the emphasis on *help, two,* and *search planes?* The pull of the natural rhythm of the sentence is so strong that it's almost impossible to get the meaning without rereading. Let's do a little transposing:

> VANCOUVER, Wash., March 24, 1948—North of here, in the snowcapped mountains, an Army plane crashed. The survivors tried frantically to signal search planes; but when help came, all but two had died.

Here is another gem—a typical press-release lead:

> An increase of nearly 50 per cent in the reliance of American business on professional industrial designers to give their products consumer appeal from an art, engineering and merchandising standpoint was indicated in a survey by the American Management Association in collaboration with the Society of Industrial Designers, released yesterday.

Transposed, this reads:

> Yesterday the American Management Association and the Society of Industrial Designers released a survey. It showed that American businessmen want to give their product consumer appeal from the standpoint of merchandising, engineering and art: their use of professional industrial designers has increased 50 per cent.

Of course, newspaper leads are notoriously anticlimactic.

For a pleasant change, let me show you a lead paragraph in which the emphasis is just right. It's from *The New Yorker*—a bit of reporting by one of its stars, James Thurber:*

> In the intolerable heat of last August, one Ezra Adams, of Clinton, Iowa, strode across his living room and smashed his radio with his fists, in the fond hope of silencing forever the plaintive and unendurable chatter of one of his wife's favorite afternoon programs. He was fined ten dollars for disturbing the peace, and Mrs. Adams later filed suit for divorce. I have no way of knowing how many similarly oppressed husbands may have clapped him on the back or sent him greetings and cigars, but I do know that his gesture was as futile as it was colorful. He had taken a puny sock at a tormentor of great strength, a deeply rooted American institution of towering proportions. Radio daytime serials, known to the irreverent as soap opera, dishpan drama, washboard weepers, and cliffhangers, have for years withstood an array of far more imposing attackers, headed by Dr. Louis I. Berg, a New York psychiatrist and soap opera's Enemy No. 1.

This is worth rereading for its perfectly balanced rhythm—from the languid beginning "In the intolerable heat of last August, one Ezra Adams, of Clinton, Iowa, strode across his living room" to the whiplash ending "soap opera's Enemy No. 1." Each sentence leads the reader up to something, with just the right number of words to give him the right impression. (There is nothing wrong with a sentence average of 33 words if you are as readable as Thurber.)

As I said, you will have done most of your revision job when you have cut your original copy to pieces and turned the sentences upside down. The rest of your morning-after work is hardly more than odds and ends.

There is punctuation, for one thing. Since you will shorten your sentences, you'll make many commas into periods. Other commas you'll take out since the better sentence rhythm will make them unnecessary. You will tie some of your short sentences together by using semicolons instead of periods between them—or colons, if the first sentence serves as a curtain-raiser to the second. You will improve the paragraphing—

---

* By permission. Copyright 1948 James Thurber. Originally published in *The New Yorker*.

usually by breaking longer paragraphs into two or three smaller ones. Your shorter sentences will force you into shorter paragraphs; there is a natural relation between the two.

You will use more punctuation for emphasis. You will underline (italicize) words and phrases to be stressed, and put parentheses around those you want to de-emphasize. You will help the rhythm of your sentences by using a dash here and there—like this.

In short, you will try at this point to see your words as the reader will see them. If your writing is to be printed, this will mean that you have to visualize it in type. You'll need to know these basic rules about readable typography:

(1) Any type size under 10 point is hard to read.

This is 10 point type.
This is 8 point type.
This is 6 point type.

This book is printed in 9 point type.

(2) Anything printed in an unfamiliar type face is hard to read.

(Imagine a whole book printed in this advertising display type.)

(3) If there is no leading (white space) between the lines, lines longer than 40 characters and spaces are hard to read. The printers' rule of thumb is "one-and-a-half alphabets" (39 characters or spaces) per line. (This book is printed with about 62 characters per line, but has 2 points leading between the lines.)

(4) Headings printed in capitals only are hard to read. It is easier to read headings in capitals and lower-case letters, particularly if printed in bold face.

You will also try to use the arrangement on the page to make reading and understanding easier. This will mean that you will tabulate information rather than bury it in running paragraphs. The remainder of the press release I just quoted is a good example:

Designers, it was learned, are employed by more than 90 per cent of companies manufacturing consumer products who responded to the poll. They are also employed by 80 per cent of companies manufacturing packages or products sold in packages and by 70 per cent of concerns manufacturing industrial goods. About 25 per cent of the companies producing consumer goods depend for their designs entirely on consultant designers.

The survey also disclosed that decision on designs is a function of top management in a majority of 133 companies that provided information and more than half of the companies surveyed use consultant designers exclusively or in addition to full-time staff designers.

In more than one-third of the companies surveyed the design of the product is recognized as so important that the choice of the designer and the supervision of his work are made the responsibility of the president or other senior administrative officers. An additional fifth of the companies assigned responsibility for design policy to committees on which all departments are represented, which is "roughly equivalent to leaving design policy to top management," the report stated.

Statistics are almost impossible to understand if presented in this fashion. Maybe you will say that you can't give a newspaper reader statistical tables or graphs. Of course not. But there is a middle way:

According to the 133 companies that answered the poll, consultant or staff designers are now used by
    70 per cent of the industrial-goods manufacturers;
    80 per cent of the package or packaged-goods manufacturers;
    90 per cent of the consumer-goods manufacturers.
More than half the companies use consultant designers, either exclusively or in addition to full-time staff designers. One-fourth of the consumer-goods manufacturers use consultant designers exclusively.

In most companies decisions on design are a function of top management: in more than one-third of the companies designers are chosen and supervised by the president or a vice-president, and in another 20 per cent by interdepartmental committees.

All this, of course, belongs to the garden variety of editing and revision. As I said, it's the kind of editing any ordinary person could or should do the morning after he has committed a piece of writing.

Things are different when it comes to tricky business like digesting or abstracting. Such editorial handicraft is beyond the call of duty of the ordinary person; but it's worthwhile to know something about the basic principles.

The first thing to understand is that abridgments are of

two kinds: the *Chemical Abstracts* kind and the *Reader's Digest* kind. One boils things down for the hurried information-seeker, the other puts it in convenient shape for the reader who is faced with an empty little chink of leisure time. The difference, of course, lies in the principle of selection: in one case you look for the inner core of facts, in the other, for the tastiest bits of reading matter.

Since most writing consists of a structure of facts and ideas covered with digressions, comments, and illustrations, this means that the same piece of writing may be shortened in two directions, so to speak, with entirely different results. The same scientific article may be digested one way for scientists and another way for laymen. On the face of it, it may look impossible that both versions were derived from the same material: but each may be just right for its readers.

Nowadays, the *Reader's Digest* type of condensation is familiar to everybody; the other type is familiar to the scientist or professional worker, but usually unfamiliar to the general public. In recent years, however, one such abridgment has become a national best-seller: D. C. Somervell's one-volume edition of Arnold J. Toynbee's six-volume *Study of History*. It is a perfect specimen of its kind: While Toynbee's original work is a fascinating maze of digressions and historical illustrations, the abridgment resembles, as one reviewer wrote, "a tree in winter." It presents Toynbee's map of world history without taking the reader on any of the author's delightful trips.

While I was reading Somervell's one-volume Toynbee, the question occurred to me what a *Reader's Digest* editor would have done with the same material. So, just for the fun of it, I took a random passage in the Somervell volume, looked up the corresponding half dozen pages in the six-volume original and then worked out a reasonable facsimile of a *"Reader's Digest* condensation" *of the same pages*. Here is the result.

This is the passage I found in Somervell: *

> Perhaps simplification is not quite an accurate, or at least not altogether an adequate, term for describing these changes. Simplification is a negative word and connotes omission and elimination, whereas what has happened in each of these cases is not a diminution but an enhancement of practical efficiency or of aesthetic

* From *A Study of History* by Arnold J. Toynbee, abridged by D. C. Somervell. Copyright 1946 by Oxford University Press, New York.

satisfaction or of intellectual grasp. The result is not a loss but a gain; and this gain is the outcome of a process of simplification because the process liberates forces that have been imprisoned in a more material medium and thereby sets them free to work in a more ethereal medium with a greater potency. It involves not merely a simplification of apparatus but a consequent transfer of energy, or shift of emphasis, from some lower sphere of being or of action to a higher. Perhaps we shall be describing the process in a more illuminating way if we call it, not simplification but etherealization.

And here is my own corresponding *"Reader's Digest* article".†

About the middle of the 19th century, in the days of the Industrial Revolution, there was an English sailing ship that used to make the voyage to China, year by year, with the same English crew and finish by going up the Yangtse, three days' sail upstream, with the same Chinese pilot.

One year the owners scrapped the old sailing ship and sent their men out in a new-fangled steamer. All the way out the crew speculated about the impression the steamer would make on the Chinese pilot. Their curiosity was titillated. As they approached the point off the China coast where the pilot always came on board they had a tense feeling of expectancy.

At last the pilot stepped onto the steamer's deck, made his customary salutation to the Captain, and walked to the wheel. "Now he will have his surprise," thought the Englishmen, "when he finds the ship moving forward with not a sail bent on the yards." But when the engines started, they were astonished to see that not a muscle moved on his face. He kept his place at the wheel without uttering a word.

"Well," the crew said, "his mind works slowly. He'll ruminate all day and tell us his thoughts in the evening." But the day passed, and the evening, and the night. The pilot said nothing, kept his place at the wheel, and quietly did his business as always. The second day and night passed likewise, and the third and last day arrived—the day on which he was to take his leave.

† Abridged from *A Study of History,* 3rd vol. Used by permission.

At this point the Englishmen forgot their resolution to leave it to the pilot to break the silence first. They asked him what impression their ship had made on him. "This ship?" the Chinese said. "Why, once upon a time we used to make ships like this in China too. Gave them up some time ago, though. Must be about two thousand years since we used them last."

The Chinese had only contempt for a steamship, or any other piece of clockwork. His own people, he meant to say, had anticipated the Western "Barbarians" in exploiting physical nature but had learned many centuries ago that this material world was not the place where human beings should lay up their treasure. So they had shifted their interest and energy from industrialism to a different sphere.

What does this comparison prove? That Toynbee's original work should have been used as the basis for a different popular version? That Somervell's one-volume edition is unreadable? But if that's true, you will say, how did it manage to stay on the best-seller lists for such a long time? Doesn't my little experiment prove just the opposite from what it was supposed to prove?

Well, I wonder. Compared with the millions who read and enjoy the *Reader's Digest* and similar magazines, the thousands of readers of even a nonfiction best-seller are only a drop in the bucket. And how many among those who bought the Toynbee abridgment ever got beyond the first hundred pages?

Chapter Fifteen

HOW TO BE A FLUENT WRITER

Some time ago I talked to a friend of mine who, like myself, had for years been teaching an evening class in writing. Being competitors, we decided to compare notes on our experiences.

"What's your main problem?" I asked him.

"My main problem," he said, "is always the same. I get swamped. During the whole period of the course, I spend every weekend buried under a mountain of papers. It's a terrific chore."

Nothing could have surprised me more. Not only were my weekends happily free of papers to correct, but on the contrary I always had just the opposite trouble: I could never manage to get my students to write enough. They just didn't produce. I tried this and that, I begged, I coaxed, I implored them—it was no use. I had long ago come to the conclusion that the average student would do anything rather than write.

What was the explanation for this enormous difference between our two writing courses? Obviously this: My friend taught creative writing and I taught the other, practical kind. People who take creative-writing courses have an urge to write, people who take practical-writing courses have a writing phobia.

Naturally, there are exceptions to this basic rule. About once every year, there appeared among my students a specimen of the "creative" type and I was handed long, wordy slices of autobiography, fictionalized experiences, and essays on philosophical themes. Thinking back over the years, I arrived at the conclusion that about one out of fifty adult Americans suffers from graphomania—which is defined in *Webster's Unabridged Dictionary* as a "morbid desire or mania for writing." The remaining forty-nine are victims of the much more common ailment of "graphophobia"—which is not listed in Webster's but certainly ought to be.

There is some statistical evidence for what I just said. In 1949 someone took a public-opinion poll in the city of Louisville, Kentucky, and found that 2.1 per cent of the voting population "wanted to write." I don't doubt that this figure is roughly true for the country as a whole. There are about 2 per cent graphomaniacs among us—people who have desk drawers full of stories and essays and unfinished novels, people who fill evening classes in creative writing, people who have the diary habit—in short, people whose nervous systems crave the activity of putting words on paper, just as those of alcoholics crave liquor.

Of course, among those 2 per cent there are a few that are successful and have made a name for themselves as authors. But they too can be classified as neurotics, just like their more unfortunate fellow writers who get nothing for their efforts but rejection slips. Dr. Edmund Bergler, well-known psychiatrist and author of the book *The Writer and Psychoanalysis,* states categorically that he has never encountered a normal writer, either in his office, or in private life, or in examining the life histories of writers. There is no such thing as a normal writer, he says; normal people just don't feel impelled to write.

I could illustrate this verdict with literally dozens of statements by famous writers who have described their neurotic attitude toward writing. I'll just quote one, which struck me as unusually pathetic when I read it. This is from the essay "Voyage with Don Quixote" by Thomas Mann, the late German Nobel prize winner, written during a slow boat trip across the Atlantic:

May twentieth. I ought not to do what I am doing: sitting bent over to write. It is not conducive to well-being, for the sea is, as our American table-mates say, "a little rough," and though I agree that our ship moves quietly and steadily, yet her motions are more felt up here on this desk where the writing-room is than they are below. Nor is looking through the window advisable, for the rising and falling of the horizon attacks the head in a way well known from an earlier experience but forgotten until now. Also it is not very healthy to gaze down upon paper and script. Curiously, obstinately persevering is the old habit of settling to composition so soon as breakfast and the morning stroll are over. It persists under the most contrary circumstances.*

Isn't that pitiful? Here is Thomas Mann, sixty years old and world-famous, and yet unable to enjoy his ten days' trip to New York without the daily dose of his writing drug. (Having no other project on hand, he decided to reread *Don Quixote* and write a long essay on *that*.)

However, this is not a book for or about "creative" writers. Chances are—about forty-nine to one, as I said—that you are *not* one of them, that you never felt "driven" to writing and can't understand the state of mind of a person who is. You don't keep a diary, you hate writing letters, and it would never occur to you to submit a story or article to a magazine. You are just an ordinary American, suffering from graphophobia like practically all the rest of us.

One of my most important jobs in this book is to prescribe a remedy for this graphophobia of yours. Here it is:

Do each writing job as if it were an informal talk to your reader. Don't start without notes—or at least specific ideas— on what you are going to say. And don't stop before you have said it.

That's all. Do this a thousand times and you'll be a seasoned professional writer. Do it for practice every day for a month or two and you'll be on your way toward getting rid of your graphophobia for good.

Let me go into a few details. As you can see, what I am trying to do here is to teach you writing by following the pattern of a course in public speaking. The most important element in such a course is the extemporaneous speech, made by one member of the group in front of the rest, who form a critical audience. The student learns public speaking by doing something he has never done before.

Take a typical student in a public-speaking course. What *did* he do before when called upon to address a group? Doubtless, whenever he was faced by such an emergency, he carefully prepared his speech in advance and *read* it to his audience, mortally afraid of injecting even one word or phrase into his prepared script.

This, in public speaking, is the number-one fault: the preparation of a speech in advance, robbing it of all personal

---

* From "Voyage with Don Quixote" in *Essays of Three Decades* by Thomas Mann, translated by H. T. Lowe-Porter. Copyright 1947 by Alfred A. Knopf, Inc.

flavor and naturalness. The same applies to writing. You have to begin by changing your basic habit, which, as of now, corresponds exactly to the prepared script and the speech that is not spoken but read aloud. If I am right—and I know I am—you go about any writing job piecemeal, slowly formulating a sentence and putting it down on paper, then stopping and thinking, preparing the next sentence in your mind, putting *that* down on paper, pausing again to think of what to say next, slowly formulating another idea, writing *it* down, stopping again, rereading what you have written, working up to the next sentence, thinking it over, searching for a transition, hesitating, inserting a qualification, writing again, stopping, thinking, searching for a word . . . etc., etc., *ad infinitum*. It's writing, after a fashion, but it's as different from the real thing as drafting a speech sitting alone at your desk is from addressing a roomful of people.

So you have to get used to the idea of "prewriting"—doing research, taking notes, organizing your material—and then writing, at an even speed, keeping up a flow of talk to your reader without any awkward pauses or hesitations.

How fast should you write? That's hard to say. Just to give you a standard—or rather an ideal to aim at—I'll tell you that a competent newspaperman, according to one estimate, averages about 1,000 words an hour. This checks with a passage from the autobiography of Anthony Trollope, the Victorian novelist, which has become rather famous among professional writers:

> All those I think who have lived as literary men—working daily as literary laborers—will agree with me that three hours a day will produce as much as a man ought to write. But then he should so have trained himself that he shall be able to work continuously during those three hours—so have tutored his mind that it shall not be necessary for him to sit nibbling at his pen, and gazing at the wall before him, till he shall have found the words with which he wants to express his ideas. It had at this time become my custom—and it still is my custom, though of late I have become a little lenient to myself—to write with my watch before me, and to require from myself two hundred and fifty words every quarter of an hour. I have found that the two hundred and fifty words have been forthcoming as regularly as my watch went.

If you write double-spaced on ordinary typewriter-size paper, you'll get about 250 words on one page—just about Trollope's output in a quarter of an hour. This, of course, as I said, would be top professional speed; you'll probably work considerably slower—even if you are a fast typist or if you dictate. However, the speed isn't too important; what's important is, as Trollope points out, the steady work and the absence of pauses for staring into empty space.

Why is this so? Because good writing must read like the author talking to the reader; and to read like that, it must be written like that. If the author has stopped in his writing for two minutes and has sat, thinking, with a vacant look on his face, then the reader is bound to feel it somehow. There is nothing on paper to show this interval, but it's there nevertheless, disturbing the communication between their minds like static. It's as if a speaker should suddenly stop talking and treat his audience to two minutes of utter silence while he is thinking of what to say next.

This sense of the writer talking without a break to his reader, this invisible mark of an easy flow of words is *the* most important thing there is about writing. It is there and will come through if you know what you are going to say beforehand and put on paper in one go, simply talking to your reader on paper; it isn't there if you write in any other way. It cannot be faked; and there is no substitute method of writing that will have the same effect.

Let's look at what this means practically. It means that if you do this talking-to-your-reader-on-paper at the top, or Trollope, speed of 250 words in 15 minutes, you'll produce in 15 minutes what the average American reader will read in about a minute and a quarter. (American adults read at about 150 to 200 words a minute. This is practically identical with the average speed of talking, which is about 180 words a minute; it therefore corresponds to the average speed of *listening* to conversation or to an informal speech.) In other words, a good professional writer will take about 15 minutes to write something that will be read in a minute and a quarter. If he does it in the way I have just described, it will be as easy to read as ordinary conversation is to listen to.

Now the amateur writer, who hasn't gained this feeling of the basic relationship between writing time and reading time, will invariably try to stuff his writing with too much material —too many facts, too many ideas, too many qualifications, too many adjectives, too many "extras." The pro, who knows in his bones that his fifteen minutes of writing time means a minute and a quarter of reading time, will automatically give the reader just as much as he can take; the amateur will fall into the trap of that blank page before him and fill it up to the brim with stuff to read. Readers like things to be brief, he tells himself; so let's condense. Let's fill every nook and cranny in each sentence with a descriptive adjective here and an allusion there; let's fit in added facts, historical side-lights, wry comment—it's amazing how much you can get into a single paragraph if you just try.

There is a kind of writing—done not by amateurs but by top professionals—where this type of condensation is done on principle and for a reason: I mean the news magazines. Look at a random sample from *Time* as an illustration:

> Setting down at New Delhi in a BOAC Britannia late one morning last week, Britain's Harold Macmillan found Union Jacks fluttering over India's capital in festive display for the first time since the British Raj moved out in 1947. Out at the airport to greet the only British Prime Minister ever to visit India while in office was an array of notables headed by Jawaharlal Nehru and backed up by thousands of cheering citizens.
>
> In the four days that followed, Harold Macmillan—who plans to visit five Commonwealth nations in as many weeks—donned festal garlands, shucked off his shoes before placing a wreath on Mahatma Gandhi's shrine, ceremonially visited the spot from which British forces launched their final assault on Old Delhi during the Indian Mutiny in 1857. . . .

I take it that you read this excerpt at your usual reading speed. Were you able to take it all in? Can you answer a set of test questions about it? When did the British move out of India? When was the Indian Mutiny? How long is Mr. Mac-millan's trip going to take? What kind of plane did he travel on? Was he the first Prime Minister ever to visit India? Or the first since India gained independence? Or the first what? How long did he stay in New Delhi? How long in Old Delhi? Where did he put on a garland? Where did he take off his shoes? Did he arrive in the morning? At noon? At night?

If you can answer all these questions without looking back at the excerpt from *Time*, then you are a very good reader indeed. Most people can't. They would read such a paragraph, getting the general sense, but forgetting most of the details as soon as they had read them.

In other words, they read with the same degree of effort and attention they ordinarily put into listening. Now just imagine what *you* would get out of it if someone told you, at normal conversational speed: "Setting down at New Delhi in a BOAC Britannia late one morning last week, Britain's Harold Macmillan found Union Jacks fluttering over India's capital in festive display for the first time since the British Raj moved out in 1947. Out at the airport to greet the only British Prime Minister ever to visit India while in office . . ." etc. (Of course, it's almost impossible to imagine that, since no one ever talks like that, every sentence starting with a modifying clause, and dozens of items of information tucked carefully into all available spaces.)

And now compare this compact, staff-researched and staff-written piece of writing with the opposite kind: a piece of writing researched by one person and written by the same person in one uninterrupted flow. This is a sample from "Inside Fashion" by Eugenia Sheppard, a woman's column appearing in the New York *Herald Tribune:*

> Anybody who is anybody seems to be getting a lift— by plastic surgery—these days. It's the new world-wide craze that combines the satisfactions of psychoanalysis, massage, and a trip to a beauty salon. The same girls who used to make a life study of detecting dark hair roots are now authorities on other girls' face repairs— how much and how often. ("I know positively. I've seen the tiny scars behind her ears.") Plastic surgery is in about the same state of repute as hair dyeing was twenty years ago, approved by the avant garde but sniffed at as slightly unholy by the conservatives. Look at what has happened to hair dyeing. Anything goes nowadays. . . . High prices of plastic surgeons and hospitalization seem to be what's holding back the mass appeal of plastic surgery in this country. Its benefits are coveted not only by women who want to look younger but by younger women who for some mysterious reason all want to look alike. Fashion models are consulting plastic surgeons to erase under-eye circles and up their bosom lines. Over in Paris the trend is more advanced and the tariff said to be less. While I was reporting the Paris collections, I ran into an old friend who had just been "done." She spoke of it with the rapture of a convert to a new faith. . . .

This, I think, is a fair example of writing with enough substance to be interesting but not so much as to overwhelm the reader. You'll find this sort of relaxed and leisurely writing in almost all the columns—they wouldn't be widely syndicated if they didn't have this quality of easy readability. You'll find it in all magazine articles—they wouldn't otherwise be accepted by the editors. And you'll find it in all books, fiction and nonfiction, that manage to become popular best-sellers.

A good place to look for masterpieces of this kind of seemingly effortless prose is in the books written by famous authors toward the end of their career—at the stage when the business of talking to a reader has become second nature to them and when the last traces of nervousness and self-consciousness have long ago disappeared. Here, for instance, is Stephen Leacock, seventy-three years old and writing his twenty-sixth book, *How to Write:*

> Suppose a would-be writer can't begin. I really believe there are many excellent writers who have never written because they never could begin. This is especially the case of people of great sensitiveness, or of people of advanced education. Professors suffer most of all from this inhibition. Many of them carry their unwritten books to the grave. They overestimate the magnitude of the task; they overestimate the greatness of the final result. A child in a "prep" school will write "The History of Greece" and fetch it home finished after school. "He wrote a fine History of Greece the other day," says his proud father. Thirty years later the child, grown to be a professor, dreams of writing the History of Greece—the whole of it from the first Ionic invasion of the Aegean to the downfall of Alexandria. But he dreams. He never starts. He can't. It's too big.
>
> Anybody who has lived around a college knows the pathos of these unwritten books. Moreover, quite apart from the non-start due to the appalling magnitude of the subject, there is a non-start from the mere trivial difficulty of "how to begin" in the smaller sense, how to frame the opening sentences. In other words how do you get started?
>
> The best practical advice that can be given on this subject is, don't *start*. That is, don't start anywhere in particular. Begin at the end: begin in the middle, but *begin*. If you like you can fool yourself by pretending that the start you make isn't really the beginning and

that you are going to write it all over again. Pretend
that what you write is just a note, a fragment, a nothing.
Only get started.

This is beautifully relaxed writing. Look at the wonderful
artistry with which Leacock produces the quotation "He wrote
a fine History of Greece the other day." There it is, in the
middle of a paragraph, having just popped out of nowhere
into Stephen Leacock's mind and used immediately to brighten
the whole page. Imagine yourself trying to "work in" such
an anecdote. You would take three paragraphs for it, awk-
wardly beginning with "This reminds me of . . ." and winding
up with a lame "Thus we see. . . ."

Or look at the content of these three paragraphs. If you
stop to analyze it, Leacock was actually sidetracked. He started
to give advice on how to begin, then got off on a tangent
about his academic friends who dreamed of vast scholarly
projects, and then had to backtrack to his original subject.
But does it matter? That's the way the old man would have
explained the business to an amateur writer who had come
to see him, and his rambling three paragraphs on how to start
a piece of writing are still meatier and more valuable than
anything ten times as compact that you would find in a textbook.

For still another example, here is seventy-three-year-old
Mark Twain, writing, writing, writing, filling his autobiography
with whatever happens to interest him. One part of it is
called "Is Shakespeare Dead?" and deals with the perennial
question of who wrote the plays. Mark Twain was convinced
that Shakespeare did *not*. Here is one chapter of his argument. (This will be the longest quotation in this book, but I
feel it's worth while to give you a few pages of Mark Twain.
To learn the art of leisurely writing, you ought to do some
leisurely reading.)

When Shakespeare died, in 1616, great literary pro-
ductions attributed to him as author had been before the
London world and in high favor for twenty-four years.
Yet his death was not an event. It made no stir, it attracted no attention. Apparently his eminent literary
contemporaries did not realize that a celebrated poet had
passed from their midst. Perhaps they knew a play-actor
of minor rank had disappeared, but did not regard him
as the author of his Works. "We are justified in assuming" this.

His death was not even an event in the little town of Stratford. Does this mean that in Stratford he was not regarded as a celebrity of *any* kind?

"We are privileged to assume"—no, we are indeed *obliged* to assume—that such was the case. He had spent the first twenty-two or twenty-three years of his life there, and of course knew everybody and was known by everybody of that day in the town, including the dogs and the cats and the horses. He had spent the last five or six years of his life there, diligently trading in every big and little thing that had money in it; so we are compelled to assume that many of the folk there in those said latter days knew him personally, and the rest by sight and hearsay. But not as a *celebrity?* Apparently not. For everybody soon forgot to remember any contact with him or any incident connected with him. The dozens of townspeople, still alive, who had known of him or known about him in the first twenty-three years of his life were in the same unremembering condition: if they knew of any incident connected with that period of his life they didn't tell about it. Would they if they had been asked? It is most likely. Were they asked? It is pretty apparent that they were not. Why weren't they? It is a very plausible guess that nobody there or elsewhere was interested to know.

For seven years after Shakespeare's death nobody seems to have been interested in him. Then the folio was published, and Ben Johnson awoke out of his long indifference and sang a song of praise and put it in the front of the book. Then silence fell *again*.

For sixty years. Then inquiries into Shakespeare's Stratford life began to be made, of Stratfordians. Of Stratfordians who had known Shakespeare or had seen him? No. Then of Stratfordians who had known or seen people who had seen Shakespeare? No. Apparently the inquiries were only made of Stratfordians who were not Stratfordians of Shakespeare's day, but later comers; and what they had learned had come to them from persons who had not seen Shakespeare; and what they had learned was not claimed as *fact*, but only as legend—dim and fading and indefinite legend; legend of the calf-slaughtering rank, and not worth remembering either as history or fiction.

Has it ever happened before—or since—that a celebrated person who had spent exactly half of a fairly long life in the village where he was born and reared, was able to slip out of this world and leave that village voiceless and gossipless behind him—utterly voiceless, utterly gossipless? And permanently so? I don't believe it has happened in any case except Shakespeare's. And couldn't and wouldn't have happened in his case if he had been regarded as a celebrity at the time of his death.

When I examine my own case—but let us do that, and see if it will not be recognizable as exhibiting a condition of things quite likely to result, most likely to result, indeed substantially *sure* to result in the case of a celebrated person, a benefactor of the human race. Like me.

My parents brought me to the village of Hannibal, Missouri, on the banks of the Mississippi, when I was two and a half years old. I entered school at five years of age, and drifted from one school to another in the village during nine and a half years. Then my father died, leaving his family in exceedingly straitened circumstances; wherefore my book-education came to a standstill forever, and I became a printer's apprentice, on board and clothes, and when the clothes failed I got a hymn-book in place of them. This for summer wear, probably. I lived in Hannibal fifteen and a half years, altogether, then ran away, according to the custom of persons who are intending to become celebrated. I never lived there afterward. Four years later I became a "cub" on a Mississippi steamboat in the St. Louis and New Orleans trade, and after a year and a half of hard study and hard work the U.S. inspectors rigorously examined me through a couple of long sittings and decided that I knew every inch of the Mississippi—thirteen hundred miles—in the dark and in the day—as well as a baby knows the way to its mother's paps day or night. So they licensed me as a pilot—knighted me, so to speak— and I rose up clothed with authority, a responsible servant of the United States Government.

Now then. Shakespeare died young—he was only fifty-two. He had lived in his native village twenty-six years, or about that. He died celebrated (if you believe everything you read in the books). Yet when he died nobody there or elsewhere took any notice of it; and for sixty years afterward no townsman remembered to say anything about him or about his life in Stratford. When the inquirer came at last he got but one fact—no, *legend*— and got that one at second hand, from a person who had only heard it as a rumor and didn't claim copyright in it as a production of his own. He couldn't, very well, for its date antedated his own birth-date. But necessarily a number of persons were still alive in Stratford who, in the days of their youth, had seen Shakespeare nearly every day in the last five years of his life, and they would have been able to tell that inquirer some first-hand things about him if he had in those last years been a celebrity and therefore a person of interest to the villagers. Why did not the inquirer hunt them up and interview them? Wasn't it worth while? Wasn't the matter of sufficient consequence? Had the inquirer an engagement to see a dog-fight and couldn't spare the time?

It all seems to mean that he never had any literary celebrity, there or elsewhere, and no considerable repute as actor or manager.

Now then, I am away along in life—my seventy-third year being already well behind me—yet *sixteen* of my Hannibal schoolmates are still alive today, and can tell— and do tell—inquirers dozens and dozens of incidents of their young lives and mine together; things that happened to us in the morning of life, in the blossom of our youth, in the good days, the dear days, "the days when we went gypsying, a long time ago." Most of them creditable to me, too. One child to whom I paid court when she was five years old and I eight still lives in Hannibal, and she visited me last summer, traversing the necessary ten or twelve hundred miles of railroad without damage to her patience or to her old-young vigor. Another little lassie to whom I paid attention in Hannibal when she was nine years old and I the same, is still alive —in London—and hale and hearty, just as I am. And on the few surviving steamboats—those lingering ghosts and remembrancers of great fleets that plied the big river in the beginning of my water-career—which is exactly as long ago as the whole invoice of the life-years of Shakespeare numbers—there are still findable two or three river-pilots who saw me do creditable things in those ancient days; and several white-headed engineers; and several roustabouts and mates; and several deck-hands who used to heave the lead for me and send up on the still night air the "Six—feet—*scant!*" that made me shudder, and the "M-a-r-k—*twain!*" that took the shudder away, and presently the darling "By the d-e-e-p —*four!*" that lifted me to heaven for joy. They know about me, and can tell. And so do printers, from St. Louis to New York; and so do newspaper reporters, from Nevada to San Francisco. And so do the police. If Shakespeare had really been celebrated, like me, Stratford could have told things about him; and if my experience goes for anything, they'd have done it.

Isn't this beautiful? Do you understand now why I called it a prose masterpiece? Did you notice how the old man goes on at his own measured pace, slowly setting forth his argument, seemingly wandering from the point, rambling, digressing, reminiscing, and yet nailing down his argument so that it becomes enormously powerful? When he is through building up his case, he simply stops and starts a new paragraph. Instead of worrying about a smooth, elegant transition, he simply says: "Now then." Later, he has to start another paragraph, containing the climax of his argument, and again he says: "Now then." That's all; but the reader is right there with him, taking in every word that is there, listening to what the old man has to say, and—perhaps—getting convinced.

Now then (to borrow a phrase). What I tried to show you with these examples is the essence of the natural, "spoken" style of writing, the kind that is produced by simply talking to your reader across the sheet of paper between you—talking slowly, leisurely, but without awkward silences, without going back to reformulate a sentence, without ever losing touch with the reader at the other end of the line of communication. This is the kind of writing you have to learn, and you can't learn it as long as you are shy, nervous, inhibited, afraid of putting your ideas on paper.

So you'll have to practice. You can overcome these inhibitions of yours only by practice in writing, just as you can learn public speaking only by practice in speaking. The exercise that follows is therefore *absolutely essential* if you want to get full value out of this book.

EXERCISE

This exercise will be the framework for the next exercises in this book.

During the period of one month (two months would be even better) write a daily 500-word letter to a close friend or relative. Pick someone who lives at a distance and is willing to help you improve your writing—your mother, brother, aunt, ex-roommate, or whoever else is the most obvious choice. Write to that person and tell him or her about this daily-letter plan, so that you'll be committed to it. (Don't substitute make-believe letters or diary entries for this exercise; it is essential that you actually send off letters to someone else.)

Here are the rules of the game:

1. Write at least 500 words every day. At first, count the words; later you'll be able to estimate the number of words on each page.

2. Set yourself a time limit of half an hour. Make every effort to write your 500 words during that half hour. That means, *do not stop to think.*

3. Know what you want to say before you start writing. You can think of what should go into your letter at odd moments during the day. Make sure you have enough material before you begin. As a rule, report on the events of the day.

4. Always write informally. Use as many contractions as possible. Underline freely for emphasis. Use parentheses for casual mention.

5. Don't be afraid to digress.

Chapter Sixteen

FIRST PERSON SINGULAR

One of the most important events in the history of writing happened on February 28, 1571. On that day Michel de Montaigne, a 38-year-old French nobleman who up to that time hadn't shown any signs of unusual literary ambitions, suddenly quit public life, left Paris and the Royal Court for good, and retired to the library of his country house to devote the rest of his life to writing. That country house with its library still stands and, for all I know, tourists can go there today on sightseeing buses. There they can look at an inscription on the wall that reads (in Latin): "In the year of our Lord 1571, at the age of thirty-eight, on the last day of February, being the anniversary of his birth, Michel de Montaigne, long weary of the service of the Court and of public employments, while still in his full vigor, betook himself to the bosom of the learned virgins; where, if the fates permit, he may pass, in calm and freedom from all cares, what little shall yet remain of his allotted time now more than half run out. This his ancestral abode and sweet retreat he has consecrated to his freedom, tranquillity, and leisure."

Why was this such an important event? Because Montaigne, in the book that he proceeded to write, picked a subject that nobody in the whole history of literature had tackled before. Montaigne's *Essays,* to the utter astonishment of his contemporary readers, dealt with—of all things—Montaigne himself.

He knew very well that this was unheard of. "Because I found I had nothing else to write about," he said, "I presented myself as a subject. When I wrote of anything else, I wandered and lost the way. . . . If the novelty and strangeness of my idea don't save me, I shall never come off with honor in this foolish attempt. It is the only book of its kind in the world. . . .

It is so fantastic and extraordinary that perhaps it will pass.
. . . I have no other aim but to reveal myself. However insignificant these essays of myself may be, I will not conceal
them any more than my old bald pate. . . .

"Custom has made it a fault to speak of oneself, and obstinately forbids it, in hatred of the boasting which always
seems to attach itself to self-testimony. . . . My trade and
art is to live my life. He who forbids me to speak of it according to my understanding, experience, and habit, may as
well expect an architect to speak of buildings, not as he himself regards them, but as his neighbor does, not from his own
knowledge, but from another's."

And so Montaigne proceeded to write about himself—
three volumes of essays about his boyhood, his family, his
education, his house, his travels, his books, his illnesses, his
friends, his dreams, his interests, his habits, his experiences,
his opinions, his religion, his sex life—a huge random collection of everything that occurred to him, put down without
any sequence or plan, just as it passed through his mind. As
the years went by, this continuing self-portrait got steadily
more intimate, more detailed, more microscopic. By the
time he was fifty-five and wrote his last essay, Montaigne
rambled on like this: "I cannot, without trying myself, either
sleep by day, or take snacks between meals. . . . I could dine
without a table-cloth, but very uncomfortably without a clean
napkin. . . . I never dine before eleven nor sup till after six.
. . . I like to sleep hard and alone, even without my wife, in
regal style, and rather well covered up. . . . I prefer to rest,
either lying or sitting, with my legs as high or higher than my
seat. . . . I mostly scratch the insides of my ears, which are
at times liable to itch. . . . I prefer bread with no salt in it.
. . . It tires me and disagrees with me to talk on a full stom-
ach. . . . My teeth have always been exceptionally good. . . .
I am not excessively fond of salads or fruit, with the exception
of melons. . . . I eat greedily. I often bite my tongue in my
haste, and sometimes my fingers."

Probably this doesn't sound to you like one of the great
classics of world literature. And yet it is. More than that, it
has set a pattern for writing that has persisted for almost four
hundred years and is today stronger than ever before. Since
Montaigne, every essayist has followed in his footsteps and
written frankly about himself. The word *I* made its appearance in literature and remained there to stay. After the essayists had taken up the first-person-singular style, the humorists
took it up, and finally practically all popular nonfiction writers

of any kind. There is a long line that stretches from Montaigne to the nineteenth-century English essayists—Lamb, Hazlitt, De Quincey, Leigh Hunt—to Americans like Thoreau and Mark Twain, to the later English essayists like Max Beerbohm, E. V. Lucas, and J. B. Priestley, and to twentieth-century American humorists like Stephen Leacock and Robert Benchley. Today there is hardly a popular nonfiction book that isn't written in the first-person style. There is virtually no newspaper column or magazine article without it. Aside from newspaper reporting, which still sticks to the traditional impersonal method, there is very little professional nonfiction writing that doesn't give the reader frequent personal glimpses of the author. (There is even a trend in this direction in reporting: as soon as a reporter graduates to a byline, he begins to rediscover the word *I*. As the years go by, his writing takes on more and more of a personal flavor.)

I hadn't realized myself to what extent this is true today until I carried on a little experiment. I went up to the attic and picked up a random copy of the *Saturday Evening Post*, dated December 15, 1956. It contained two serials, four short stories, and seven articles. I analyzed the seven articles and found that five of them were written in the first-person-singular style. The remaining two did not contain the word *I*, but their style was so personal that this seemed to be more by accident than by design.

I repeated my little experiment with dozens of articles, taken from many different magazines. The result was always the same: the standard magazine article in the United States today is written in the first person. Even articles based on long interviews with nonwriters are now usually bylined "By A. B. [the source of information who can't write] as told to X. Y. [the professional who can]."

Clearly, if you want to learn to write like a professional, just about the first thing you have to do is get used to the first person singular. Just plunge in and write "I" whenever "I" seems to be the word that is called for. Never mind the superstitious notion that it's immodest to do so. It just isn't so. Professor Bergen Evans, in his *Dictionary of Contemporary American Usage,* puts it well when he says: "Anyone who is interested in the person he is speaking or writing to may use the word *I* as often as he likes. No one will ever see anything egotistical in *I like what you did and I wish you would tell me how I can pay you for it.*"

However, there is a catch to this. You have to learn to refer to yourself without any awkward inhibition or shyness, but you must also learn never to be pompous either. Most people, whenever they venture onto a piece of paper with their ego exposed, try to cover it up quickly with some dignity or authority, or anyway something that will make them appear competent, well informed, and superior. You may be an ignoramus, a bumbling fool, a pretty miserable specimen of humanity, but you certainly can't be induced to put that in writing, for everyone to read.

Or can you? Can you train yourself to do just that, to sacrifice your pride and admit all your mistakes and faults and shortcomings, your ignorance, your weakness, your poverty, your irresponsibility? Can you, in other words, write about yourself like a professional writer? Like Montaigne, like Charles Lamb, like Hazlitt, like Mark Twain? Could you bring yourself to write down things like these?

Montaigne: "I was born and bred in the country and among field-laborers; I have been in the business of husbandry ever since my property was left to me. And yet I can add up neither with counters nor with a pen. Most of our coins are unknown to me. I cannot tell the difference between one grain and another, either in the ground or in the barn unless it is too striking to miss; and I can hardly distinguish between the cabbages and lettuces in my garden. I don't even know the names of the chief implements of husbandry, nor the rude principles of agriculture, which every boy knows. I know still less of the mechanical arts, of trade and merchandise, of the nature and varieties of fruits, wines and foodstuffs. And, to complete my disgrace, only a month ago I was caught in ignorance of the fact that leaven is used in making bread, and of the meaning of allowing wine to ferment. . . . Of music, either vocal, for which my voice is very inept, or instrumental, they never succeeded in teaching me anything. At dancing, tennis, wrestling, I have never been able to acquire any but very slight and ordinary ability; at swimming, fencing, vaulting and jumping, none at all. My hands are so clumsy that I cannot even write so I can read it; so I would rather do over what I have scribbled than give myself the trouble of unscrambling it. And I read hardly any better aloud. I feel that I bore my listeners. . . . I cannot close a letter the right way, nor could I ever cut a pen, or carve at table worth a rap, or saddle a horse. . . ."

Charles Lamb: "My reading has been lamentably desultory and immethodical. Odd, out of the way, old English plays, and treatises, have supplied me with most of my notions, and ways of feeling. In everything that relates to *science*, I am

a whole encyclopaedia behind the rest of the world. . . . I
know less geography than a schoolboy of six weeks' standing. . . . I do not know whereabout Africa merges into Asia;
whether Ethiopia lie in one or other of those great divisions;
nor can form the remotest conjecture of the position of New
South Wales, or Van Diemen's Land. . . . I have no astrono-
my. I do not know where to look for the Bear, or Charles's
Wain; the place of any star or the name of any of them at
sight. I guess at Venus only by her brightness—and if the
sun on some portentous morn were to make his first appearance in the West, I verily believe, that, while all the world
were gaping in apprehension about me, I alone should stand
unterrified, from sheer incuriosity and want of observation.
Of history and chronology I possess some vague points. . . .
I am entirely unacquainted with the modern languages. . . .
I am a stranger to the shapes and texture of the commonest
trees, herbs, flowers . . . and am no less at a loss among purely
town-objects, tools, engines, mechanic processes."

J. B. Priestley: "I have no knowledge whatever of the
sciences, in which I once received a thorough if rudimentary
instruction. . . . I once knew German and read Goethe and
Heine. Now I doubt whether I could ask for a bed or a cigar
in that tongue. I have forgotten nearly all the history and
philosophy I once knew. . . . I never knew anything about
Nature, flowers and birds and trees and so forth, and if I
lived to be a thousand I could never become one of those
persons who can tell you what anything is at a glance. . . .
My piano-playing is gone; I cannot dance now or play foot-
ball; my billiards and chess are contemptible; I could draw
a little once, but that too has gone; even my French is vile, and
I puff and pant, grow fat, and creep about in the shadow
of a liver."

Robert Benchley: "I have tried to know absolutely nothing
about a great many things, and, if I do say so myself, have
succeeded fairly well. . . . I am never upset when I find that
I know nothing about some given subject, because I am
never surprised. The names of birds and flowers, for example,
give me practically no worry whatever, for I never set out
to learn them in the first place. I am familiar with several
kinds of birds and flowers by sight, and could, if cornered,
designate a carnation or a robin as such. But beyond that
I just let the whole thing slide. . . ."

Well, you may say, these are all professional humorists
and essayists; the ordinary person is not called upon to do
all this confessing and self-abasing in print. But that is just

the point. The principle holds in practically all nonfiction today. If you want to write well, about anything at all, you must be prepared to face the consequences and portray yourself quite mercilessly whenever the occasion arises. Good writing should sound like one human being talking to another on an equal footing—that's why it must show, one way or another, that the human being that is talking is just like the human being that is reading: imperfect, not too well informed, ignorant of vast areas of human knowledge, physically weak, sometimes a coward, and often ridiculous.

To prove my point, let me describe in detail the five first-person articles that I found in my random copy of the *Saturday Evening Post*. Here they are:

The first was an article by Joseph N. Bell, "New War on Hit-and-Run Killers." Mr. Bell writes: "I spent several weeks watching the Chicago police unit in action. . . . I traveled with the Hit and Run Unit while they interrogated suspects, and I listened to all the pat excuses from every walk of life and prefabricated alibis. . . ." etc., etc.

This doesn't tell us anything unfavorable about Mr. Bell, but it does show that he doesn't claim to be the world's expert on what he is writing about, but to have worked long and hard at collecting his information.

Next: "Personal . . . From Budapest" by Noel Barber. Mr. Barber, an English journalist, was an eyewitness of the Hungarian Revolution of October, 1956. He begins: "This is my personal testament of what happened in the bloodstained streets of Budapest, of how men and women, boys and girls died in the thousands, and of how I myself fought with a group of insurgents, until a direct hit from a Soviet tank all but wiped us out. . . . Two days later I was twice shot in the head by a Soviet sentry. For days I lay desperately ill in hospital, after blood transfusions and an operation. . . ." And so on, a heartbreaking story of suffering and tragedy.

Next: "I'm Glad I Bought a Toupee" by Fred Sparks. You can figure out for yourself in what light the author appears in this article. For example, he writes at one point: "My mother often said, 'Don't worry; bald men can be handsome.' That's true of citizens like President Eisenhower, Jim Farley or Yul Brynner, who have well-shaped skulls. But millions of bald men under fifty years of age are miserably self-conscious, particularly if their bone structure is odd. The top of my head is like the top of a bent knuckle, my chin drops suddenly, my cheeks puff out and my complexion is very red. I was once described as looking like a hot-water bag with eye-glasses."

Next: "Suddenly He Was a Genius," part of a series of articles by Diane Disney Miller as told to Pete Martin. This is written in the first person by Mrs. Miller, but the real hero of the story is her father, Walt Disney. Surely this article was read and approved by him before it was printed. Yet the first sentence reads: "The nervous breakdown my father suffered in 1931 . . ."

Finally: "Deadliest Fighter in the Air" by Frank Harvey. This is an eyewitness description of a mock missile attack on a B-52 bomber by a supersonic interceptor F-102A, as seen from a TF-102A trainer plane. Mr. Harvey describes how he went up in the trainer, carefully showing to the reader that he is something less than a hero:

"We hurried out into the sun glare and climbed into the airplanes, and a crew chief crawled up the ladder and leaned in to help me with the buckling-down details. I always hate to go through this with a crew chief. I feel the rascals have a streak of sadism where writers are concerned. They always explain the ejection procedure in minute detail and with great relish—also with a touch of sadness, as if they felt that this was probably the last time they would be seeing you about. They point out little items like the fact that there is a solid iron bar directly overhead in the canopy of a TF-102A.

"'Too bad you aren't flying in some other jet, sir,' the chief says wistfully. 'Other jets don't have that bar. In an emergency, if the canopy fails to jettison, you can blow yourself up through the plastic glass with ease. But not in a TF, sir.' . . . 'Know how to use an oxygen mask?' my boy asked, peering beadily from his perch on the ladder. 'Oh, sure,' I said doubtfully . . ." etc.

And there you have it. Five people are self-described here, and as you leaf through the magazine, you read about their ignorance, suffering, ugliness, nervous breakdowns, and cowardice. And yet, all of this does not detract from the quality of these articles. On the contrary, it is essential. It's what makes them good writing—good enough to have been bought for good money by the *Saturday Evening Post* and printed for millions to read. Without this humble, self-depreciating attitude on the part of the writers, these articles wouldn't have been worth publishing. A piece on police methods can only be properly done by a reporter who doesn't know too much about such matters and puts in the time and legwork necessary for getting the information. An eyewitness report on a bloody war and revolution becomes memorable if the writer himself has fought and been injured. An article on toupees is good only if written by someone who wears one. A profile of a celebrity must cover the ups and downs of his life—especially the downs. A true adventure story seems even truer to life if it is written by someone like you and me— someone who would be afraid.

This is the great paradox of writing—the thing about it that you have to understand before you can make a decent job of it. If you want to convey information, you must first show the reader the extent of your ignorance before you began to learn. If you want to describe an adventure, you must first confess that you were afraid of the danger before you went into it. If you want to write about health, your point of view must be that of someone who has known sickness; if your subject is beauty, you must be familiar with ugliness; if it is money, you must first tell your reader that your own financial troubles are just as bad as his own.

Readers are, on the average, average. To reach them, to write for them in such a way that they will understand and remember, you must show them that you are average too. And so you are, of course, in almost all respects, but you hate to admit it. Well, you'd *better* admit it. Among many other things, it will help you write better English.

Since in most of what you write, the main purpose is to convey information, it's particularly important that you learn the technique of *admitting ignorance*. Not present ignorance of your subject, of course, but past ignorance before you went to work collecting your information. It's no good telling the reader that you are an expert; he doesn't believe in experts, instinctively. He has known too many so-called experts who turned out to be phonies. What he knows and has faith in is a person like himself who doesn't know anything but what he reads in the papers. Whenever he does want to get information on a subject, he goes and finds out.

So did you, of course, and to gain your reader's confidence you'd better tell him how you did find out. Truth is what has been established. How did you establish it? Who did you see? What did you read? Tell him exactly in so many words. Don't rely on your position and title to qualify you as an expert. Possibly you are one; but the reader may not be impressed. He'll be more impressed if you state loudly and clearly that you were once utterly ignorant but made it your business to learn.

Here are two beautiful examples—two famous writers who weren't afraid to admit their ignorance.

First, here is John Gunther, world-famous author and political reporter. I quote from the foreword to his *Inside U.S.A.*, which was published after *Inside Europe, Inside Asia,* and *Inside Latin America,* and therefore had a ready-made nation-wide audience, presumably trusting John Gunther as an expert reporter. And yet, he wrote candidly:

> I visited all forty-eight states of course, and of cities in the country greater than two hundred thousand in population, of which there are forty-three, I saw all but five. Also I visited a great many smaller communities. Most of these I had never seen before; it often occurred to me that the only virtue I brought to the job, aside from curiosity, was ignorance. Until my trip (1944-46) I had never in my life been in Denver, New Orleans, Rochester, Atlanta, Memphis, Salt Lake City, Portland, Oregon or Portland, Maine; except to pass through on a train or fly over, I had never seen Arkansas, Oklahoma, Kentucky, Delaware, Mississippi, the Dakotas, or Montana. All this did, at least, serve to give me the advantage of a fresh eye and an unprejudiced approach. Not only was I writing for the man from Mars; I was one.

Second, here is Dorothy Canfield Fisher, first lady of the state of Vermont, which she had known and loved for a long lifetime. In her book *Vermont Tradition* I find the following charming admission of ignorance:

> Every Vermonter with old-time roots here knows something about potash. . . . My own interest was aroused almost by chance, when I happened to notice in a dry county history the fact that in 1791, a thousand tons of potash were sent out of Vermont. . . . That was surprising. I had no answer to the question, "Who in the world could possibly have wanted to buy as much as that?", so the next time I was in Montpelier I stepped into the fine library of our State Historical Society and asked the librarian for information.
>
> He answered readily, "Potash was used in making soap—same thing as lye."
>
> That much I knew already. . . . "But," I objected, "the amount of potash you come across in old account books and commerce reports couldn't have been for making

soap to wash with. Enough was sent out of Vermont every year to wash the clothes and faces of humanity all around the globe ten times a day. . . ."

The librarian . . . suggested, "It was mostly taken, you know, to cities outside of Vermont. . . . The local records say, 'Mostly for export.' "

We looked at each other nonplussed. . . .

Whereupon Dorothy Canfield Fisher devotes a chapter of her book to the history of Vermont potash, which was of enormous world-wide economic importance in the manufacture of woolen cloth.

That's why the word *I* is so essential in all nonfiction writing. The advertising people always talk about "believability." But "believability" goes further than advertising. Everything that is presented as fact must be believable if it is to make any impression on the reader. In face-to-face conversation or in an informal speech "believability" is established because the personality of the speaker comes through—by way of his voice, his expression, his gestures, his manner, his eyes, his hands, his arms, his legs, everything about him. Facts are believed because the speaker looks like a person who knows.

In writing, all this is absent. The writer is hidden behind a sheet of paper. If he says, "Ten per cent of all Americans are suffering from nervous or mental diseases," you may or may not believe him, even if he is an expert in psychiatry with half a column in *Who's Who*. But if he writes, "I was a complete ignoramus in the field of psychiatry, but I wanted to know how many neurotics there are in this country. So I went to the library and studied the following twenty-nine sources. . . . Then I interviewed seventeen leading psychiatrists, belonging to nine different schools of thought. . . . Then I carefully checked this information. . . . etc., etc."—if he writes like that, he will be automatically believable. He has gained your confidence as a fellow ignoramus who has simply done what you yourself would have done if you'd had the time and the curiosity to look into the matter.

Moral: Always confess your ignorance. If you write a report, begin by showing what you didn't know, and go on to explain how and what you found out. Even if you write a simple letter, based on a routine check of the files, start by saying that, to make sure of the answer, you checked the files.

Which brings us to the question of the pronoun *I* in a business letter. This, as I have discovered, is one of the great problems in American life. Most business letters are written by employees of large corporations—usually by a minor employee a little further down for the signature of a major employee a little higher up. Where does the word *I* fit into such a letter? Usually it doesn't. If it's an older, more traditional company (or a branch of the government), the writer happily settles in the impersonal, passive-voice style, and the third-person pronoun reigns supreme. "It is suggested . . . Reference has been made . . . It should not be inferred . . . The policy has been established . . . The question arises . . . An early reply will be appreciated." If it's a modern, more progressive corporation, the letters are being written in the first person plural. "We regret to say . . . It gives us great pleasure . . . One of our customers has written us concerning . . . We are now in a position to reply . . . We are looking forward to hearing from you." The little word *I*, first person singular, appears nowhere. The letter writer can't use it in speaking of himself because he doesn't sign the letter; the signer can't use it because he didn't write it; nor can the writer use it in referring to the signer, because that's an awkward and unnatural thing to do.

Does this mean that this whole chapter is useless for the ordinary business-letter writer? I don't think so. There are some compromise solutions. In the first place, it's a good thing to know and have learned that the first-person style is better English and that the impersonal style should be avoided if at all possible. At least, if you know *that,* you have a standard and a direction in which to go.

Secondly, it is always possible, in any organization, to use the first person *plural.* This is not as good as the first person singular, but it is still better than saying *it* all the time. The passive-voice style, which has been denounced in every single course and textbook on writing for some fifty or seventy-five years, is really inexcusable today. So if you can't say *I,* say at least *we.*

However, if you do use the first person plural, be careful. Use *we* in referring to the organization for which you write, but don't use it in any other way. Don't write pompous sentences like "We know today," if by *we* you mean mankind, or "every thinking American" or, most likely, your own inflated ego. Mark Twain said, "Only presidents, editors, and people with tapeworm have the right to use the editorial *we.*" I would go further than that, demoting even editors to plain, ordinary *I.* The word *we* should mean a group of two or more people that can be identified, or else it shouldn't be used. And now let's drop this subject—and by "us" I mean exactly two people: you and me.

Third compromise: It is possible to use both *I* and *we* in a business letter. You can say *we* whenever you refer to something done by the company, and *I* whenever you mean the writer (or signer) of the letter. In practice, this means that you can—and should—use *I* when you express feelings and emotions, and *we* for everything else. There are, after all, emotions that come up in a business letter. The news it contains is usually either good or bad. Therefore, as a matter of ordinary courtesy, you'll want to express pleasure or regret. Don't write "We are pleased" or "We regret"; instead, write "I am happy" or "I am sorry" (or, more informally, "I'm happy" or "I'm sorry"). In this way, you will manage to make clear that the information given in your letter comes from the organization but the feelings expressed are your own. (If you write "We regret the delay in answering your letter of February 26, 1958," you don't really mean that your 10,000 fellow employees share your regret. You mean that you are sorry—just yourself.)

As I said, these are compromise solutions. Ideally, letters like everything else should be written in the first person singular throughout, with the word *I* appearing naturally wherever it fits in. Writing, after all, is just a substitute for speech. And there is no speech without a speaker.

EXERCISES

These exercises are meant to be done within the framework of the continuing exercise described on page 139. At any rate, they should always be given to someone else to read and criticize.

1. Describe, in about 500 words, your general ignorance of subjects most people are expected to know.

2. Describe, in about 500 words, your lack of skills most people are expected to have.

3. Describe, in about 500 words, your physical weaknesses and disabilities.

4. Describe, in about 500 words, your financial status and past ups and downs.

5. Describe, in about 500 words, some situation in which you were defeated or failed.

Chapter Seventeen

TO BE EXACT

There are some 100 or 150 free-lance writers in this country who make a living by writing articles for magazines. Some years ago, this brave band of independent spirits joined together to form the Society of Magazine Writers. In 1954 they published a book, *A Guide to Successful Magazine Writing,* which was in part a handbook and in part an anthology of a few dozen minor masterpieces of the species. It's a fascinating book, full of highly valuable information.

Each of the reprinted articles is prefaced by a detailed statement by the author in which he tells how the article was written, how he got the idea, how long he worked on it, what obstacles he ran into, how he managed to place it in a magazine and, in most cases, how much he was paid for it. On the average, the articles run to three thousand words or more, the average price (around 1950) was $1,500, the average time spent was usually about two weeks of research and one more week for the actual writing.

Often, however, the work was far more. Here are statements on what it amounted to in three cases:

Jack Harrison Pollack: "I spent an intensive month doing live research. My notes show that I talked to 58 individuals in person or by telephone."

Edith M. Stern: "After about three months I arrived at that half-joyful, half-terrifying point where your material seems to be duplicating itself and you know you should stop research and get at the writing. Before me lay some forty solid single-spaced pages of typewritten notes, in addition to a small library of printed material I had picked up in the course of my travels and answers to requests for information I had sent to various states I had not visited. By what I call the iceberg method, in which eight ninths of your research doesn't show,

I had to boil down this formidable mass into the *Companion*-set limit of 4,000 words."

Robert Froman: "Altogether I had spent about four weeks on the research, had interviewed some two hundred individuals, made a few more than one hundred pages of notes, and had collected a five-foot shelf of books, pamphlets, press releases and technical papers. . . . It took me a week to choose the useful items in my collection, to read them, and to discard the useless ones. By then the main points of the story were clear in my mind. . . . At that point I pushed the whole thing out of my conscious mind and spent several days sawing and splitting wood. When I was ready to go back to work, I ignored the material I had collected and made first a rough, then a detailed outline sort of in free-hand. Then I went through all the useful material again and made note of items which I had left out of the outline but which seemed to belong in the story. When I had fitted them in, I started writing. . . ."

If you labor under the common superstition that a magazine article is written by looking up a few data and then knocking off a digest of your ideas and opinions in an afternoon, then these quotations may serve as an antidote. An article, as Mrs. Stern rightly says, is like an iceberg: to get the three thousand words which the subscriber will read in fifteen minutes, the writer must take at least twenty thousand words of notes.

This is the aspect of writing that is almost impossible to teach in a class—or in a book, for that matter. A class in writing naturally creates the optical illusion that writing consists primarily, or wholly, of putting words on paper. The same with a textbook or handbook: the reader expects it to deal with vocabulary, sentence structure, and paragraphing, and that's usually all it does. So the student concentrates on expressing his ideas in words. He writes essays and themes on some assigned subject, setting down whatever he knows about it, or thinks about it, or vaguely feels about it. No wonder all of these exercises produce thin, empty stuff, without substance and without interest for anyone in the world but the writer himself. No wonder so many teachers despair and arrive at the conclusion that "writing cannot be taught." It can't be taught, that is, in a vacuum; it can be taught only if the student has things to write about—real, live facts he has assembled by hard work rather than ideas he has simply thought up. The unpleasant truth, as I always tell my students, is that *nobody is interested in your personal opinions.*

So you have to go out and get facts. How do you do that?

There are two ways: the amateur way and the professional way. The amateur prepares for a writing job by getting together the relevant facts; the professional goes out and gets *all* the facts. In other words, if you are not a trained writer, you consider yourself the best judge of what facts are relevant; you assemble those and think you are ready to write. The old pro—the seasoned reporter or magazine writer—knows that this isn't good enough. The only thing that's good enough is to soak yourself in all the facts you can lay your hands on, to become a temporary expert on the subject. You go after the more obvious sources, then after the less obvious sources, and finally you follow up all the stray leads that you can possibly uncover. You never can tell. In principle, you have to know everything there is to know about a subject so that you can write a short piece a few people will bother to read. Legwork is nine-tenths of the job.

There is no better illustration of the meaning of the word *legwork* than this story about the late O. K. Bovard, managing editor of the St. Louis *Post-Dispatch:*

When Bovard was city editor, Charles G. Ross, who years later became President Truman's press secretary, was a cub reporter. One day Bovard sent him out to get the facts about the fall of a painter from a high smokestack in the extreme southwestern part of St. Louis.

It was a hot summer day. The trip to the scene of the accident consisted of a streetcar ride to the end of the line and a long walk from there. Finally Ross got to the factory and collected his information—name, address, and age of the painter, the place where he fell, how he happened to fall, the extent of his injuries, and so on. He took the long walk back to the end of the streetcar line, rode back to the office, sat down and composed a short item about the accident. Feeling rather proud of it, he turned it in to the city editor.

Mr. Bovard glanced over the few lines and called his cub to the desk. "Ross," he asked, "how tall is this smokestack?" Ross couldn't say. Quite tall, he said. About so-and-so-many feet.

But Bovard wasn't satisfied with this. "Ross," he said, " 'tall' is a relative term. I want you to go back and find out the exact height of that smokestack."

So Ross took again the long, hot trip to the factory. When he returned to the office, it was night. But he had the precise height of the smokestack in feet and inches.

This sounds legendary, but it isn't. Only a cub reporter or

an amateur would forget to put down the height of that smokestack. A pro would do it automatically. Thousands of stories that you read in your paper every day testify to that fact. Here is one, an insignificant little item that I picked at random from the *New York Times*, Sunday, February 2, 1958:

PRIEST RUNS CAFE TO COUNTER EVIL

His Puerto Rico Shop Sells
No Liquor but Lures Trade
From Drinking Places

By PETER KIHSS

VILLALBA, P.R., Jan. 25—There is a new cafetin—a typical Puerto Rican bar and grocery—here, and the Rev. Salvatore Ruffolo, a Roman Catholic parish priest, started it.

Thirty men of the Holy Name Society bought shares and the Church of Our Lady of Carmel purchased 10 per cent. Three church women operate it seven days weekly from 7 A.M. to 11 P.M. When the store ends its first year next month the guess is that it may have paid back 20 per cent of its $2,825 capital investment.

One non-typical aspect is that the cafeteria La Fé does not serve alcoholic beverages, relying instead on soft drinks. But, like other Puerto Rican grocery-bars, it is a neighborhood meeting place.

Around its central square counter are six tables where neighbors gossip and buy meals. The cafetin sells fruit, milk, bread, biscuits, instant coffee, canned goods and candy.

It serves children of a near-by Government school with sandwiches from 5 cents for ham and cheese. Meals include rice with meat and vegetables at 35 cents.

Father Ruffolo had to be prevailed upon to explain why he started the cafetin. Villalba had many alcoholic bar-groceries—"barbarity," one parishioner said—with fourteen in two blocks alone.

Churchgoers said they went there to meet friends but had to buy liquor. Women said that neither they nor their children dared go to such places. Father Ruffolo, less than five feet tall but willing to try anything, arranged to rent a former drygoods store—and scored a success as a bar operator. He said it was a "moralizing diversion."

The 47-year-old priest came to Puerto Rico from Italy in May 1954, responding to a papal appeal for service in Latin America.

Puerto Rico is nominally 90 per cent Roman Catholic but has only one priest for every 7,000 inhabitants as against perhaps one for 700 in the New York Archdiocese. It has sixty-five Catholic parishes for its 3,400 square miles; New York Archdiocese has eighty-nine with Spanish-language services.

Father Ruffolo serves a parish of 17,000 inhabitants in the rugged southern slopes of central Puerto Rican mountains. He regularly says mass in thirty-two places, of which thirteen have chapels. Services elsewhere are in tiny mountain huts.

He travels in a bright red jeep, by horseback or afoot to get through his parish, sometimes needing an hour and a half even though the limits are only twenty-five by thirty-five miles.

Under papal regulations he can say mass twice on weekdays, provided this is in two different places, and three times on Sundays. Once he spent $400 of his own money to bring another priest from Italy; the other priest endured the mountain rigors just a few weeks and left.

It is staggering to think of the amount of work Mr. Kihss put into this routine item, which appeared on page 38 of a *New York Times* Sunday issue, to be glanced over sleepily by a few subscribers while they were munching their eggs and toast. There it is, the small part of the iceberg of facts and figures—the price of rice with meat and vegetables (35¢), the capital investment ($2,825), the limits of the Villalba parish (25 by 35 miles), the color of Father Ruffolo's jeep (bright red), his height (under 5 feet), his first name (Salvatore), the number of tables around the lunch counter (6), the number of chapels in the parish (13), the number of alcoholic bars (14 in 2 blocks), the hours the café is open (7 A.M. to 11 P.M.), its name (La Fé), how often a priest can say mass under papal regulations, how Puerto Rico compares with New York in its Spanish-language Catholic services, what kind of store was there before Father Ruffolo opened his café, when it opened (a year ago next month), and so on and so forth.

It's impossible to guess at all the other facts Mr. Kihss must have assembled that *didn't* get into the story as it appeared in the paper. He probably took complete notes on Father Ruffolo's previous career, maybe a few anecdotes about his service in Puerto Rico, more details about the operation of the La Fé cafetin, more statistics about the Catholic Church in Puerto Rico, perhaps something more about the drinking problem there, plus all sorts of other things that are hard to guess. At any rate, he probably got ten times as many facts as he needed—and about a hundred times as many facts as an amateur writer or casual tourist would have collected. And by doing so, he managed to write a story that does a superb job in conveying truth. After reading it, the *New York Times* subscriber has a notion of what life is like in central Puerto Rico—the mountains, the poor roads, the masses said maybe once every two weeks in a little hut, the long struggle for the government school and the five-cent sandwiches for the children, and the men drinking in bars that are crowding each other on Main Street.

Or take another example, one of the routine masterpieces by Meyer Berger, the *New York Times* Pulitzer prize-winning reporter, who wrote a daily column called "About New York." This is from his column of February 5, 1958:

In a few weeks or so the wreckers will come. They will tear down the two venerable brick and brownstone mansions that have stood hard by the First Presbyterian Church in West Twelfth Street for more than 100 years.

No. 12, nearest the churchyard, was built in 1849 for James W. Phillips, son of the Rev. William Wirt Phillips, who held the pulpit next door from 1826 to 1865. No. 14, built at the same time as a twin, except for the interior, was the home of Charles C. Taber, a prosperous cotton merchant.

The two dwellings are the last remaining two town houses in this city of the many designed by Alexander Jackson Davis. A modest man, he conceded that the interiors of his Twelfth Street designs were "remarkable." Even in their last stages of neglect the unpracticed eye can see that. They are lovely.

The buildings had famous tenants, too, at one time or another. Thurlow Weed, nineteenth-century Warwick—he was called that in his own day for his genius in moulding political careers—lived in No. 12 from 1866 to 1882. Most of the important men and women of his time were his guests there. Down the street lived Gen. Winfield Scott.

Probably the chief feature of the old Weed house was the octagonal stairwell with the stained-glass skylight at the top. The stairwell in the other house is oval, but it has the same glowing dome skylight. In both dwellings you find rich stucco molding, handsome fireplaces, magnificent woods.

Just outside the old Weed study there stood, in his lifetime, a handsome willow brought from St. Helena near the grave of Napoleon. It was uprooted long ago to make play space in the churchyard for the children of the church school. Incidentally, after the old mansions come down, a new church school will rise on the spot. The Davis mansions are now a firetrap.

The most famous dweller in No. 14 was John Rogers, a nineteenth-century sculptor, a kind of Edgar Guest who worked in stone. His studio was on the second floor. It looks today pretty much as it did when he worked in it from 1888 to 1895, turning out such groups as "Checkers Up at the Farm," "Fetching the Doctor." A pair of his works are in the church office. Each has the Twelfth Street house address worked into it.

Though church folk dislike the idea of having the old mansions torn down, and architects in town frown on the notion, too, they know they must go. The space is sorely needed for the children. So, one by one, the master works of the great architects vanish from the city—Davis did preliminary sketches for the old Tombs, worked on the old Custom House, on many hospitals and colleges. All that will remain of his dreaming on paper, when the Twelfth Street mansions go down in rubble, will be a few villas up in Hudson River Valley.

Here again you have the mass of facts, the enormous accumulation of details, the feeling that Mr. Berger's column is just the top of the iceberg that's visible. He probably had in his notes *all* the inhabitants of No. 12 and No. 14 ever since 1849, and the names of the hospitals and colleges built by Davis, and the number of the house on Twelfth Street where General Winfield Scott lived, and the names of half a dozen more of Rogers' sculptures, and more details about the interiors of both houses. Notice that even within the brief space of his column, he *does* give you the most prominent inhabitants of both houses, the exact dates of their stay there, the floor on which Rogers had his studio, and the fact that the stairwell in No. 12 is octagonal, whereas that in No. 14 is oval. And note how Mr. Berger, the famous reporter, carefully records his ignorance of art and architecture: "The unpracticed eye can see that they are lovely," he says, right in the spirit of the literary tradition that started with Montaigne in 1571.

Perhaps you think that these two examples from the pages of the *New York Times* represent the ultimate in detailed reporting. They do not. There is no end to what you can do once you start with the business of collecting facts.

In 1894 a man by the name of Shuman published a textbook in journalism in which he described the now-famous 5-W formula: Who, What, When, Where, and Why. It was the business of every reporter, he said, to get these five W's of each story and to tell them in the opening paragraph. But this was sixty-five years ago. Today the trained reporter gets not only the five W's, but also dozens and dozens of minor W's—what middle initial, what street address, what floor, what age, what occupation, what amount in dollars and cents, what height, what weight, what bust measurements, what price, what annual income, what injuries, what hour and minute of the day, what birthplace, what for lunch, what to drink, what brand smoked, what nickname, what hobbies, what mannerisms, etc., etc. It's like the scientific study of the atom. Every year the search extends to smaller and smaller particles. In exactly parallel fashion, a writer who fifty years ago would have been satisfied with the general facts about Lincoln's assassination now has to know precisely what he ate for breakfast on the morning of April 14, 1865.

This happens to be an actual example. Some time ago I watched a television interview with Mr. Jim Bishop, author of the best-selling book *The Day Lincoln Was Shot*. He was asked about the problems he ran into while writing the book, and told that he had the greatest trouble in finding out just what Lincoln had for breakfast on the morning of the day he was shot. He spent months and months in research on this nagging little item and was finally forced to give up. (His book *doesn't* tell what the breakfast consisted of.) He did find out, though, that Lincoln's *usual* breakfast was one egg and one cup of coffee.

As an example of Mr. Bishop's fantastically meticulous research, which took in such items as this one, I'll quote a few paragraphs from his book:

The Washington police force consisted of fifty police-
men who worked by day and were paid by Washington
City, and a night force of fifty more who were paid by
the Federal Government. The night men were not paid
to protect citizens; their job was to protect public buildings. The Fire Department was paid by the city, but it
was controlled by politicians and often refused to go out
to fight fires. The criminal code of the District of Columbia was archaic and was enforced largely on political
grounds. Crimes punishable by death were murder,
treason, burglary, and rape if committed by Negroes.
Only a few years before this day, many of the politicians
who fought for the abolition of slavery made extra
money by selling freedmen back into slavery. Until the
Emancipation Proclamation had been signed in 1863, a
weekly auction of Negroes was held in the back yard of
Decatur House, a block from the White House.

There was a great difference between "permanent"
Washington and political Washington. A clerk earning
$1,500 a year in the new Treasury Building found it
difficult to feed a wife and children and his quarters were
little better than what the Negroes had. He was at his
desk at 7:30 A.M. and, in the evening, he left it after 4.
Political Washington functioned between November and
June, when Congress was in session. It convened late and
it did not convene every day.

The hotels, which understood the legislators, served
breakfast between 8 A.M. and 11. A good breakfast consisted of steak, oysters, ham and eggs, hominy grits, and
whiskey. Dinner was served at noon and ran to six or
eight courses. Supper was disposed of between 4 P.M.
and 5. Teas were common at 7:30 P.M. and cold supper
was eaten between 9 and 10 P.M.

I am sure these quotations are enough to make the point
that legwork is all-important in writing. And legwork may
take many forms: Young Charlie Ross making his second hot
trip to get the exact height of that smokestack; Mr. Kihss of
the *New York Times* walking along the main street of Villalba,
Puerto Rico, and counting the number of bars and drinking
places; Meyer Berger climbing the stairs in both the old
Davis houses on West Twelfth Street to compare their interior
décor; Jim Bishop ransacking libraries for months and months
to find out whether Abraham Lincoln had an egg for breakfast on the morning of April 14, 1865. It's up to you to go

and do likewise. Use the iceberg method. Whatever you are writing, fill it with facts—detailed facts, minute facts, utterly, absurdly trivial facts—and collect ten times as many of those facts beforehand as you are ever apt to use.

Of course I know that this is counsel of perfection. I *know* you are not going to work like that. But at least I want to go on record as having said so. These are the facts of writing. This is the way it's done if it's done right. The way to better English is through mountains of picayune details.

But, you say, this doesn't apply to everything. What about writing that *isn't* reportorial—what about argument, debate, opinions? My answer is that the principle holds for every kind of writing. If you want to argue, do it with facts. If you want to state your opinions, do it by way of facts. If you feel the urge to write an essay, set down facts. Which means, of course, don't write an essay, write an article.

Anyway, essays are extremely hard to find nowadays. Topics that used to be discussed in finely chiseled literary essays are now given the facts-and-figures treatment in articles. For example, here is how Agnes Repplier treated the topic of "Leisure" in the *Atlantic Monthly* in 1893:

A visitor strolling through the noble woods of Ferney complimented Voltaire on the splendid growth of his trees. "Ay," replied the great wit, half in scorn and half, perhaps, in envy, "they have nothing else to do"; and walked on, deigning no further word of approbation.

Has it been more than a hundred years since this distinctly modern sentiment was uttered,—more than a hundred years since the spreading chestnut boughs bent kindly over the lean, strenuous, caustic, disappointed man of genius who always had so much to do, and who found in the doing of it a mingled bliss and bitterness that scorched him like fever pain? How is it that, while Dr. Johnson's sledge-hammer repartees sound like the sonorous echoes of a past age, Voltaire's remarks always appear to have been spoken the day before yesterday? They are the kind of witticisms which we do not say for ourselves, simply because we are not witty; but they illustrate with biting accuracy the spirit of restlessness, of disquiet, of intellectual vanity and keen contention which is the brand of our vehement and over-zealous generation.

"The Gospel of Work"—that is the phrase woven
insistently into every homily, every appeal made to the
conscience or the intelligence of a people who are now
straining their youthful energy to its utmost speed.
"Blessed be Drudgery!"—that is the text deliberately
chosen for a discourse which has enjoyed such amazing
popularity that sixty thousand printed copies have been
found all inadequate to supply the ravenous demand.
Readers of Dickens—if any one has the time to read
Dickens nowadays—may remember . . . etc. etc.

Mind you, this is not a poor example of a literary essay.
On the contrary, I think it's one of the best essays ever written, well worth reading even today, after some sixty-five years.
(It is one of Agnes Repplier's *Essays in Idleness*.) And yet,
now that I have copied out these opening paragraphs, I
realize that one cannot ask anyone today to work his way
through all this stately prose, the elaborate adjectives, the
elegant phrasing, the precious thoughts—the whole hopelessly
old-fashioned literary bric-a-brac of a past age. If you want
to talk or write about leisure today, you have to give the
reader facts, figures, statistics—yes, statistics. Like Mr. David
Dempsey in the *New York Times Magazine* of January 26,
1958:

If we are to take literally the findings of the statisticians, ours is a civilization that works less and plays
more than any since the Roman Empire declined and
fell. No less than sixty million of us belong to the new
Leisure Class, a group whose hands have been freed by
technology and whose minds are now being liberated by
automation. We are men and women, manual workers
and white-collared, old and young, all with plenty of
free time (theoretically at least), a steady income and,
most important, an abundance of available credit.

On paper, there is no argument about it. Salaried em-
ployes and wage-earners work an average of forty hours
a week where, as recently as 1929, their fathers worked
fifty, and congratulated themselves on not having to
work sixty, as *their* fathers did in 1900. (Today's workers also produce six times as much as their grandfathers
produced for every hour on the job.) What is more, as
the work week shrinks, the vacations get longer—a
month is no longer unusual for an employe with seniority.

On paper, too, this huge dividend of extra time made

possible by modern technology is an unmixed blessing. We spend more money on recreation and amusement than we did a generation ago on food and clothing. Including travel and the do-it-yourself movement, some $34 billion a year finances what is represented to us as a longer and longer pause in the day's occupation.

One student of the subject, for instance, credits the average American with about 3,000 "free" hours a year. . . . etc., etc.

The moral of all these examples is clear: Don't write anything without a firm foundation of facts—details, specific data, figures, statistics, incidents, names, addresses, biographical material, anecdotes, measurements, lists, descriptive matter— surely you know by now what I mean. Yes, you know, and then, at the next opportunity, you'll go ahead and inform the world of your personal prejudices and opinions, things you have read somewhere, things you think you know, basic principles that have to be put down, and so on. I say, forget it. *Nobody is interested in your personal opinions.* That's too bad, but there it is. Stick to the facts. If you haven't got the facts, go out and get them. You'll be surprised at what you'll find. Maybe—who knows?—the facts that you'll have learned will even make you change your opinions.

EXERCISES

I am still assuming that you are doing the continuing exercise described on page 139. The following exercises are meant to be done within the framework of that daily-letter-writing scheme. At any rate, they should always be submitted to another person for his or her reaction.

1. Describe, in about 500 words, a significant event in your life (landing first job, marriage proposal, etc.). Be as specific as you possibly can. Try to recall what the weather was like, exactly what was said, what was eaten at meals that day, what people wore, etc.

2. Describe in equal detail, in about 500 words, a recent family event (birthday, holiday celebration, etc.).

3. Describe in equal detail, in about 500 words, your room or office.

4. Write a detailed biographical sketch, of about 500 words, of someone you know very well.

5. Describe, in about 500 words, as exactly as you can, a familiar short trip (e.g., from your home to your office).

6. Describe, in about 500 words, with as much detail as possible, a recent sport or hobby activity of yours (a game you played, something you made yourself, etc.).

Chapter Eighteen

QUOTE . . . UNQUOTE

The other day I read an interesting article about "Parole and the Prisons" in *The Atlantic*. It was by Erle Stanley Gardner, the famous mystery writer, who is also a serious student of crime and penology.

In the article, Gardner told about two New York judges he knew who had worked out a system of their own in re-regard to probation. The article went on:

> I asked them about the percentage of failure and was startled to find that they had virtually no failures. I wanted to find out the secret.
>
> One of the judges told me, in effect, "There isn't any secret about it. We know that these men got up against conditions that were too much for them and they committed a crime. We know that if they get up against another set of similar conditions they're apt to commit another crime. The thing to do is to see that their troubles and temptations don't pile up to such a point that they lose their perspective.
>
> "Every so often we send for one of those fellows . . ." etc.

I quoted this brief passage because it's an example of a professional author of popular fiction discussing a serious topic in the pages of one of our leading literary magazines. It shows, I think, that professional experience in writing goes deep. Gardner, who day in day out produces the machine-gun prose of the Perry Mason stories, can't be sedate and dull even if he tries. Even in the midst of an earnest, high-minded article in *The Atlantic* he has to dramatize what he says by telling the reader that he met two judges who had a powerful secret. (In the next line it turns out that there isn't any secret.)

However, the operative words in this passage, the really telling phrase revealing the hand of the old pro, is the two words "in effect." Observe how Gardner, by using these two innocent-looking words, has turned his not particularly exciting piece of information into the highly dramatic revelation of a new system "out of the horse's mouth." To be sure, the two judges told him *something;* but, as is clearly shown by the words "in effect," they certainly did *not* tell him what is printed in *The Atlantic* between quotation marks. Erle Stanley Gardner, the old pro, just couldn't help himself: when he has something important to say, he naturally, almost unconsciously, slides into dialogue.

This, as I have found out after fourteen years of dealing with amateur writers, is the decisive difference between the amateur and the pro. The pro has an itch to go into dialogue and, by hook or crook, surrounds large chunks of his material with quotation marks. The amateur, on the other hand, has a quotation-mark phobia. He has, as I said earlier, his general "graphophobia" anyway, but the classic, outstanding symptom of his disease is his total inability to put spoken words on paper. The writing of such a simple sentence as "He said, 'O.K.' " presents almost insuperable psychological difficulties to the average American.

This is very odd. Somehow, at the end of a long historical development, we have arrived at a situation that is completely upside down. Writing is essentially nothing but recorded speech. And yet, people nowadays are willing to use it for anything *but* recorded speech. The normal, natural function of writing—putting down something that has been *said*—has now become a specialty performed only by experts.

I have a hunch that we, in the twentieth century, have arrived at some sort of turning point in this matter of writing and speaking. Look at the historical facts. Some three thousand years ago, when the alphabet was invented, writing was a highly difficult and cumbersome affair. Only a few people mastered the technique, and even those had to struggle with poor, inefficient writing materials. The best they could do was to slowly and elaborately put down one letter after another. The first real progress in the field of writing was the invention of printing in the fifteenth century. But even that was a special process for books and, later, newspapers and magazines. The bulk of literate mankind kept on with their goose quills and inkwells and sandboxes. Then, only some eighty years ago, the typewriter came on the market and it became possible for people like you and me to write reasonably quickly and efficiently by machine. Finally, just a few years ago, photocopying came in in a big way, so that tedious copying was eliminated.

My point is that writing, for thousands of years, has been an awkward and time-consuming business, a miserable makeshift substitute for getting ideas across by talking. Talking is as easy as breathing; writing is—or has been—a chore. No wonder it is natural for most people to shy away from writing as they would from a nasty medicine.

Because of this situation, there is a tradition to put down on paper only *a highly condensed version of what the writer would have said*. Human beings, on the whole, do everything they do with a minimum of exertion; therefore, they tend to write down in a hundred words what they would have *said* in a thousand. (Don't start arguing that most people are verbose and don't know how to boil things down. That's true, but it's also true that hardly anyone has the gift of freeflowing, 100 per cent conversational style.)

Now, in the middle of the twentieth century, the time has come to change these ancient writing habits. We don't write the way we talk because it *used to be* practically impossible to do so. (A man laboriously forming curlicued letters with a goose quill—bending down over his paper with the tip of his tongue showing between his pursed lips—can't be expected to produce an exact image of rapid, fluent talk.) But we don't write that way any longer. We now have fast typewriters and Dictaphones and tape recorders and there is no reason any longer why we shouldn't write conversational English.

So let's use this new opportunity and put dialogue into our everyday writing. Don't tell me that it's impossible to work quoted speech into your business letters and reports. It's the easiest thing in the world—if you really want to do it. For instance, suppose you write in a letter: "A thorough investigation was made and it appeared that the delay in delivery was due to heavy absenteeism in our shipping department because of the snowstorm and the subway strike. As soon as normal conditions returned . . ." etc.

Why not write it this way? "We checked with Arthur Smith, who's in charge of our shipping department, and he told us, 'That was the week of the snowstorm and the subway strike. Only half of the men came in and we simply couldn't handle the load. After the strike was over . . .' " etc.

After all, most of the information that goes into a letter or a memo is the result of talking or listening to people—either personally or by telephone. So why not say so in a letter? If you go by the typical business correspondence today, all office work is performed in utter silence: people receiving letters, silently studying the files, silently going over previous correspondence, silently assembling data, silently drafting a reply. Nothing ever stirs except the rustling of paper. You know very well that this isn't so. Letters are the result of talk, just as all other business activity is essentially the result of talk. Quotation marks belong in a business letter because the natural way to write is to set down what was *said*.

But that's only the beginning—the minimum essential, so to speak. After you have trained yourself to use quoted speech wherever possible, you then ought to go ahead and learn from the professionals the use of dialogue as a fine art. There is a tremendous difference between the simple use of quotation marks and the writing of talk that feels and sounds like talk.

The professional writers have been perfecting their technique for a long time—ever since that memorable day, May 16, 1763, when young James Boswell returned home from his first meeting with Dr. Samuel Johnson and wrote in his journal: "I shall mark what I remember of his conversation." Boswell of course was a born genius at this sort of thing, but there have been many writers since his day who have been blessed with a remarkable ear and memory for the inimitable sound of talk.

One of the best current performers of this highly specialized art is Mr. Harvey Breit, who for several years used to write weekly interviews with writers for the *New York Times Book Review*. They were later collected in a book, *The Writer Observed*. Here are a few samples:

From an interview with Aldous Huxley:

"For a long time," Mr. Huxley said, "I have been thinking of doing the impossible job of writing a historical novel, and I've been thinking of collecting my material on the spot. It would be fourteenth-century Italy. It fascinates me. Why! Well, it has the fascination of the impossible task—I still don't know how it's to be done—of indicating that people are always the same and awfully different."

Why did fourteenth-century Italy fascinate Mr. Huxley? "It's awfully good," he said. "It's really human nature with the lid off of it. It really is wonderful. The

violence and picturesqueness; and I must say it's fun
when one reads a life of the Middle Ages and the intimate life emerges. All kinds of things that we regard
as very, very strange they took for granted. There is
that passage from extreme sanctity to extreme brutality
—things we consider incompatible go on in the same
breath. Men ate off gold plate and were monstrously
filthy. Beautiful women painted their teeth, which ate
away the enamel. [Mr. Huxley said "et" away.] Women
made themselves so revolting that the men were driven
to sodomy. No, I must say it's fascinating—and then
you get into the early humanists: Petrarch, Boccaccio
and that extraordinary woman, St. Catherine, rushing
about and bawling out the Pope."

From an interview with E. E. Cummings:
    Why did Mr. Cummings turn his back on the con-
ventional upper-and-lower-case system and employ nearly
exclusively the lower-case letter? "Sure, I'll tell you,"
Mr. Cummings said, serenely and simply. "Sam Ward,
a New Hampshire farmer and a dear friend of mine,
used to write to me. I remember once he wrote: 'we
had a Big snow.' He'd write 'i' not 'I'—because I wasn't
important to him. I got letters and letters from him. It
is the most natural way. Sam Ward's way is the only
way. Instead of it being artificial and affected, it is the
conventional way that is artificial and affected. I am
not a scholar but I believe only in English is the 'I'
capitalized."

From an interview with Angela Thirkell:
    ". . . I think we're rather lucky to have the English
language. There are so many good novels in English.
There are a few good novels in French and a few in
German, but the real flowering of the novel was in
England."
    INTERLOCUTOR: Isn't there one exception?
    MRS. THIRKELL: You're not going to say *War and
Peace?*
    INTERLOCUTOR: Yes, I am. But I mean the whole great
nineteenth-century Russian novel—Pushkin, Gogol, Tolstoy, Turgenev, Dostoevsky.
    MRS. THIRKELL: Oh, Russian novels are *so* dull! They
make me squint!

These snatches of recorded talk are, I think, examples of high art. What makes them so good is the trained precision with which Mr. Breit recorded all the peculiarities of speech, the unconventional grammar and special inflections of his interviewees. Aldous Huxley, he noticed, used "Why" as an exclamation, and said "human nature with the lid off of it," and pronounced *ate* as "et" in the British fashion. E. E. Cummings said "I got letters and letters from him," which is something of a prize example of English as it is spoken but never written. And Angela Thirkell said that "Russian novels are *so* dull," emphasizing the word *so*, which means something quite different from "Russian novels are so dull," with the emphasis on *dull*.

If talk is recorded with that much exactness, then you get some meaning beyond the meaning of the individual words. Something of Aldous Huxley's fascination comes through by the sheer rapidity with which he jumps from gold plate and painted teeth to St. Catherine bawling out the Pope. And you understand, perhaps for the first time, the inner meaning of those funny-looking poems by E. E. Cummings, because his simplicity shows in the way he talks about his lower-case *i's*. As to Angela Thirkell's remark about Russian novels—well, it somehow tells more about upper-middle-class England than pages of sociological analysis.

And yet, even an interview artist like Mr. Breit can give us only a substitute. The real thing—the actually spoken words, as they fell from the speaker's lips—is still beyond the reach of even the most gifted writer. You need a tape recorder if you want to catch some of the extraordinary things people say and their wholly unorthodox ways of saying them.

There used to be two easily accessible sources of printed tape-recorded interviews: Mike Wallace's daily TV interview in the New York *Post* and the weekly Q.-and-A. interview feature in *U.S. News & World Report.* Here is a specimen from Mike Wallace. He was interviewing Mrs. Gwen Caffritz, the well-known Washington hostess:

Q. Do your parties really do some good?

A. Well, I do think you do a certain amount of good bringing significant people together.

Q. What's a significant person, Mrs. Caffritz?

A. Practically anybody in an important position in Washington is a significant person.

Q. You've never met stupid people in important positions?

A. Oh, no!

Q. You're said to be a king-maker, Mrs. Caffritz. Are you?

A. Oh, modestly, I wouldn't say so. But these top-rate people come here and when they think they're going to run for the Senate, then I usually give a dinner for them, and we toast to the future Senator.

Q. You always pick winners?

A. We pick them well. They usually get to be Senators.

Q. What are your politics?

A. My husband and I like to have friends on both sides at all times. I'm bipartisan.

Q. How can one person be bipartisan? Don't you have definite political opinions?

A. Yes. It wouldn't be any fun if I didn't.

Q. Well, for example, what do you think of Mr. Reuther's profit-sharing plan?

A. I'm afraid I don't know much about Mr. Reuther. Economics are out of my field. What I'm really interested in is the future of Western civilization.

Q. Do you really worry about the future of Western civilization without worrying a little bit about economics?

A. I'm afraid I do.

Q. Does this make sense?

A. I don't know. . . . I think people should discuss the things they know about. I know about Western culture. . . . I simply love Fra Angelico and things like that.

Only a genius—or a tape recorder—could have set down Mrs. Caffritz's last two sentences in just this way. If an ordinary person had recorded them from memory, they would doubtless have sounded incredibly stupid. But this way, somehow they don't; at least they don't seem so to me. How would *you* define Western civilization, sitting under glaring lights and fending off a hostile interviewer who is trying to score off you? As far as I can see, Mrs. Caffritz's declaration that she "simply loves Fra Angelico and things like that" isn't a bad answer at all. It seems rather likely that she does—in contrast to lots of people who are all in favor of Western civilization but whose acquaintance with Fra Angelico is slight.

And what about the rest of the interview? Somehow, the Q's seem to be more interesting and revealing than the A's. Here, as clear as daylight, is the nasty undertone with which the words "Does this make sense?" were spoken—with which, in fact, all the questions were asked. Could this be brought out on paper except by the exact reproduction of every single word of the interview? I don't think so. I think the tape recorder has added another dimension to written English. (The only editing of a tape that's required is the removal of some of a speaker's "ers" and "ahs.")

U.S. News & World Report, as I mentioned, has for several years been running a weekly tape-recorded interview—a highly successful feature that many subscribers read word for word every week. The interviews are a gold mine for the student of language and writing. I shall quote a few of the most instructive ones.

Here is one (February 7, 1958) that shows nicely the creative power of conversation. It's an interview that was designed to produce a certain effect but developed a powerful drift of its own. The interviewee was Dr. Donald J. Hughes, a nuclear scientist who had just returned from a trip to Russia. The interviewer tried to show the readers that the United States was still ahead of the Russians in basic research and that there was no reason for being panicky. At one point Dr. Hughes said: "I made quite an effort when I was in Russia to find out what books they used at the university level. It was somewhat of a surprise to learn that their main textbooks in advanced nuclear physics are American books translated into Russian."

Q. Are any of your books being used over there?
A. Yes. Here on the desk is the Russian version of a book of mine on neutron physics.
Q. Do they give you credit for it?
A. They didn't at first. My book appeared in the United States in 1953, and I think the next year it was printed in Russia, but they didn't tell me about it.

One interesting point is that a Soviet book always contains a notation giving the number of copies printed. You can see here in the back of this Russian translation of my book that 20,000 copies were printed.
Q. And how many were printed in this country?
A. Probably a quarter of that number.

You see? The interviewer neatly steers Dr. Hughes into telling about how the Russians use his book as a textbook, and suddenly, without warning, Dr. Hughes drops his bombshell about the comparative number of copies printed. There is no way this effect could have been produced except by the Q.-and-A. method.

Next, here is an interview (November 1, 1957) with Dr. Edmund Jacobson, widely known expert on techniques of relaxation. What's the best way for executives to relax? After a while the questions and answers take an unexpected turn:

Q. What about sports? A lot of businessmen take up golf, for instance. Is that a good form of relaxation?

A. It is not necessarily relaxing at all. It's a fine sport, and good exercise. It develops muscles. But that doesn't teach you tension control. It doesn't show you how to quiet your nerves when you've got five different people calling for you, as in the case of a busy executive. . . .

. . . By all means play golf. I can remember Grantland Rice, 25 years ago, having me tell him about this very matter, although I've never played a game of golf. I know one or two professional golfers who have come for a little special training in relaxing. I think sports are wonderful, but I believe that sports are one thing and technical training in relaxing is another.

Q. Well, then, should you take five minutes off every so often during your working day and just sit back and relax?

A. That won't do much good either, unless you use the right procedure in relaxing.

Q. What about wandering into a bar and having a few quiet drinks?

A. That might do more good than what you've just mentioned, because there you've got the alcohol, which is a depressant. . . .

Again, this is much more illuminating than straight exposition could possibly be. What happened here, it seems to me, is that the *U.S. News* editor tried to have Dr. Jacobson comment on the commonly used means of relaxing tension, but got unexpected "no" answers, except in the case of alcohol, where you *would* expect a scientist to say "Lay off it." And why was Dr. Jacobson so bearish on all the things executives usually do to relax their nerves? The reason is clearly visible, somewhere between the lines of his answers. According to Dr. Jacobson, nothing relaxes you "really" except relaxation according to the Ten Commandments of Dr. Jacobson. You may kid yourself and have a fine time on the golf course or take splendid afternoon naps but you can't get any official credit for it "unless you use the right procedure in relaxing." Could this have been brought home to a reader except by means of a tape recorder? I doubt it.

Next: Here is Charles E. Wilson, former Secretary of Defense, interviewed on January 10, 1958. This was shortly after the first unsuccessful attempt of getting the Navy Vanguard satellite into orbit. Mr. Wilson was asked:

> Q. There is a report that 17 billion dollars has been spent or committed on guided missiles up to now. Do you think the money has been well spent?
>
> A. Some of it was. Not all of it.
>
> Q. Do you mean there was some waste?
>
> A. Of course, people don't understand the research and development thing very well. If everything you started was bound to be successful, it wouldn't be research and it wouldn't be development. It would be just straight engineering.
>
> Take all this disappointment over this first little Vanguard outfit that was put up to launch a satellite a few weeks ago and then didn't work. It would have been a near miracle if it had worked.
>
> The whole Vanguard thing was projected on the basis of six, hoping that one of them would work. And I think it is wrong to talk too much about experimental things as if they're proven and as if somebody made a mistake just because it didn't work the first time.

This is an excellent example of the way people really talk. Mr. Wilson is quoted as having said "the research and development thing" and "this first little Vanguard outfit" and "the whole Vanguard thing" and "experimental things." Not exactly the kind of smooth, orderly English students are encouraged to use in their compositions, is it? And yet, Mr. Wilson's point could hardly have been made as well as he made it if he'd prepared an article, say, for *The Atlantic,* and had informed "thinking Americans" of his views on "the underlying philosophy of research and development projects" or "the basic differences between experimental procedures and applied science and technology." Something of this order would have appeared on paper if he had translated his offhand remarks into statelier English, but the force—in fact, some of the meaning—of what he said would have been lost in the process.

For the fact is that Mr. Wilson did say something rather

important here. He practically coined a phrase: "If everything you started was bound to be successful, it wouldn't be research and it wouldn't be development. It would be just straight engineering." These two sentences make you think, don't they? They certainly made *me* think. There is a fine quality of paradoxical logic about them, with their casual disdain for success and for "just straight engineering" and their emphasis on development. You might do worse than copying this quotation and putting it framed on your desk, to look at and ponder from time to time.

Finally, here is an excerpt from a long interview with Mr. Frederick H. Ecker, ninety-year-old honorary chairman of the Metropolitan Life Insurance Company (December 27, 1957):

Q. A friend has this formula: When he gets worried about a document or a memorandum, he does something about it, or else he puts it aside in his drawer and does something about it five days later. He takes a definitive step and puts it out of his mind. Do you ever try that?

A. I do it all the time—always have.

Q. Different men apply it in different ways—

A. If you worry about a thing, it takes half an hour and you get all upset and forget the other things you ought to be doing. I say, "I'll look at that tomorrow," or two hours from now, and I get so busy with something else I forget it.

Q. You wait until you can do something about it, and then dispose of it?

A. It helps to do it just that way. I won't say one is always successful in doing it. If you have something on your mind and turn to something else, the first thing you know, you are thinking of the other.

Q. Do you feel that the thing they call "tension" today is a form of worry, or is it overactivity?

A. It goes along with another thought that occurs to me. In your body, where there is pain there is tension. If you can relieve the tension, you relieve the pain. If you can find the tension before the pain comes, that is really preventive.

Q. Are you a fatalist? Do you believe that what is going to happen will happen, and that there is nothing you can do about it, and do you accept it?

A. I have faith in an all-merciful Providence and the divinity of God, but with that faith I have a realization that, while I can't do things which determine courses for myself without interference, I am responsible for what I do, and I can accomplish things if I make the effort.

If I were to die tomorrow, I wouldn't worry. I am like the Irishman who was talking about death. He said, "If you will tell me where, I will never go near the place." Well, at my age, if I were going to die next Tuesday, I wouldn't change anything. I would carry on just as I am doing, but, then, I am an old man.

Q. Is that based upon a philosophy that you have a job to do and it is not finished until you are ready to go? Is it possibly like someone undertaking a job—that, if that is the time it ends, it ends then?

A. Fatalistically, you mean? I give no thought to it.

Q. That is probably the real answer—you don't think about it—

A. "Consider the lilies, how they grow; they toil not, neither do they spin." I don't think about it. I just think about the things I am doing.

Q. That, then, is the training and discipline of someone who has work to do?

A. Yes. You can't put it in a book. I don't know that you can teach it. You can't make your son understand it. You can guide him a little bit, to help him understand things for himself, but you can't decide it for him.

"You can't put it in a book," Mr. Ecker says. Well, here I *have* put it in a book, and I think it's quite an extraordinary thing to read. The tape recorder has performed something close to a miracle. Here is the thing you can't write, the thing you can't teach, the thing you can't pass on to your son. And it is true that no one, sitting in front of a typewriter and composing an orderly succession of English words and sentences, could possibly put on paper what ninety-year-old Mr. Ecker here murmurs and hints at and leaves finally unsaid. Nobody could possibly write it, but the tape recorder has somehow caught it—the attitude of a man who can say, "If I were going to die next Tuesday" without a flutter in his heart, of a man who can say quietly, "You can't make your son understand it," though this son happens to be Mr. Frederic W. Ecker, current president of Metropolitan Life. This is how it feels to be ninety years old. You can't write it, but you can *say* it, and, if there is a tape recorder handy, it can be printed for other people to read.

The moral of all this is clear: If you want to say something that's hard to put into words, use dialogue. Dialogue somehow has a wider reach than ordinary prose. It can, and often does, express the inexpressible. Use it as much as you can. Drag it into your writing with a deliberate effort. Give those quotation marks a real workout. Of course, ninety-nine times out of a hundred the difference between straight exposition and the dialogue you produce won't be anything very exciting. But the hundredth time something is going to happen. Suddenly you will see on paper something that you didn't know you were going to say—something that you didn't know you knew.

EXERCISES

I am still assuming that you are carrying on with the basic daily-letter exercise on page 139. Now use this exercise to train yourself in using dialogue.

1. Tell about a movie or TV play you saw recently, quoting as much dialogue as you can. If you can't remember the exact words, try to come as close as possible.

2. Describe a recent party or social event you went to, using as much dialogue as possible.

3. Do the same with a business conference, luncheon meeting, etc.

4. Write down the ten best funny stories you know—using lots of dialogue, of course. Make them as funny as you know how.

5. Describe, from memory, an important conversation you had years ago—"the best advice you ever had," for instance. Use straight dialogue, even though you may have to invent all of it.

6. Describe, from memory, the most memorable scene you ever saw in a play or movie. Again, use dialogue, though the actual words may be your own.

Chapter Nineteen

HOW TO WRITE LIKE A PRO

Mr. Morton Sontheimer tells us, in the introduction to *A Guide to Successful Magazine Writing* (the book I mentioned on page 152): "As much of the article as possible is told in narrative style. The fuel that keeps this narrative style running smoothly is anecdotes. Not just any anecdotes . . . The article demands anecdotes that make a given point, that illustrate, that tell the story. Ideally, the anecdotes will not merely supplement but substitute for description or exposition in the article. Anecdotes are far and away the favorite device for sustaining reader interest in nonfiction subjects. . . . Certainly they have become the overriding fetish of our magazine editorial rooms. Many a story has been ordered, many a long trip taken, on the basis of a couple of anecdotes alone. Hardly any idea can be put over without one. . . ."

This is no exaggeration. On the contrary, the introduction to the official handbook put out by the magazine writers' association is just about the best source on what is accepted technique. If Mr. Sontheimer says so, then we may take it for granted that anecdotes *are* the chief element in all popular nonfiction today.

You don't need to look very far to find out that this is so. Open any popular magazine, pick any article at random and you'll find that it consists of about a dozen or so anecdotes, spaced more or less evenly and strung together with swatches of dry subject matter. This is the famous "sandwich" method. Without anecdotes, popular nonfiction would be unsalable and free-lance magazine writers would starve.

To prove my point—and to provide you with some mild entertainment—I picked two articles at random, one from the *Ladies' Home Journal* (April, 1957) and one from the *Saturday Evening Post* (February 22, 1958).

Here are some of the anecdotes I found in "Who Are America's Ten Richest Men?" by Margaret Parton (*Ladies' Home Journal*):

"After the first hundred million, what the heck?" asked Clint Murchison, discussing his friend and fellow Texan, Sid Richardson.

• • •

Richardson, a large, barrel-bodied man with thinning brown hair, a rolling walk and a Texas drawl, has been a bachelor all his life. Whenever he is teased about this, which is often, he remarks amiably, "Why, I been thinkin' about a wife for forty years now."

• • •

The acquisition of property and business, particularly in Dade County—which means Miami and its suburbs —is his [Arthur Vining Davis'] current absorption. He owns one eighth of the county, and many of its banks, hotels and skyscrapers. "Arthur Vining Davis is a large body of money surrounded by Dade County," quipped one observer.

• • •

Howard Hughes carries most of his business in his head, and does business by telephone, often calling associates in the middle of the night. "I don't know whether Howard is a genius or crazy," says one of them. "Maybe he's a little of both. I know I sometimes feel like blowing my top when I hear the phone ring at four A.M. But then he's always so polite and apologetic for waking me up, I forget about it."

• • •

Generally considered hot-tempered but fair, [August] Busch often bellows at his family or at members of his board, "Let me finish! Then you can blow *your* top!"

And here are a few of the things I learned by reading

"The High Price of Art" by Ernest O. Hauser in the *Saturday Evening Post*:

> "I own no stocks," a well-known Hollywood producer confided as he led me past the glittering walls of his Paris establishment. "My savings go into my paintings."

• • •

> [Mr. Basil P. Goulandris bought a still life with apples by Gauguin at a Paris auction for a quarter million dollars.] "Your face showed no excitement," a friend said to the winner afterward.
> "You should have seen my hands," was the reply.

• • •

> "If you brought me a Raphael today," one leading art dealer said recently, "I would have trouble selling it. But let me have a Renoir, and I'll dispose of it"—he pointed to his phone—"in fifteen minutes!"

• • •

> "We've always made our living selling impressionists," says Jean d'Auberville, third-generation owner of the house of Bernheim Jeune, which, in the last half century, has sold some 27,000 canvases. "But we made our fortune with the ones we kept."

• • •

> "No truly good collector ever bought with an eye on appreciation," one veteran art dealer states. "Buy what you like, not what is fashionable, spend only what you can afford to lose, and your reward will be in your enjoyment. If you must speculate, buy stocks!"

There are a few more anecdotes in both Miss Parton's and Mr. Hauser's articles, but basically it is true that without the ones that I have quoted neither of them could have sold the article—or rather, neither of them could have written it, because there simply is no other way nowadays of presenting information to the general public.

Of course, you are not interested in writing articles for

mass-circulation magazines. (If you *are* interested, let me warn you: it's a long, hard road.) But you can and should learn from the technique of the successful practitioners. If you write anything—a letter, a memo, a pamphlet, a company brochure, a report—never underestimate the power of anecdotes. If you come upon one in your preliminary research, don't just smile and go on. Take it down carefully: it's valuable stuff—in interest, in reader appeal, in forcefulness, in general all-purpose usefulness for written presentation.

The magazine writers usually use the most telling one of their anecdotes as the "lead"—the opening paragraph of the article. That's good practice for article writing; for other kinds of writing other types of leads are often preferable. The best model for you—for your letters and memos and reports—is the standard newspaper lead, which is simply a capsule summary of the story.

We're all reading the daily paper every day, but I know from experience that very few people are aware of the rigid, standardized form of the newspaper story. Open your morning paper of the day you are reading these words, and you'll find that every story on the front page, without exception, begins with a summary lead and goes on from there, anti-climactically, into less and less interesting details.

For instance, here is the *New York Times* (Monday, March 24, 1958):

WASHINGTON, March 23—Three of the nation's leading scientists and educators outlined today a six-point program to improve high school education.

JAKARTA, Indonesia, March 23—The Indonesian Army announced tonight that a new victory over rebel forces had established Jakarta's control over all the major oil centers operated by United States companies in Central Sumatra.

WASHINGTON, March 23—Democratic leaders of Congress have been quietly exerting their influence, with apparent success, against rank-and-file agitation for tax reduction.

CAIRO, March 23—The abrupt removal today of Lieut. Gen. Afif Bizri as Chief of Staff of the Syrian Army was regarded here as proof that President Amal Abdel Nasser had taken over complete control of the Syrian forces.

ALBANY, March 23—Several major clashes between Republicans and Democrats were in prospect tonight as the Legislature headed for a final adjournment of this year's session on Wednesday.

Frankfurt, Germany, March 23—Erich Ollenhauer, Social Democratic leader, called today for a general strike to upset the Government's decision to accept nuclear arms.

New Haven, March 23—The first undergraduate co-eds in Yale's history will be living and studying on the campus here in September.

And so on. There are a few more stories starting on the *Times* front page, but the pattern of the lead is always exactly the same. Read the first paragraph and you know the gist of the story. (In fact, read the headline—which the copyreader has distilled from the first paragraph—and you have the gist of the gist of the information.)

This pattern, which has been established in American journalism for a good many years, is, I think, invaluable for *all* ordinary, practical writing. *Every* business letter, to be fully effective, should start with something like "The widgets you ordered on March 23 are under way" or "Sorry, but we can't give you the $100 refund you asked for."

Traditionally, of course, half the letter is spent on elaborately acknowledging the receipt of the incoming letter and leisurely paraphrasing its contents. Then, in the third or fourth paragraph, the poor addressee is given his first inkling of whether the answer he is waiting for is going to be yes or no. Well, I think it's time to learn something from the professionals and be a little quicker on the uptake.

I don't mean to say, however, that the average lead paragraph in the daily paper is a particularly good model for an opening summary. It is not. It's possible to do better than the average lead on a random front page of the *Times*. (The lead on the story from Albany, for instance, is *not* informative.) If you really want to learn how to summarize information, study the front page of the *Wall Street Journal* for a few weeks. There are two regular features—"What's News" and "Business Bulletin"—that contain series of summarized items, written with high professional polish. (Sir William Osler once said, "It is often harder to boil down than to write." I would say, it is *always* harder.)

Look at these gems, for instance:

Billy Mitchell's conviction for violating military law 33 years ago was upheld by Air Force Secretary James H.

Douglas. He turned down a petition by William Mitchell, Jr., to void the court-martial conviction of his father—a champion of American airpower. Douglas ruled the late general conducted himself to the prejudice of good order and military discipline. But he added Mitchell's views "have been vindicated" and his vision on airpower has proved "amazingly accurate."

* * *

A Japanese team launched a plastic rocket, believed to be the world's first. The inventor said it cost about a fifth less than a metal rocket and should give more accurate observations of electrical phenomena. The 78-pound missile was nine feet long, 51 inches in diameter and carried a radio transmitter.

* * *

Rosie the Riveter has had it. Even another full-scale war, say defense manufacturers, will find much less use for this lady and the thousands of other unskilled or semi-skilled hands of World War II. Intricate new missiles require higher skills; one defense contractor suggests training present unskilled hands now in these finer arts.

* * *

An 11-year-old New York boy, George Jones, admitted to police that he pushed two of his playmates into the Hudson River. He shoved a 4-year-old girl off a 62nd Street pier last June 28—for no reason which officers could determine. His other victim, he said, was a 7-year-old boy he pushed off a 27th Street pier last Sunday in a dispute over a dime.

An enormous amount of time, money and effort could be saved if the average business letter or report started with a brief summary of this type. A brief letter or memo, as I said, should begin with a simple newspaper-type lead, conveying immediately the essence of the information. A longer paper or report should be preceded by a separate summary somewhat along the lines of these *Wall Street Journal* examples. Good writing, as I explained in Chapter 15, often requires length and a leisurely pace; on the other hand, a busy executive shies away from thick bundles of typewritten pages. The compromise solution is the opening summary, followed by the detailed full story.

Most of the trade journals, in fact, have arrived at the same solution and their typical pattern today is a combination of newsletter pages and "briefs," introducing a series of fairly lengthy articles. (*U.S. News & World Report* runs half a dozen variegated newsletters side by side with their leisurely rambling Q.-and-A. features.) Here are a few well-written items I picked from *Chemical Week* (January 4, 1958):

Foods with built-in protection against tooth decay may be possible, say University of Wisconsin researchers. Fumito Taketa and Paul Phillips have investigated the decay-prevention properties of oat hulls. They previously had found a diet with 10% finely ground oat hulls that could cut decay in half. Their latest work indicates that 0.5% partly purified hull extracts can turn the trick.

The two biochemists are trying to find out which compounds are responsible for the results. They've zeroed in on 10 phenolic compounds and fatty acids, theorize that one or more of them protect the teeth through their bactericidal action.

They feel that, once the material is identified, it could be manufactured at a modest cost, incorporated into food the way vitamins are. It might be possible, they say, to use the compounds in items such as candy and chewing gum that are normally hard on the teeth.

Now it's "cloud poisoning" to prevent snow. Geophysics Research Directorate, Air Force Cambridge Research Center (Bedford, Mass.), has found in laboratory tests and in preliminary atmosphere tests that monoethyl amine prevents snow crystals from growing, apparently by coating the seed crystals. The "poison" is floated into the cloud in gaseous form. In test cases, none of the treated clouds have "snowed." Some control clouds have, others have not.

• • •

Some new mathematical formulas to speed up molecular analysis have been polished up by three physicists at the Illinois Institute of Technology. After two years' work, they have come up with new formulas that give values to constants in several large molecules, eliminate cumbersome cut-and-try methods of determining thermodynamic data.

Let's analyze these *Wall Street Journal* and *Chemical Week* examples. What exactly *is* this modern technique of boiling things down? What are the rules of the game?

As far as I can see, they are as follows. If you want to become a first-rate boiler-downer, do this:

1. Save every unnecessary comma and every unnecessary *that*. ("Douglas ruled the later general conducted himself . . .")

2. Don't spell out words that can be implied. ("A plastic rocket, believed to be the world's first" . . . "Some control clouds have, others have not.")

3. Use terse colloquial phrases to convey your ideas. ("Rosie the Riveter has had it" . . . "Now it's 'cloud poisoning' to prevent snow.")

4. Use the most expressive verbs you can think of. ("He shoved a girl off a pier." . . . "They've zeroed in on 10 phenolic compounds.")

5. Let the names, numbers, specific data, and verbatim quotes carry the story.

And now, let's do a couple of excursions into the higher reaches of professional writing. By this I don't mean fiction or poetry or drama or any of the creative types of writing—far from it. No. The real test of good writing comes when you are called upon to explain rules and regulations to an ordinary reader. If you can translate legal language into English so that both lawyers and laymen will be satisfied, then you can really write.

I am indebted for my first example to Mrs. Jean Whitnack, editor of the Columbia University catalogues of information, and to her assistant, Miss Marjorie Malcolm. Some time ago these two ladies decided that it ought to be possible to put out catalogues that contained neither gobbledygook nor academic jargon—in other words, to rewrite the rules so that a student could read them and know what was meant. Here is a specimen (from the old catalogue) of what Mrs. Whitnack and Miss Malcolm were up against:

Subject to the approval of the appropriate deans, an undergraduate student in Columbia University whose academic record has been good and who, in the final session of his candidacy for a Bachelor's degree, is within twelve points of that degree may register for graduate courses with a view to offering such courses in partial fulfillment of the requirements for residence for a higher degree, provided, however, that he shall not receive graduate credit in excess of the difference between fifteen points and the number of points that he needed for his Bachelor's degree at the beginning of such session.

The two brave ladies waded into this horrible mess and came up with the following version in English:

An undergraduate student in Columbia University may register for graduate courses and offer them in partial fulfillment of the residence requirement for the advanced degree. Provided: (a) He is within twelve points of the Bachelor's degree. (b) He is in the final session of his candidacy for the degree. (c) His academic record has been good. The amount of "excess credit" may not exceed the difference between fifteen points and the number of points he still needs to fulfill the requirements for the Bachelor's degree.

Let's compare: The old version is exactly 99 words long and is all in one sentence. Its score, according to the test described in Chapter 35, is 10 (assuming that the sentence formed a complete paragraph and counting two extra points at the beginning and the end). The revised version consists of six sentences (counting the very effectively used word *Provided* as a separate sentence, since it is preceded by a period and followed by a colon). It scores 31 points within 85 words, or 36 points per 100 words. As rated by our scale, the revision changed the writing from "formal" to "very popular."

How was it done? To begin with, Mrs. Whitnack and Miss Malcolm broke up that 99-word sentence and gave a complete sentence to each separate idea. Note that they went all out and formed really complete sentences for each one of the conditions. They did *not* write—like all bureaucrats in good standing—". . . provided he is (a) within twelve points of the Bachelor's degree, (b) in the final session of his candidacy for the degree, and (c) has had a good academic record." No. They wrote the way human beings talk and put *He* and *His* after (a), (b), and (c).

Next, please note that the two ladies exactly reversed the sequence of the three conditions. That's typical if you try to translate legal lingo into English. Lawyers, for some reason or other, always put the exception or the least important condition first, and proceed step by step from the exceptional and insignificant to the general and important. The ordinary person, naturally, does it the other way round. Therefore, whenever you do any such job of rewriting, you have to start at the bottom and work your way *up*.

Next, the rewrite team had the good sense to start with the main point: "An undergraduate student in Columbia University may register for graduate courses." The original version has 26 words between *an undergraduate student in Columbia University* and *may register for graduate courses*. Why? Because the legal mind has a basic horror of setting down *any* statement that could conceivably be lifted out of context so as to get away with something. "An undergraduate student may register for graduate courses"? Why, of course not, perish the thought! Who ever heard of such a thing? No one—absolutely no one—is allowed to register in the graduate school . . . except, of course, if he fulfills the three conditions "as herein stated." So let's not be rash; let's stop anyone who is apt to jump to conclusions by putting 26 words in his way. Result: Gobbledygook instead of English.

Finally, the two ladies explained the business about the "excess credit" in a separate sentence rather than working it in by way of "provided, however." Also, they called it by its usual handle ("excess credit") rather than sticking to the formal "shall not receive graduate credit in excess of." (This is fine, but here they ought to have gone a step further and added an example or two, e.g.: "If the student needs 12 points for his Bachelor's degree and takes 15, he gets 3 points extra credit" or "If he needs only 10 points for his Bachelor's degree and takes 16 points, he still gets only 5 points excess credit.")

After this rather tricky problem let's climb the Mount Everest of all writing problems. I mean, of course, the world-famous, forbidding peak of U.S. income-tax prose. On March 19, 1958, the Associated Press carried the following story:

WASHINGTON, March 19—Senator Arthur V. Watkins is offering a prize to anyone who can figure out the meaning of a 212-word sentence in the Government's latest income-tax instructions. He said a puzzled constituent had written him, asking what the sentence meant.

An Internal Revenue Service spokesman said its experts had "done their best to make this instruction readable and understandable" but were handicapped by the complications in the law, as passed by Congress.

He said the questioned section came from the Internal Revenue Code, and was not a regulation laid down by the service.

Senator Watkins said later he probably had voted for the law himself. He said that if Congress were at fault, maybe some of its members could enter his contest and help clarify things.

Earlier, the Utah Republican said he had read the sentence several times "without getting anywhere—save for a state of aggravated thirst, induced by repetitive reading of the 212-word sentence."

"I even exposed it to some of my colleagues in the Senate, a group not normally nonplussed by long-winded and obscure phrases," he said. "They too were stumped —and dehydrated."

In his statement, Senator Watkins said that as a prize for the best explanation of what the sentence meant he would give a copy of the book "Simplified English."

He suggested that the winner could autograph the book and give it to the Internal Revenue Commissioner, Russell C. Harrington.

The Senator said he would also present to the winner a copy of the Bible, "an all-time best seller, known for the simplicity and lucidity of its prose."

A few contest rules were set. Professional tax experts and Internal Revenue Service employees are ineligible. Entries must be typewritten, not over 300 words in length, and be submitted by April 16.

And he had one more admonition: "No 212-word sentences, please."

The sentence to be interpreted is from Page 8 of the Internal Revenue Service Booklet "How to Prepare Your Income Tax Return on Form 1040."

It is entitled "Additional Charge for Underpayment of Estimated Tax," and says:

"The charge with respect to any underpayment of any installment is mandatory and will be made unless the total amount of all payments of estimated tax made on or before the last date prescribed for the payment of such installment equals or exceeds whichever of the following is the lesser—

"(A) The amount which would have been required to

be paid on or before such date if the estimated tax were whichever of the following is the least—

"(1) The tax shown on your return for the previous year (if your return for such year showed a liability for tax and covered a taxable year of 12 months), or

"(2) A tax computed by using the previous year's income with the current year's rates and exemptions, or

"(3) 70 per cent (66⅔ per cent in the case of farmers) of a tax computed by projecting to the end of the year the income received from the beginning of the year up to the beginning of the month of the installment payment; or

"(B) An amount equal to 90 per cent of the tax computed, at the rates applicable to the taxable years, on the basis of the actual taxable income for the months in the taxable year ending before the month in which the installment is required to be paid."

Before offering a brief interpretation of the 212 words, the spokesman noted that the words applied only to those required to file an estimated return, a comparatively small minority of individual income taxpayers. The great majority has to file returns only for income received in the previous year.

The sentence, he said, sets forth the applicable rules and tells when the penalty will be assessed for failing to pay a sufficient amount.

It also states the exceptions, or "outs," that apply even though the affected taxpayer hasn't paid the required 70 per cent of his liability for the year.

A 6 per cent penalty is imposed, the spokesman continued, but not on the difference between what a taxpayer has paid and what he was supposed to pay.

The penalty is assessed against the difference between what he paid and the 70 per cent he was supposed to pay. And the penalty on this is prorated quarterly because the tax is payable in quarterly installments.

Then the sentence attempts to explain certain conditions under which no penalty will be assessed even though 70 per cent of the tax has not been paid, the spokesman said.

One exception is when a declaration is filed and a tax paid on the basis of the individual's actual tax for the previous year. If the tax paid in 1956 was $100, for example, and $100 was paid in 1957, there is no penalty even though the 1957 liability might be greater.

The spokesman said another exception applied when one has filed a declaration and paid a tax on the basis of his previous year's income but has taken advantage of the current year's exemptions and deductions.

A third exception arises, the spokesman went on, if a taxpayer files a declaration and pays his estimated quarterly tax on the basis of actual income for the year up to that date, prorated on the annual basis. He's in the clear, the spokesman concluded, even though he's not up to the 70 per cent minimum at the end of the year.

This is quite a long story to read, but I think it's invaluable for anyone who wants to improve his English. Here is a sentence of absolutely unreadable English, so ridiculous that it makes a front-page story if a Senator happens to look into it. The Senator, properly appalled, offers a mock prize for contestants trying to rewrite the sentence (I still don't know whether the book on "Simplified English" is mythical or real). Newspapers all over the country print the story, and everybody has a good laugh. Six weeks later it is announced that lots of people tried for the prize, but not a single contestant in the whole United States managed to come up with a version that satisfied a panel of tax experts. And that's the end of the story: it's officially impossible to translate income tax prose into readable English.

Or is it? I don't think so. For the thing that nobody noticed, the miracle of American everyday journalism, was the fact that the AP story itself contained an excellent rewrite of the 212-word sentence. Senator Watkins' prize by right belonged to the unknown reporter who had written the story. As a matter of course, as part of the routine of the day's work, he had performed the impossible.

What happened was simply this: After the AP man got the story from Senator Watkins, he did what any good newspaperman would have done and got in touch with the Bureau of Internal Revenue. There he got hold of someone who explained to him what the unreadable sentence was supposed to mean, and asked a few questions to make sure he fully understood the explanation. Then he went back to his office and sat down to write the story in time for the morning-paper deadline. The result of this perfectly normal routine of news writing was the solution to the seemingly insoluble problem: an understandable explanation, in 277 words (not counting "the spokesman said," etc.), of what the sentence meant.

If you analyze the unknown AP hero's work, you'll find that he pretty much followed the principles I just derived from Mrs. Whitnack's and Miss Malcolm's simplification of the Columbia University rules. First, he broke up the monster sentence and used a separate sentence for each separate idea. (Altogether, he used eleven sentences for his explanation.) Second, he too reversed the sequence of the conditions, starting —rightly—with Point (A) (3), which happens to be the basis of the whole penalty system. Third, he too started with the main point: "A 6 per cent penalty is imposed . . . on the difference between what the taxpayer paid and the 70 per cent he was supposed to pay." However, the AP man, more seasoned than the two Columbia University ladies, did two more things: He went out of his way to forestall any possible misunderstanding (". . . but not on the difference between what a taxpayer has paid and what he was supposed to pay"), and he added an example where one was called for ("If the tax paid in 1956 was $100 and $100 was paid in 1957 there is no penalty even though the 1957 liability might be greater").

So, if you ever find yourself faced with the tough problem of rewriting rules and regulations, here are five points to remember:

1. Put each idea in a separate sentence.
2. Start with the most general condition and end up with the most exceptional case.
3. State the main point first.
4. Forestall possible minunderstandings.
5. Give illustrative examples.

EXERCISES

It has been said that everybody considers himself an expert on marriage, education, and politics. So, take the subject of marriage and imagine that you are preparing an article on it, stating your views and experiences. Do the following:

1. Write down six anecdotes that illustrate your point of view. Tell them as effectively as you can.
2. Pick as the lead of your article the one among the six anecdotes that will serve best to get a reader interested.
3. Write a one-paragraph summary of the article. Make it as meaty as possible.
4. Do the same three things for an article on education.

5. Do the same three things for an article on politics.

6. Write your own simplified version of the 212-word sentence from the income-tax instructions on pages 187 to 190, using the AP version as a guide.

Chapter Twenty

DANGER! LANGUAGE AT WORK

In the fall of 1786, Goethe went on his famous trip to Italy. Three weeks after he got there, he wrote in his diary:

> We northerners can say *Good night!* at any hour of parting in the dark. But the Italian says *Felicissima notte!* only once: at the parting of day and night, when the lamp is brought into the room. To him it means something entirely different. So untranslatable are the idioms of every language: from the highest to the lowest word everything is based on national peculiarities of character, attitudes, or conditions.

Goethe's casual observation contains a profound truth. Every word in every language is part of a system of thinking unlike any other. Speakers of different languages live in different worlds; or rather, they live in the same world, but can't help looking at it in different ways. Words stand for patterns of experience. As one generation hands its language down to the next, it also hands down a fixed pattern of thinking, seeing, and feeling. When we go from one language to another, nothing stays put; different peoples carry different nerve patterns in their brains, and there's no point where they fully match.

Of course, Goethe wasn't the only one who noticed this. Everybody who comes in contact with foreign languages sooner or later runs into the same thing. In recent years, UN meetings have furnished many examples. When the UN charter was written, Latin Americans protested that the phrase "sovereign equality" didn't mean a thing to them; they preferred "personality of states," a phrase meaningless to everyone else. The French, it turned out, had no word for "trusteeship," the Chinese had trouble in translating "steering committee," the Spanish-speaking members couldn't express the difference between "chairman" and "president." The Russians had trouble with "gentlemen's agreement" and had to fall back on semi-English, making it *gentlemenskoye soglasheniye.*

Russian is filled with words showing the Russian "character, attitudes and conditions." The critic Edmund Wilson found that out when he read Tolstoy in the original. He came upon such beauties as *dozhidat'sya* (to attain by waiting), *propivat'sya* (to squander all one's money on drink), and *pereparyvat'* (to whip everybody all around). And in *Anna Karenina* he found no fewer than fifteen words that meant different expressions of the eyes.

The more exotic the language, the odder the thinking pattern to us. In Hindustani the same word, *kal*, stands for yesterday and tomorrow. In Lithuanian there is a word for gray when you speak of eyes, another when you speak of hair, a third when you speak of ducks and geese, several more for other purposes, but no word for gray in general. In Balinese there is a lovely word, *tis*, that means "to feel warm when it's cold or cool when it's hot."

We don't even have to go that far to realize differences in language patterns. They are brought home to every first-year French student when he is asked to translate a simple sentence like "The girl is running down the stairs." Naturally, he tries to translate word for word: *La petite fille court bas l'escalier.* Then he learns that that's all wrong. A Frenchman says: *"La petite fille descend l'escalier en courant"*—the girl descends the stairs in running.

Or take German. Everybody has heard of the three German genders, which make tables, chairs, coats, and spoons masculine; cats, roads, bridges, and forks feminine; and horses, sheep, girls, and knives neuter. Or the two German forms of *you*—familiar *du* and formal *Sie*—whose subtle difference may spell the loss of a job or the acceptance of a marriage proposal.

German has all sorts of the fine distinctions that don't exist in English. A German isn't satisfied with a word meaning "to know"; he needs two, *wissen* and *kennen*. One means "to have knowledge of," as in knowing a secret; the other means "to be acquainted with," as in knowing a place or a person. A German woman doesn't just "put on" a dress, an apron, or a hat; she "pulls a dress on," "ties an apron around," and "puts a hat on top of herself." A German horse has a different name depending on whether it's white or black: if it's white, it's a *Schimmel;* if it's black, it's a *Rappe*.

Even more subtly, German writers come in two grades. They may be either *Schriftsteller* (professionals who make a living by writing) or *Dichter* (poets in verse or prose; literary figures). Thomas Mann is a *Dichter*, but Vicki Baum is a *Schriftstellerin*. In German translation, Ernest Hemingway doubtless is a *Dichter*, but Erle Stanley Gardner is a *Schriftsteller*.

To a German, of course, some of our English distinctions are just as odd. *Braten*, in German, covers roasting, baking, grilling, broiling, and frying. *Reise* means travel, journey, voyage, cruise, tour, and trip. So don't get me wrong—don't consider the English language pattern natural and all others perverse. It all depends on where you sit.

Just for the fun of it, I drew up a short list of German "untranslatables" (with explanations in English of what they mean almost but not quite). Here they are:

Lebenskünstler	one who knows how to live
Sehnsucht	great longing or yearning
Zeitgeist	spirit of the age
Weltschmerz	world-weariness
Rausch	drunkenness, delirium, passionate glow, ecstasy, mad fit
verscherzen	to lose something through folly; to trifle away
Gemütlichkeit	good-natured, sanguine, easy-going disposition; good nature; cheerfulness; comfortableness; sentiment; freedom from worry about money
Schadenfreude	malicious joy at another's misfortune; gratification of pent-up envy; joy over the misfortune of those one has formerly cringed to and envied
Übermut	wild spirits; excessive joy or merriment; cockiness; sauciness; uppishness; arrogance

Naturally, English has its share of "untranslatables" too. They don't seem any different from other words to us, but foreigners have an awful time with them. Examples: "to humor someone," "a bargain," "a pet."

On the other hand, there are quite a few useful words that other languages have but we have not. We have no single

word that means "his or her" and have to make shift with
sentences like "Everybody put on their hats and coats." We
have no word for "brother or sister" and our sociologists had
to invent the word "sibling" for the purpose.

And, as John T. Winterich noted in the *Saturday Review*
a while ago, we have no noun "to denote the relationship of
one father-in-law (or mother-in-law) to his (or her) opposite
number." You may doubt—looking at the world through
your own culture-and-language spectacles—whether any people ever went to the trouble of coining a word for such a
complex relationship. But you'd be mistaken. As soon as
national "peculiarities of character, attitudes or conditions"
make a relationship important and meaningful, a label for it
will appear. Yiddish, for one, is a language equipped with
Mr. Winterich's word: the father-in-law is to his opposite
number a *mekhoótn,* the mother-in-law a *mekhtáynesta.*

Words for family relationships, in fact, are the pet examples
of the anthropologists to show cultural differences among
languages. The variations are endless. To you, an uncle is an
uncle; to millions of people there is a tremendous difference
between a father's brother and a mother's brother. In English,
the word *cousin* covers both girls and boys; in practically all
other languages, such an idea would be utterly unthinkable.

Consider, for instance, the fantastically complex system of
the Vietnamese. They wouldn't think of using the term for the
father's elder brother, *bac,* for the father's younger brother,
who is called *chu,* not to speak of the mother's brother, who
is called *cau.* The father's sister is *co;* the mother's sister is *di.*
On the other hand, one word, *chau,* is all they use to refer to
grandchildren, great-grandchildren, nephews, nieces, grand-
nephews, grandnieces and so on of either sex. A son, when
he grows up, is suddenly called *cau,* like the mother's brother;
so is a wife's brother after he gets married. Before that, he is
called *anh,* "elder brother," which is also the term used by a
wife for her husband's elder brother, as well as for her husband himself. If this sounds utterly confusing to you, please
remember that our system is probably just as confusing to
the Vietnamese.

Anthropologists soon learn not to be bewildered by varieties
of words. The Eskimos have one word for "snow on the
ground," another for "falling snow," a third for "drifting
snow" and a fourth for "a snow-drift." They have a general
word for "seal," another for "seal basking in the sun," a third
for "seal floating on a piece of ice," and any number of others

classifying seals by age and sex. To the Chukchee, a tribe that lives at the far eastern tip of Siberia, reindeer are what seals are to the Eskimos. They have twenty-six different words for reindeer skin colors, and sixteen words for reindeer of various ages and sexes. For instance, a *qlikin*, a male baby reindeer, is different from a *penvel*, a male reindeer one to two years old; a *krimqor* (female, two to three years old) is not the same as a *rewkut* (female, five to six years old); and so on through sixteen different names—a system which comes perfectly naturally to even the dumbest Chukchee boys and girls. Halfway around the globe, the Lapps of northern Scandinavia also live of, by, and for reindeer. *They* call them *patso, sarves, hierke, svaljes, vateuvaja, stainak, ratno, tjnoivak, kiepak, pajuk* or *tjousek*, depending on sex, color, fertility, tractability and whatnot. Of course their classification has nothing to do with the Chukchee system; no reason why it should.

If you feel superior to all this and insist that a reindeer is a reindeer (except for specially famous ones like Donder, Blitzen, or Rudolph), that just shows you don't realize the close relation between language and life. For Lapps or Chukchees, a single word for reindeer would be the height of inconvenience; they *have* to make all these distinctions to get on with the business of living. To them, the sentence "I saw a reindeer" would be as absurd as if *you* said, "I live in a dwelling with family members and own a vehicle."

Anthropologists also often run into a single word used by a primitive tribe that seems almost impossible to define exactly. One of them once spent fourteen months in the Solomon Islands, using most of that time trying to pin down the meaning of the word *mumi* in a Papuan dialect. It was easy to see that a *mumi* was a chief headman, wealthy, a born leader, and owned a clubhouse filled with wooden gongs, which was used ever so often for big parties. But it took much research to find some of the other connotations of the word *mumi:*

> He is given preference over other natives in pig-buying; the choicest cuts of pork go to him; he need never climb palms for drinking nuts if someone else is around. . . . He can sit in his clubhouse and listen to the flattery of his followers, he can call upon supernatural aid whenever he needs it, and he can rest assured of a comfortable place in the afterworld.

Quite a word, isn't it?

All of these examples, however, are nothing compared to

the brilliant researches of our own anthropologists into the structure of American Indian languages. Fortunately for the science of linguistics, the Indians live right among us, while their languages are as far removed from ours as they can possibly be. They are full of eye-opening examples of the enormous range and flexibility of the human mind. Better than anything else, they show that the very nature of facts and events changes as soon as another language is used to state them.

Here are some of our anthropologists' finding:

In the Kwakiutl language, there is no single word that means "to sit." There are only words that mean "sitting on the ground," "sitting on the beach," "sitting on a pile of things," "sitting on a round thing," or "sitting on the floor of the house."

In Dakota, there is one word meaning "to be gripped" that covers a wide range of situations that seem utterly different to us. Depending on the context it may mean "to kick," "to tie in bundles," "to bite," "to be near to," "to pound" and so on.

Dakota verbs are equipped to express subtle degrees. *Slecha,* for example, means "to split something easily"; *shlecha* means "to split something with some difficulty"; *hlecha* means "to split something with great difficulty." *Zezeya* means "dangling"; but *apazhezheya* means "right on the edge, almost falling over."

In Hupa, nouns have present, past, and future tenses. *Xonta* means "house now," *xontaneen* means "house past (in ruins)" *xontate* means "house to be (planned)."

The Shawnee translation of the English sentence "I pull the branch aside" is *nilthawakona.* Broken down into its elements, this means "Fork tree by-hand I do." The Shawnee translation of "I clean it (a gun) with a ramrod" is *nipekwalakha*—which means "I dry-space inside-hole by-moving-tool do."

In Nootka, there are no parts of speech whatever. The difference between nouns and verbs, or between subjects and predicates, simply doesn't exist. There is a word for "house," for instance, but it's something indefinite between a noun and a verb and means "it houses." Or take the simple English sentence, "He invites people to a feast." In our language, this has a subject ("he"), a verb ("invites"), and a neat logical progression—that is, according to *our* logic, the way of thinking embodied in our language. A Nootka Indian looks at this situation in an entirely different way. He starts *his* sentence with the main thing about a feast—the event of boiling or cooking: *tlimsh*. Then comes *ya*, meaning "result": *tlimshya*, "cooked food." Next comes *is*, "eating," which makes *tlimshya-is*, "eating cooked food." Next: *ita*, "those who do." Now he has *tlimshya-isita*, "cooked food eaters." Finally he adds *itl* ("go for") and *ma* ("he") and comes up with the sentence *tlimshya-isita-itlma*, "cooked food eaters he go for" or, in English, "he invites people to a feast."

And then there is the most fascinating of all Indian languages, Hopi. By now you won't be surprised when I tell you that a Hopi classifies things differently from us. For water he has two words: *pahe* and *keyi*. *Pahe* is a lot of water running wild, so to speak—the sea, a lake, a waterfall; *keyi* is "tamed" water, water in a container—a panful or a glassful. The word *masaytaka* takes in everything that flies except birds. It doesn't bother a Hopi that *masaytaka* may at different times mean an airplane, a pilot, a butterfly, or a mosquito.

Hopi verbs don't have present, past, or future tenses; it is a "timeless" language. Instead, its verbs have forms that show whether something is (or was) *actually* happening, whether it is *expected* to happen, or whether it is merely apt to happen *in general*. When a Hopi says *wari* ("running"), it may mean "he is running, I see him"; but it may also mean "he was running, you and I both saw him." When he says *warikni*, it means "I expect him to run," which isn't quite the same as "he will run." And when he says *warikngwe*, it means "he runs" (in general, say, on the track team).

A unique feature of Hopi is that verbs can express one big action or a series of little ones. A suffix ending in *ta* takes care of that. *Yoko* means "he gives one nod"; *yokokota* means "he is nodding." *Ripi* means "it gives one flash"; *ripipita*, "it is sparkling." *Wukuku* means "he takes one step without moving from his place"; *wukukuta*, "he is dancing up and down." *Hochi* means "it forms a sharp angle"; *hochichita*, "it is zigzag."

All of this is as odd as can be, but again I must remind you that it seems odd only to us who are used to thinking in English. Hopi and English are just two of thousands of languages actually spoken today. Each of them, as the late Edward Sapir put it, is a particular *how* of thought; and the speakers of each consider all others as more or less inferior, absurd, and illogical.

The knowledge of this basic fact is essential to clear thinking. To be sure, we can't help using our native (or adopted) language in our thoughts; but we can try to remember that ours isn't the only way to think.

Does this mean that the practice of translation will help you think? Maybe it does. Let's go into that question in the next chapter.

Chapter Twenty-One

THE PURSUIT OF TRANSLATION

Some time ago I wrote a *Reader's Digest* article that was translated into German and Spanish. One of the expressions I used was "fancy words." It turned out that you can say that neither in German nor in Spanish. In German the phrase becomes *geschraubte Ausdrücke* ("screwed-up expressions"); in Spanish, *palabras rebuscadas* ("farfetched words").

What surprised me even more was that the common word "executive" has no counterpart in either German or Spanish. In German it's *leitende Männer* ("leading men"), in Spanish *directores de empresas* ("directors of enterprises").

These are, after all, simple words. Quite another problem came up when Billy Rose's *Wine, Women and Words* had to be translated for the French *Reader's Digest* edition. Maurice Chevalier was hired to do the job and did himself proud—considering what he was up against. He translated "it was a seven-day wonder" into *époustoufla* ("it blew them over"), "it was a cinch bet" into *c'était du nougat!* ("it was candy"), and "razzle-dazzle and razzmatazz" into *plaisanter sur des plaisantries plaisantes* ("having fun with fun").

Translation problems of this sort are not exceptional. Do you think translating means taking the dictionary translations of each word and putting them together? This is a widespread notion; it's the theory of automatic translation. And I mean automatic: in California there is a machine, the Bureau of Standards Western Automatic Computer, that's supposed to translate on just that principle. I haven't seen any of its translations, but I am skeptical. Equivalent words in two languages are not the rule, but the exception.

In 1949 Monsignor Ronald Knox wrote a little book about Bible translation problems. Among his illustrations are such apparently simple cases as the English word "danger." Surprisingly enough, it doesn't occur once in the Authorized

Version of the Old Testament. Now, says Knox, "it is nonsense to suppose that the Hebrew mind has no such notion as danger; why is there no word for it? The answer can only be, that in Hebrew you express the same idea by a nearly-allied word which has to do duty, also, for slightly different ideas; a word like 'affliction,' 'tribulation' or 'trouble.' " Or take the word "land": "Neither Hebrew nor Greek nor Latin has two separate words for 'earth,' in the sense of the terrestrial globe, and 'land' in the sense of a particular region of it. When we are told that there was darkness all over the *terra* at the time of our Lord's Crucifixion, how are we to know whether that darkness was world-wide, or was only noticeable in Palestine?"

Then there is the simple word "know," which, according to Knox, "is a constant problem to the translator, all through the New Testament. Nine times out of ten you want to translate it 'realize' but unfortunately that use of the word 'realize' is modern slang." Even more basically, "Hebrew has one word that does duty for 'and' and 'but'; and wherever the translator comes across that word in the Old Testament he must decide between them, sometimes at the risk of making nonsense of a whole paragraph."

On top of all that, translation, like woman's work, is never done. It has to be done all over again for each succeeding generation. How many English translations of the Bible there are by now, I don't know; but there are over thirty translations of Homer's *Odyssey*, for instance. You'll immediately understand why when you compare different versions of the same passage.

In the standard translation by Butcher and Lang (1879) the famous scene in which Odysseus is recognized by his old dog looks like this:

> Thus they spake one to the other. And lo, a hound raised up his head and pricked his ears, even where he lay, Argos, the hound of Odysseus, of the hardy heart, which of old himself had bred, but had got no joy of him, for ere that, he went to sacred Ilios. Now in time past the young men used to lead the hound against wild goats and deer and hares; but as then, despised he lay (his master being afar) in the deep dung of mules and kine, whereof an ample bed was spread before the doors, till the thralls of Odysseus should carry it away to dung therewith his wide demesne. There lay the dog Argos, full of vermin. Yet even now when he was ware of

Odysseus standing by, he wagged his tail and dropped both his ears, but nearer to his master he had not now the strength to draw.

Now let's go back to 1725, to the most famous English translation of the *Odyssey*, by Alexander Pope:

Thus, near the gates conferring as they drew,
Argus, the dog, his ancient master knew:
He not unconscious of the voice and tread,
Lifts to the sound his ear, and rears his head;
Bred by Ulysses, nourish'd at his board,
But, ah! not fated long to please his lord;
To him, his sweetness and his strength were vain;
The voice of glory call'd him o'er the main.
Till then in every sylvan chase renown'd,
With Argus, Argus, rung the woods around;
With him the youth pursued the goat or fawn,
Or traced the mazy leveret o'er the lawn.
Now left to man's ingratitude he lay,
Unhoused, neglected, in the public way;
And where on heaps the rich manure was spread,
Obscene with reptiles, took his sordid bed.
He knew his lord; he knew and strove to meet:
In vain he strove to crawl and kiss his feet;
Yet (all he could) his tail, his ears, his eyes,
Salute his master, and confess his joys.

T. E. Lawrence (Lawrence of Arabia) translated the *Odyssey* in 1932. His version is this:

As they talked, a dog lying there lifted his head and pricked his ears. This was Argos whom Odysseus had bred but never worked, because he left for Ilium too soon. On a time the young fellows used to take him out to course the wild goats, the deer, the hares: but now he lay derelict and masterless on the dung-heap before the gates, on the deep bed of mule-droppings and cow-dung which collected there till the serfs of Odysseus had time to carry if off for manuring his broad acres. So lay Argos the hound, all shivering with dog-ticks. Yet the instant Odysseus approached the beast knew him. He thumped his tail and drooped his ears forward, but lacked power to drag himself ever so little towards his master.

You probably feel that the third version is the best. So do I. But all such judgments are relative. When Pope's translation was published, a contemporary critic wrote: "To say of this noble work that it is the best which ever appeared of the kind, would be speaking in much lower terms than it deserves." Sixty years later, in 1788, William Cowper said flatly: "There is hardly a thing in the world of which Pope is so entirely destitute as a taste for Homer." As to T. E. Lawrence, Professor Gilbert Highet of Columbia University casually remarked in a book review: "T. E. Lawrence's caricature of Homer's *Odyssey* is clever but cheap, like a mock-Victorian drawing-room."

Another paradox of translation is this: The simpler the words of the original, the harder it is to translate them. That's why simple lyrics are the toughest translation problem in the world. Compare, for instance, four English translations of Goethe's *Wanderers Nachtlied,* which is generally considered *the* most beautiful German poem. Here is the original—all twenty-four words of it:

> Über allen Gipfeln
> Ist Ruh,
> In allen Wipfeln
> Spürest du
> Kaum einen Hauch;
> Die Vögelein schweigen im Walde.
> Warte nur, balde
> Ruhest du auch.

Here is Longfellow:

> O'er all the hill-tops
> Is quiet now,
> In all the tree-tops
> Hearest thou
> Hardly a breath;
> The birds are asleep in the trees:
> Wait; soon like these
> Thou too shalt rest.

Aytoun and Martin:

> Peace breathes along the shade
> Of every hill,
> The tree-tops of the glade

Are hush'd and still;
All woodland murmurs cease,
The birds to rest within the brake are gone.
Be patient, weary heart—anon,
Thou too, shalt be at peace!

George Sylvester Viereck:

Over the tops of the trees
Night reigns. No breath, no breeze.
Never a voice is heard
Of rustling leaf or bird
    The forest through.
Hush! But a little ways
From where your footstep strays
    Peace awaits you.

John Rothensteiner:

Over all the hill tops
    Is peace;
In all the trees' still tops
    Gentle cease
The breaths from the blue.
The birds in the forest are sleeping,
    Soon in God's keeping
Sleepest thou too.

Which is best? The one that's printed in all the anthologies is Longfellow's, of course; the one that's nearest to the letter and spirit of the original, I think, is Rothensteiner's. But it doesn't really matter: none of the four comes anywhere close to the original with its magically soft and soothing German words.

If you don't know German, I can't very well ask you to appreciate that. In fact, it seems almost impossible to talk understandably about translation to a person who may not know any foreign language. Therefore, I want to add here one more example, this time the other way round: I'll show you an English passage and describe the various words that have been used to translate it into German. (I apologize for drawing so much on my native language.) My example is the famous lines from *Macbeth*:

Out, out, brief candle!
Life's but a walking shadow, a poor player

That struts and frets his hour upon the stage
And then is heard no more: it is a tale
Told by an idiot, full of sound and fury,
Signifying nothing.

The Germans have about as many Shakespeare translations as we have Homer translations. I compared eight different versions of this passage and found eight different expressions for "struts and frets," five for "idiot," and six for "sound and fury." For "struts and frets" a German reader gets something like: makes a noise and raves, swaggers and gnashes, labors and raves, stilts and gnashes, parades and raves, rages and storms, stilts and brags, and boasts; for "idiot": blockhead, fool, madman, simpleton and ninny; for "sound and fury": pomposity, noise and rage, flood of words, storm and urge, tone and fire.

Reading this, you probably sympathize with the poor Germans who get only a vague inkling of Shakespeare's immortal words. But remember that most of these translations are excellent: one is by Schiller, one is by the famous team of Schlegel and Tieck, and so on. On the whole, they are just as good as *our* translations of Goethe—or of Homer, Plato, Horace, Dante, Cervantes, Balzac, Tolstoy, and all the rest. You just have to accept the fact that translations are always approximations; as Don Quixote said, they show us the wrong side of the tapestry.

But even that isn't all. Often a complete shift is necessary in order to convey anything at all in another language. Two famous Broadway plays furnish good examples.

In his translation of Jean Giraudoux's *Madwoman of Chaillot,* Maurice Valency completely changed a great many passages that meant a lot to Frenchmen but would have left Americans cold. For instance, a character, in the role of a billionaire, says: "I have flowers sent from Java, where they are cut from the backs of elephants, and if the petals are the least bit crushed, I fire the elephant-drivers." In English he says instead: "I dispatch a plane to Java for a bouquet of flowers. I send a steamer to Egypt for a basket of figs. I send a special representative to New York to fetch an ice cream cone, and if it's not exactly right, back it goes."

And when Arthur Miller's famous play *Death of a Salesman* was produced in Vienna, the leading part, believe it or not, was played as a sort of petty official. Otherwise the Viennese wouldn't have understood what it was all about.

What does all this mean to *you?* It means that translating is the ideal form of intellectual exercise. Whenever we translate, we are forced to abandon the mental patterns we are used to and get the hang of others completely alien to our thinking. There's nothing quite like it to gain mental flexibility —which, as you'll see later on, is practically *the* main ingredient of clear thinking. If foreign languages didn't exist, we'd have to invent them as a training device for our minds.

This looks like a plug for the study of foreign languages, but I don't quite mean that—at least not in the usual sense. Usually foreign languages are played up either because they are practical ("You ought to know how to order a meal in Paris") or because they are cultural ("Latin makes you think more logically"). The way I look at it, all that's neither here nor there. Let Schopenhauer make my point for me:

> In learning any foreign language, you form new concepts, you discover relationships you didn't realize before, innumerable nuances, similarities, differences enter your mind; you get a rounded view of everything. Which means that you think differently in every language, that learning a language modifies and colors your thinking, corrects and improves your views, and increases your thinking skill, *since it will more and more detach your ideas from your words.*

Schopenhauer, who was an intellectual snob, goes on to say that everybody ought to know Latin and Greek—in fact, that people who don't are only half human. I don't think that follows from his argument. If language study is good because it detaches ideas from words, any language will do—Chinese, Swahili, Navaho—the farther removed from our own culture the better. To be sure, some languages have richer literatures than others, but that's another story.

Probably you'll be skeptical about all this; interest in foreign languages doesn't come naturally to an American. But before you shrug it off, let me remind you that ever since the Romans, Western civilization was built and run by people who knew at least one foreign language; that until not so long ago, Latin and Greek were part of every educated person's mental equipment. As the famous quotation goes, the battle of Waterloo was won on the playing fields of Eton; it's equally true that the British Empire was won in the *classrooms* of Eton, where future colonial administrators were forced to compose little Latin poems.

Well, then, do you have to go to a Berlitz school to learn the art of clear thinking? Not quite. As I said, the important thing is not the learning of foreign languages, but the activity of translation. Fortunately, you can practice translation—to a degree—even if you don't know a single foreign word. You can translate from English into English. You do this whenever you detach ideas from one set of words and attach them to another. You do it whenever you write a letter and make your ideas clear to the addressee; whenever you make a speech and present your thoughts to your audience; whenever you carry on an intelligent conversation. You can learn to do this sort of translating better and better, and you can use it consciously "to detach your ideas from your words."

Otherwise you never can tell whether you *have* any ideas —or just words.

Chapter Twenty-Two

WHY ARGUE?

Logic is the science of argument.

This was true in the fourth century B.C., when Aristotle started it all; it is still true today, when the teaching of logic is being justified by the fact that it helps students win an argument.

But what does it mean—"win an argument"? When you argue with someone, you pit your opinion against his. Your opinion is the result of past experience; so is his. If you win the argument, it means that your opponent has to realign his ideas so that they parallel yours.

This is unpleasant for him. Everybody's established opinions are as comfortable as an old shoe; they have acquired exactly the right shape and form through continued use in all sorts of conditions. If you are forced to accept a different opinion, it's like getting used to a new pair of shoes: the change may be for the better, but it's always a somewhat uncomfortable experience.

Winning an argument is therefore, to begin with, doing something unpleasant to someone else.

But does that matter, you say, if you are right and the other fellow is wrong? Well, does it? Let's take a simple example. Someone has used the quotation from *The Ancient Mariner,* "Water, water everywhere, and not a drop to drink." Knowing better, you speak up and say that it is ". . . nor any drop to drink." An argument follows and, with the aid of Bartlett's *Familiar Quotations,* you win. Your opponent is embarrassed. Was it worth doing that to him? Is the truth so important?

Oh well, you say, that's a trivial example—an argument turning on a simple question of fact. What about really significant arguments about deep-going differences of opinion? Aren't such arguments worth winning?

All right, let's take another example from literature—a famous controversy this time. Not long ago, I was reading the letters of Maxwell Perkins, the late, great editor of Thomas Wolfe, Ernest Hemingway, and F. Scott Fitzgerald. I came upon the sentence: "It is certain, to my mind, that the man Shakespeare was not the author of what we consider Shakespeare's works." Suppose you belong to the minority Perkins belonged to, and find yourself in an argument with an orthodox Shakespearean. What would happen if you won that argument?

Naturally, your opponent would resent it terrifically. You'd have upset many of his most cherished beliefs, you'd have made his mind acutely uncomfortable, you'd have filled his brain with sore spots.

And after some time, it would turn out that you haven't won the argument after all. Your opponent's old, strongly held ideas would gradually overcome all your arguments, by and by the balance would be restored, and his mind would settle back in the old grooves. If you won the argument because of your logically trained, superior debater's technique, this would happen even sooner. "Why," your opponent would say to himself, "that fellow put something over on me. Everybody knows that all this business about Shakespeare not being the author of Shakespeare's plays is nonsense. Can't understand what came over me when I agreed with all that stuff."

The trouble is, you see, that big questions cannot be settled by looking up the facts; you may be able to win an *argument* about a big question, but you'll hardly ever win a *person* over to your side. (Even facts won't always do the trick: plenty of people would still believe in Shakespeare's genius if it were proved that he never wrote a line.)

Of course, I'm not talking here about arguments you are trying to win for a purpose: if you are out to make a sale, that's a different matter. Or if you are out for votes. Or if you want to win a law suit (I'll go into that in the next chapter). In all those cases it will obviously profit you to win your argument and hold on to your point of view regardless.

But when it comes to purposeless argument, argument for argument's sake, that's something else again. There's no profit at all in hanging on to your point of view for dear life, just because it's yours. It's not as precious as all that.

Most dinner-table or living-room arguments are hardly arguments at all. You stick to one opinion because it's been part of your mental furniture for years, and the other fellow sticks to another for the same reason.

Conversations of this sort aren't taken down in shorthand, which makes it hard to give examples. But "sidewalk interviews" by newspaper photographers are a reasonable substitute. Here is one from the New York *Post*.*

QUESTION: Who are the biggest gossips—men or women?

MISS FLORENCE C. (bookkeeper): The men are the biggest gossips. They can't keep anything under their hats. They are always telling their friends the things that they should keep to themselves. And women are the main topic they gossip about.

DR. MAX O. (dentist). The men have the women beat by far. They are always talking about the other fellow's business life. And many times by their tales they put a man in an awkward situation.

MISS JEAN P. (division manager): Both of them are just as petty and gossipy. I wait on them all day long and I know. There is no difference in either sex. Both men and women gossip to me about things I never should be told or even know about.

MR. PASQUALE T. (barber): The feminine sex takes the prize on that subject. They are always chattering. They don't need a hint of anything, just let them surmise something and they are capable of building it into nice juicy gossip.

MRS. MAUREEN M. (housewife): Women definitely. They have a tendency to be very jealous and will gossip about other women whether it is necessary or not. Just give them the opportunity and they'll never miss it.

Imagine these people sitting in a living room and you have the perfect pattern of an ordinary conversational argument. A general question is raised and five people give five different answers—each according to his or her experience or general pattern of living. The girl who works in an office remembers all the men she has heard gossiping about women, the girl who waits on customers meets men and women gossips all day long, the housewife recalls the chatter at canasta games, the barber has listened to women under the dryer, and the dentist sums up *his* experience with anguished, open-mouthed businessmen. If these people started to argue among themselves, they would each repeat and elaborate what they have

* Reproduced from the New York *Post* of September 18, 1950. Copyright 1950 by New York *Post* Corp.

said. After a while, the argument might get heated—Mrs. M. insisting that only a married woman really knows anything about gossip, Dr. O. announcing that only a dentist can arrive at a detached, objective point of view on the subject, and so on. Is it possible for anyone to win the argument? Hardly. The question could only be settled by a complete statistical survey—and even then you'd have trouble defining a gossip and agreeing on what makes one gossip bigger than another. For all practical purposes, the question is unanswerable and to argue about it is rather silly.

Now you are protesting against my choice of an example. Of course, you say, these are idle, aimless arguments. But there are topics worth talking about, and people who are intelligent and well-informed. Should *all* arguments be dismissed as useless?

Before I answer that question, let me give you a few more examples—serious arguments this time, debates between experts. The first deals with the newspaper I have just been quoting, the New York *Post*. In 1949 that paper was taken over by a new young editor, Mr. James A. Wechsler, who successfully built up circulation by a heavy dose of crime and sex. Many old readers of the *Post* were disgusted by the sudden switch. In June, 1950, the *Saturday Review of Literature* ran a lengthy debate between Mr. Wechsler and Mr. August Heckscher, editorial writer on the New York *Herald Tribune*. Mr. Wechsler said that you can't get an audience without using showmanship; Mr. Heckscher said that was "a false formula."

Nobody reading that debate could possibly say that either of the two men won the argument; each stated his point of view, presented excellent reasons in support of it, and proved that he knew what he was talking about. But in the end it was clear that the basic patterns of experience of the two debaters simply couldn't be reconciled.

Mr. Wechsler faced the job of selling a New Dealish paper to millions of potential readers who strangely preferred papers with whose political views they disagreed. He looked at the circulation figures of New York City papers and found the answer to his problem: "The meaning of these numbers is not mysterious. They prove beyond dispute that newspapers which displayed the deepest interest in crimes of passion and passionate crimes have remained far out in front in New York. . . ." His business was to sell a liberal newspaper to liberal readers in Manhattan, Brooklyn, and the Bronx. To do that, he had to put sex on page one.

Mr. Heckscher felt that emphasis on sex degraded a paper, regardless of what it printed on the editorial page. He made an excellent case for his point of view. But the telling sentence that gave flavor to his whole argument was one that was obviously based on direct experience:

. . .

> If friends of the *Post* object to the emphasis of sex, it is on the practical grounds that they do not like being compelled to leave their favorite evening newspaper on the train, or otherwise dispose of it, before entering homes where growing children are entitled to be protected against at least the most brutal and the most sordid facts of life.

Let's turn to another debate which appeared in *The New Yorker*. On one side we have Mr. Lewis Mumford, well-known authority on city planning, contending that the new housing developments in New York City are bad because they add to congestion. Over on the other side is Mr. Herman T. Stichman, New York State Commissioner of Housing, defending the projects because they are what people want. Again, the argument can be reduced to two irreconcilable pictures in the minds of the debaters.

Writes Mr. Stichman:

> By and large, Americans appear to aspire to high buildings as the Swiss do to mountains, and to love to congregate in groups. . . . If all our tall business and residential structures were to be replaced by buildings of two and three stories, New York City would stretch from here to Hartford. . . . Actually people are commuting almost that far today in their eagerness to enjoy the view from an office on the fortieth floor in Manhattan when they might just as well be doing business on the ground floor of a building on Main Street in their home towns. What we need is not better planners but better psychologists to help us understand why people are so gregarious and why they seek the heights.

Answers Mr. Mumford:

> Mr. Stichman says that the people of New York have a passionate desire for high buildings. That singular passion exists only in the minds of the authorities. . . . Every honest poll of housing preferences shows that the

popular ideal for people with families is single-family houses with a patch of garden around them, an ideal for the sake of which people who can afford it put up with the all but intolerable handicaps of commuting.

I think that Mr. Mumford has a slight edge in this argument, just as I think that Mr. Heckscher had a slight edge in the other one. After all, neither Mr. Stichman nor Mr. Wechsler was a disinterested debater: one defended his agency, the other his paper. So the pictures in their minds were necessarily biased. But the fact remains that an argument of this sort cannot really be won. A man who sees people attracted by skyscrapers like moths by a flame can't convince another who sees the picture of a little bungalow etched in each heart.

In our next example we can safely say that both sides are completely disinterested. Here are two academicians debating a question in *Science* magazine. One is Dr. Bernhard J. Stern, a Columbia University sociologist, the other is Dr. Curt Stern, a University of California biologist. The argument is over the old question of heredity *vs.* environment—more specifically, over the low birth rate among higher-income people and whether it means that our nation is in danger of getting more stupid. Dr. Curt Stern of California thinks there may be something to this; Dr. Bernhard J. Stern of Columbia thinks not. The remarkable thing is that both base their conclusions on exactly the same data: the results of intelligence tests.

Stern of Columbia is not impressed at all by differentials in intelligence tests.

> The tests [he says] use chiefly words, situations, pictures, and experiences which are much more familiar to individuals who have grown up in middle and upper socio-economic groups. The conventional tests measure, therefore, not the real intelligence of the child or adult, but the cultural and economic opportunities they have had.

Stern of California thinks otherwise.

> Even with these imperfections of the tests in mind, the results strongly suggest hereditary influence. . . . I found it hard to avoid the conclusion that there *are* differences in the genetic endowment of the different socio-economic groups.

And there the argument comes to a standstill. The two Sterns look at the same figures and graphs; one thinks something may have to be done about differences in our birth rate, the other sees the need to provide more educational opportunities for the poor.

Finally, an example I ran into the other day when I bought the latest revision of H. G. Wells' forty-year-old *Outline of History*. The introduction tells how the original edition was written, how Wells called in four eminent authorities to help him—Sir Ray Lankester, Professor Gilbert Murray, Sir Harry Johnston, and Mr. Ernest Barker—and how they ran into innumerable differences of opinion, which found their way into a mass of footnotes. Mind you, these were not differences as to facts, but *different ways of looking at the same facts*.

Wells, for instance, thought that Napoleon I was the quality of Mussolini and intellectually inferior to Napoleon III. Mr. Barker disagreed. "Put me down of the opposite opinion," he wrote.

Wells wrote that Athens wasn't a democracy in the modern sense. "The modern idea, that anyone in the state should be a citizen, would have shocked the privileged democrats of Athens profoundly." A footnote adds: "I feel strongly that the text is unjust to Athens. E.B."

Wells tells of the wretched social conditions in Africa in the days of the late Roman Empire. "Manifestly," he writes, "the Vandals came in as a positive relief to such a system." A footnote reads: "E.B. disagrees with this view. He regards it is as the pro-Teutonic view of the German historians."

Later in the book, Wells writes about eighteenth-century England. "The poetry, painting, architecture, and imaginative literature of later eighteenth-century England is immeasurably below that of the seventeenth century." There is a footnote signed G.M. (Gilbert Murray): "But Sir Joshua Reynolds, Hogarth, Gray, Gibbon for instance! And the golden age of the great cabinet-makers!" A footnote to the footnote is signed H.G.W.: "Exactly! Culture taking refuge in the portraits, libraries and households of a few rich people. No national culture in the court, nor among the commonalty; a steady decay."

What do all these examples prove? That it's always futile to argue? Not quite. Only that the same facts often create different patterns in different people's brains, and that it's extremely hard to change them—even if you have all the facts at your finger tips and are a whiz in the technique of debating.

Yet I am not going to end this chapter by telling you that you should never argue. Arguing is too much fun for that. Why shouldn't you jump into the fray if you have a strong opinion of your own and feel that you can convince your opponent? It's good mental exercise, it's a much more intelligent pastime than television or canasta, and there's always the chance that you'll win.

If you do, you'll feel a pleasant glow of satisfaction.

And if you lose, you'll have discovered your hidden bias, added to your mental flexibility, looked at things from another point of view, learned something you didn't know before, and gained some new understanding.

Chapter Twenty-Three

LEGAL RULES AND LIVELY CASES

A month or so ago I was on jury duty. For two weeks I heard lawyers address each prospective juror with the time-honored question: "Are you going to take the law neither from me nor from my adversary but only from the judge?" And for two weeks I heard jurors solemnly pledge that they would.

Whereupon the jurors were duly selected, swore their oaths, listened to the lawyers' arguments, listened to the testimony, listened to the judge's charge, and went to the jury room to consider the verdict.

They did exactly what they had pledged to do, and took the law only from the judge.

And then, in most cases, they didn't apply it.

What do I mean by this? Am I accusing all juries of stupidity or willful malice? Not at all. Let me explain.

When you, as a layman, think of the law, the application of a legal rule to a specific case looks like a simple matter. Once you know what the law is—or once the judge has explained it to you if you sit on a jury—all you have to do is make sure of the facts. When you *have* the facts—or when the jury has agreed on them—you apply the rule, and your verdict follows almost automatically. You may have your doubts about the application of abstract rules to concrete situations in other fields; but not in law. That's what the law is, isn't it?—a body of rules and a procedure for applying the rules to cases.

Or so you think. But lawyers know better. "The assumption," one of them writes, "that the application of a law is merely . . . matching the rule against the case . . . is naïve and misleading."

Another lawyer, in a well-known book on legal reasoning,

217

is even more explicit. "It cannot be said," he writes, "that the legal process is the application of known rules to diverse facts. . . . The rules change as the rules are applied." He then goes on to explain what happens in the application of case law, statutory law, and the Constitution. Case law is applied by "classifying things as equal when they are somewhat different, justifying the classification by rules made up as the reasoning or classification proceeds." As to statutory law, "it is only folklore which holds that a statute if clearly written can be completely unambiguous and applied as intended to a specific case." And the Constitution? "The Constitution permits the court to be inconsistent."

Are you outraged? Does this offend your sense of justice? Wait a minute before you answer yes.

For one thing, you have to realize that justice doesn't necessarily mean the application of laws. That idea is just part of your unbringing in our Western civilization. The Chinese, for instance, whose civilization is a good deal older than ours, have a different notion. Confucius said he was for government by wise and just men and *against* government by laws. So, in traditional Chinese law, it's considered an *injustice* to base a decision on a general rule; the only fair thing, from the Chinese point of view, is to decide each individual case strictly on its own merits.

When it comes down to it, you are not as far removed from the Chinese point of view as you think you are. You don't *really* think that the law should be applied in each case. You see no harm in settling a case out of court, in compromising, in submitting to mediation or arbitration. You don't consider it an injustice if a policeman lets you off without a ticket. You are a concrete Chinese thinker in practice, but an abstract Western thinker in theory.

Even in theory, however, your faith in the application of rules to cases is hard to justify. There's the awkward fact that there seem to be *two* possible rules applying to each case, depending on which side you're on. And higher courts, every so often, apply different rules from lower ones. And judges on the same bench have a habit of dissenting in their opinions. In fact, if a case comes to court at all, there is always some doubt as to what rule applies.

Here are, at random, a few cases I picked from the newspapers some time ago. Each could have been plausibly decided either way. Each is a slap in the face of the theory that the law means applying rules to cases.

Item: The C. F. Mueller Company made—and still makes

—macaroni; all the money it made went to the New York University School of Law. So, the company said, it was a "corporation organized exclusively for educational purposes" and didn't have to pay income tax. The Internal Revenue Bureau said it had to pay taxes just like everybody else, since the macaroni business isn't education regardless of who gets the profits. The Tax Court sided with the Revenue Bureau.

Item: Irma Smith was employed by her father. According to the books, she drew a salary of $15,000, and that's what she paid income tax on. Then the government went over the company's books, thought $15,000 was too much, and decided that what Mr. Smith really paid his daughter was $9,000 at most. So Miss Smith asked for a refund of her personal income tax on the difference of $6,000. The Revenue Bureau said no; the change on the company's books had nothing to do with Miss Smith's personal taxes. In this case the Revenue Bureau lost. The U.S. District Court of New Jersey turned them down. (But later a higher court decided the case the other way. See what I mean?)

Item: Another businessman, Mr. Bernard Glagovsky, also had a daughter. When Miss Glagovsky got married, her father thought he'd invite his customers and business acquaintances to the wedding. All in all, there were 350 guests and the bill was $9,200. Mr. Glagovsky felt that about 60 per cent of the amount was strictly a business expense and therefore deductible on his tax return. The Revenue Bureau, as always, disagreed. If Mr. Glagovsky liked to have two hundred customers and prospects join the celebrations, that was his own affair. The Tax Court felt the same way.

Item: Thomas Petro was born in Oklahoma in 1900. When he was ten, his parents moved to Canada. Petro senior became a naturalized Canadian. Automatically, Thomas became a Canadian citizen too. He grew up as a Canadian and voted in five Canadian elections. Then, in 1942, he went back to the United States, claiming he was still an American. The case came to court, and the court said he had to go back to Canada: a 1941 law said anyone voting in a foreign election lost his American citizenship. Whereupon Petro appealed to the U.S. Court of Appeals and won: the higher court looked at the *same* 1941 law and discovered another provision in it that made him an American. It said that if you lose your U.S. citizenship because your parents were naturalized abroad, you get it back as soon as you return.

All of which should effectively cure you of the notion that

you can apply a legal rule to a case and that's that. Trouble is, there are always at least *two* rules.

But then, where do the rules come from? In the bulk of our law, they are derived from previous decisions in similar cases. And since no two cases are ever exactly alike, this means that in case law, strictly speaking, there *are* no rules.

The law books are full of illustrations to prove this point. The most famous is the story of the so-called "inherently dangerous" rule. This deals with the question of whether the manufacturer of an article has to pay damages if the article injures someone who bought it from a retailer. The rule used to be that he was liable if the article was "inherently dangerous"—like a loaded gun—and wasn't if it was not. The distinction was first made in an English case in 1851 when a housewife was hurt by an exploding oil lamp; the court said then a lamp wasn't like a loaded gun and the manufacturer wasn't responsible.

In the horse-and buggy days, of course, there was no trouble in applying this rule to vehicles: carriages, just like a lamp, were not "inherently dangerous." But then the automobile came in and things began to look different. The old rule didn't fit the times any more. So what happened? Very simple: The courts suddenly discovered there wasn't any such rule after all.

Before that discovery, in 1915, a Mr. Johnson bought a Cadillac whose wheel broke, and sued the Cadillac company for damages. He didn't get a penny because, as the court said,

> . . . one who manufactures articles dangerous only if defectively made, or installed, e.g., tables, chairs, pictures or mirrors hung on the walls, carriages, automobiles, and so on is not liable to third parties for injuries caused by them, except in cases of willful injury or fraud.

A year later, in 1916, a Mr. MacPherson bought a Buick whose wheel broke, and sued the Buick company for damages. Mr. MacPherson was luckier than Mr. Johnson. Somehow, between 1915 and 1916, the old rule had melted away and Judge Benjamin Cardozo found that the Buick Motor Company had to pay.

> The defendant argues [he wrote] that things inherently dangerous to life are poisons, explosives, deadly weapons, things whose normal function is to injure or destroy.

But whatever the rule may once have been . . . it has
no longer that restricted meaning. . . . If the nature of
a thing is such that it is reasonably certain to place life
and limb in peril, when negligently made, it is then a
thing of danger.

And with these words of Cardozo, the old rule vanished
forever.

This famous example shows what can happen in case law,
where rules are derived from court decisions. Surely, you'll
say, things are different in statutory law, where rules are
spelled out in so many words by legislators. But are they?
Take the Displaced Persons Act of 1948. That law said that
40 per cent of all DP's must come from "de facto annexed
countries and areas," meaning Estonia, Latvia, and Lithuania.
It turned out that this made it practically impossible to fill the
annual quota of 205,000. So a year later the State Department
discovered that "de facto annexed countries and areas"
meant not only those three Baltic states, but also all territories
administered by Russia or Poland under the Potsdam Agreement of 1945.

Usually, when there is a question about the meaning of an
act of Congress, the lawyers say that you have to find the
intent of the legislature. But that's a fiction. What it really
means is that statutes are changed by suddenly declaring that
Congress meant something different from what everybody
thought it meant. This is easy because doubtful cases are
exactly those that Congress either didn't foresee or deliberately
left up in the air. For instance, in the 1949 revision of the
minimum wage law, the law was narrowed to cover fewer
workers. This is the way it was done. Congress can make
laws only in connection with goods produced for interstate
commerce; so the original law had referred to workers "necessary to" the production of goods for interstate commerce.
The House of Representatives felt that these words had been
interpreted too broadly by the Wage and Hour Administration and proposed to replace them by "indispensable to." The
Senate wanted to stick to the old phrase "necessary to."
Finally the House and the Senate compromised and settled
on "workers engaged in a closely related process or occupation *directly essential to*" the production of goods for interstate commerce.

Now what does this mean when it comes to deciding a
specific case? Does it mean that a man washing the windows
of a firm engaged in interstate commerce has to be paid at

least 75¢ an hour? Nobody knows. What was the intent of the legislature? Well, the congressmen who were for "indispensable to" obviously didn't mean to include the window-washer; those who wanted to stick to "necessary to" probably did. And those who finally voted for the compromise? Sometime in the future a judge will decide they meant one thing or the other.

That judge will do well to look at the circumstances of the case rather than search for what was in the minds of the congressmen who debated the bill. Otherwise he'll get confused by exchanges like this in the House:

> MR. LUCAS: . . . substituting the word "indispensable" for the word "necessary." These changes are needed in order to stem, and in some cases, reverse the action of the administrator and the courts in bringing under the act many businesses of a purely local type by giving to the word "necessary" an all-inclusive construction. . . .
>
> MR. DONDERO: Mr. Chairman, will the gentleman yield?
>
> MR. LUCAS: I yield to the gentleman from Michigan.
>
> MR. DONDERO: . . . What does the gentleman do in this bill in regard to caddies on golf courses, boys and girls who are in high school or now out of school during their vacations working and earning a little money picking fruit or picking vegetables, pulling weeds, and things of that kind? What does the gentleman do with them?
>
> MR. LUCAS: Well, sir, it is going to be difficult to find them in interstate commerce, but I do not question the ability of the administrator, the present administrator, to find that caddies are in interstate commerce, if they are handling golf balls which were produced across the State line, or if they are carrying golf clubs which are produced in another State, or if they are working for a traveling man. The administrator may well find them in interstate commerce.
>
> MR. JACOBS: Mr. Chairman, will the gentleman yield?
>
> MR. LUCAS: I yield to the gentleman from Indiana.
>
> MR. JACOBS: Has the administrator held caddies to be in interstate commerce?
>
> MR. LUCAS: I will answer the gentleman by saying that if he has not done so, it is because the problem has not yet been presented to him.

Does this sort of thing help in deciding a case by ascertaining the intent of the legislature? It does not. No wonder Senator Elbert D. Thomas came out of the House-Senate Conference telling reporters that the new law was an invitation to litigation. It might be ten or twelve years, he said, before the courts would interpret the meaning of *directly essential*.

So the rules of statutory law are just as open to shifts and changes as the rules of case law. There is even a famous case where a statute said one thing and a court said exactly the opposite. In 1885 Congress passed a law forbidding "the importation of foreigners . . . under contract . . . to perform labor in the United States." A few years later, Trinity Church in New York picked an English minister as its new pastor. A contract was signed, and the minister came to the United States. Whereupon the government sued the church for breaking the law. The Supreme Court pondered, found that the law applied to the case—and decided in favor of the church. Otherwise the result would be absurd, the court quietly explained.

The Trinity Church case is mentioned in the book *Courts on Trial* by Jerome Frank, in connection with Judge Frank's theory of legal interpretation. The courts interpret the law, Frank says, the way a musical performer interprets a composition. Until it is performed, a composition exists only on paper; it is the performer's vision and imagination that brings it to life. The law, too, is only a dead letter until a court interprets it in the light of an actual case.

For the ordinary layman, even this elegant analogy doesn't go far enough. What he wants is fairness and justice, and if the law doesn't seem fair and just, then he is all for playing by ear. The layman's legal heroes are not the master interpreters of the law. His heroes are Erle Stanley Gardner's Perry Mason and Arthur Train's Ephraim Tutt, who do right by their clients and let the niceties of the law go hang.

And this brings us back to the question of what happens to the law when it is put in the hands of laymen—the question of how a jury decides a case. You'll agree now, I hope, that they don't just apply the law to the facts of the case. But what do they do instead? What actually does happen in a jury room?

Well, in a case I helped decide on last month, a housewife sued a storekeeper because she had been injured by a defective piece of merchandise. The storekeeper swore she had never been in his store. The woman swore she had bought the article from him. The jury had to decide which one to believe.

It so happened that nine of us believed the woman and three the storekeeper. By the strict rules of law, that meant a hung jury and a new trial. Actually, it didn't mean any such thing. We compromised and awarded the woman a fraction of what she had asked for.

Typical? I think so. Not long ago a magazine writer described *her* experiences in a jury room. It was an automobile accident case. A boy riding a bicycle had been injured by a car after he had darted from a side road onto a busy highway. The law calls this "contributory negligence" and legally the boy wasn't entitled to a thing. But three jurors disagreed. One thought the driver had been speeding; one remembered a case in California where the driver had to pay $10,000; and a woman insisted that "that poor woman ought to have enough to send her boy to college." The jury tried to compromise but couldn't agree because the magazine writer was the only one who stuck to the letter of the law.

That experience was even more typical than my own. According to a statement by an experienced judge, Mr. Joseph N. Ullman, juries *always* disregard the law of contributory negligence. And, Judge Ullman adds, that's not at all unreasonable: the "illegal" law that the juries apply on the highways has always been the accepted law for accidents on the high seas.

Many people have come to the conclusion that juries are a good thing just *because* they often don't apply the law. James Gould Cozzens, in his novel *The Just and the Unjust*, has stated the case beautifully. In that novel, two men are on trial for murder because they have admittedly taken part in a kidnaping in which a man was killed. The actual murder was committed by a third man who is not on trial in that court. The judge explains to the jury that they can either find the two men guilty of first-degree murder (for participating in the kidnaping that led to murder) or else acquit them. The jury, however, disregards the law and returns a verdict of second-degree murder, saving the two men from execution. As one of the characters remarks, "The jury was jibing at executing two men for something they argued a third man had really done."

To which old Judge Coates (the author's spokesman) replies:

"A jury has its uses. That's one of them. It's like a

cylinder head gasket. Between two things that don't give any, you have to have something that does give a little, something to seal the law to the facts. There isn't any known way to legislate with an allowance for right feeling. . . . The jury protects the court. It's a question how long any system of courts could last in a free country if judges found the verdicts. It doesn't matter how wise and experienced the judges may be. Resentment would build up every time the findings didn't go with current notions or prejudices. Pretty soon half the community would want to lynch the judge. There's no focal point with a jury; the jury is the public itself. That's why a jury can say when a judge couldn't, 'I don't care what the law is, that isn't right and I won't do it.' It's the greatest prerogative of free men."

He might have added that it's also the greatest prerogative of *intelligent* men: to rise above the abstract rules of law, formal logic, or mere convention, and meet each new problem on its own terms.

Chapter Twenty-Four

ENTER A BRIGHT IDEA

Let me tell you the story of a bright idea.

In 1949 a Congressional fight broke out over federal aid to education. The debate didn't center on the principle of aid to public schools, but on the question of whether private schools should get it too. Catholic congressmen, thinking of their parochial schools, felt they should—not for religious instruction, to be sure, but for collateral services such as health, transportation and nonreligious books. Other congressmen insisted that, as a matter of principle, private schools should get no federal money whatever.

The debate went on for weeks and months. Neither side was willing to give an inch. Legislation was stalled.

At this point, Senator Paul H. Douglas of Illinois hit upon an idea. He described it later in a magazine article:

> Whether children are in public or private schools, and whether they are Protestant, Catholic or Jewish, children present a uniform health problem, and what is done to improve their health has a beneficial effect upon the community as a whole. In consequence, it appeared to me that a distinction could be drawn between health services on the one hand and transportation and books on the other; that federal aid for these health services should be furnished to all children, whether they were in private or public schools. Under this view, the school-house at certain hours in the term would have the status of a convenient neighborhood dispensary.

Senator Douglas drafted a bill along these lines, which was promptly approved by the proper Senate Committee. The

226

debate went on in the House, however; in fact, the issue is still unresolved.

But this doesn't concern me right now. What interests me is that we have here a simon-pure, test-tube specimen of what is usually called a bright idea. It has all the earmarks: a seemingly insoluble problem, a neat, simple solution, and that feeling of "Why, that's it, of course! Why didn't *I* think of that!"

If there is any secret of clear thinking, this is it. What is the nature of a bright idea? How do you get one? Where does it come from?

Ask anybody these questions, and the answer is apt to be: "A bright idea comes to you out of nowhere in a flash of inspiration."

Very simple. Very unsatisfactory, too. Doesn't tell you a thing.

Do psychologists have a better answer? They do, in a way. Their answer is far from simple, and not quite satisfactory either. But it's fascinating and well worth knowing.

Psychologists don't study bright ideas, they study "problem-solving"; and they like to strip things down to essentials. To them, a Senator wrestling with a knotty problem in legislation is essentially the same thing as a chimpanzee trying to get at some bananas that are out of reach. Both are examples of problem-solving behavior; one situation is a thousand times more complex than the other, but basically there's no difference.

The first step in problem-solving is a thorough study of the problem situation. The chimpanzee looks through the bars of his cage at the bananas, sees that he can't reach them, surveys the inside of the cage, focuses on all the objects inside—including a stick—and ponders. The Senator looks at federal aid to education, sees that a compromise seems impossible, surveys Catholic and non-Catholic reasoning, focuses on schools, children, teachers, buildings and collateral services—including health—and ponders. Both consider all the elements in the situation before they are ready to solve the problem.

Next come two steps. They are taken simultaneously or one after the other.

One is an effort to find the factor that can be moved or changed. If that factor were obvious, there'd be no problem but a routine operation. (If you want to ring a bell, you push the button.) A problem arises whenever the key factor is hidden; you don't see it because it looks like an inconspicuous bit of background. The stick is one of many things inside the cage; it *looks* like just another object that happens to be around. Health services are lumped together with transportation and books under the heading "collateral services"; they *look* like just another minor part of school expenditures. To solve the problem, you have to focus on the key factor and mentally "pry it loose." You have to see the stick as something that can be pushed through bars; you have to realize that health services may serve as a basis for a compromise.

The other step is not a survey of the situation before you, but a survey of your mind. You search among your memories for a pattern that would fit the situation. Again, if that pattern were obvious, there'd be no problem. You have to find a pattern that is usually *not* applied to this sort of problem. The chimpanzee thinks of games he played and remembers how he used a stick to "make a long arm"; the Senator thinks of community services and remembers health centers and dispensaries. Is there a parallel? Does that mental framework fit the situation? Would it change it so that the problem can be solved?

As I said, the two steps may come at the same time. One psychologist, Dr. Duncker, calls them the approach "from below" and the approach "from above." Basically, they are two ways of doing the same thing: you try to look at the situation in a different light.

And then—after you have pried loose a key factor or found a new pattern—something clicks and the bright idea appears. It isn't a flash of inspiration, psychologists insist. It's what happens in your brain when a remembered pattern matches the pattern of the situation before you. If you want a picturesque phrase, the best psychologists have to offer is the word *Aha!-experience*.

So there you are. Disappointed? Did you expect a magic formula, a big wonderful secret? If so, I'm sorry; psychology doesn't seem to work that way. It'll be a long time until psychologists can produce miracles.

Meanwhile, I think their researches in problem-solving are highly valuable. If you want to know how to get bright ideas, by far the best thing is to look closely at their experiments and illustrations. Let me describe two, one showing a solution "from below," the other a solution "from above."

The first is one of Dr. Duncker's ingenious experiments. It's one of a series in which he asked people to solve simple mechanical problems.

Here is the situation: You are led into a room with a table in it. You are told that the room is to be used for visual experiments and you're supposed to put three small candles side by side on the door, at eye level. On the table there are all sorts of materials for you to work with: paper clips, paper, string, pencils, tinfoil, ash trays, and so on. There are also three little cardboard boxes; the first contains a few short, thin candles, the second contains tacks, and the third contains matches. How are you going to put up the candles? (If you want to, put the book down at this point and try to figure out the answer.)

Stumped? If you are like Dr. Duncker's test subjects, you probably are. Only 43 per cent of them solved the problem. Fifty-seven per cent looked at the door and the candles, spent two or three minutes picking up this or that object from the table, and then gave up. They couldn't think of a possible way of getting those candles up on the door.

The solution is very simple once you know it. You empty the three boxes and tack them into the door as platforms for the candles.

Now why is this so difficult to think of? The answer is clear: the three boxes are "fixed" in the problem situation; to solve the problem, you have to "pry them loose." Dr. Duncker proved this neatly by slight changes in the experimental setup. First he repeated the experiment, but left the boxes empty. Result: The problem was solved by *all* subjects. Then he filled the boxes not with candles, tacks, and matches, but with buttons—that is, he pushed the key factor even farther into the background. Result: The percentage of those who *failed* rose from 57 per cent to 86 per cent.

The ability to solve problems this way is the ability to spot things that are hard to distinguish from their background. Psychologists have devised several tests to measure this ability; one of them, the "Gottschaldt Figures Test," is referred to in Dr. Duncker's work. You will find it on pages 230 to 234.

I can see you looking at these little geometrical designs and wondering. Seems like a children's game, you say. Is there really a connection between these figures and the art of thinking?

There certainly is, and I can prove it. During World War II, Dr. L. L. Thurstone of the University of Chicago gave a group of Washington administrators a battery of seventy tests to find out what mental abilities are most important for

<u>PART I</u>

In each pair of figures below, mark that part of the second figure which is the same as the first.

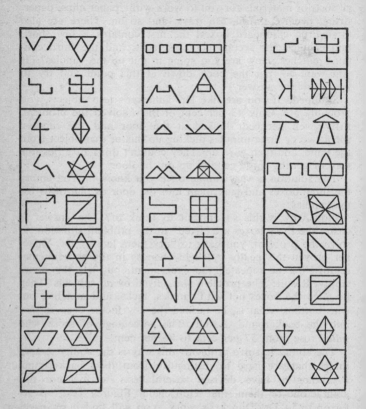

executives. He worked out the statistical relationship between these tests on the one hand and salaries and ratings for professional promise on the other. *Of all seventy tests, the one most closely related to administrative success was the Gottschaldt Figures Test*. Which seems to mean that an executive is essentially a problem-solver, and problem-solving means being able to spot the key factor in a confusing situation.

If you want to take this test, all you need to do is take a pencil and trace each of the "hidden figures." Before you start

PART II

Look at the adjacent figure.

It is contained in each of the drawings below. Find it in each drawing and then mark it. Mark only one figure in each drawing.

each page, look at your watch. Part I is easier than the rest; an average person takes about five minutes to mark all twenty-seven figures. Parts II to V are more difficult; an average person takes about fifteen minutes to do all thirty-four figures. (If you're a whiz, you may be able to do Part I in two minutes and Parts II to V in six.)

And now let's look at another example of problem-solving —this time a solution "from above," through using a different mental framework. I take this illustration from *Productive Thinking,* the brilliant book by the late Dr. Max Wertheimer. The example is not as ingenious as Dr. Duncker's box problem, but far more illuminating.

Dr. Wertheimer tells how he was looking out the window one day and saw two boys playing badminton in the garden. (He calls the boys A and B, but I'll call them Andy and Bill.) Andy was twelve, Bill was only ten. They played several

<u>PART III</u>

Look at the two adjacent figures. One of them
is contained in each of the drawings below.

In each of the following drawings, mark that part
which is the same as one of the adjacent figures.
Mark only one figure in each drawing.

sets, but Bill was a much poorer player and lost all the games.

Dr. Wertheimer watched and listened. Bill got more and
more unhappy. He had no chance at all. Andy often served
him so cleverly that he couldn't possibly return the bird.
Finally Bill threw down his racket, sat on a tree trunk and
said: "I won't play any more." Andy tried to talk him out
of it, but Bill didn't answer. Then Andy sat down too. Both
boys looked unhappy. They were faced with what seemed
an insoluble problem.

What would *you* have done in Andy's place? Dr.
Wertheimer says he asked many people the same question, but
hardly anybody arrived at Andy's intelligent solution. What
actually happened was this:

PART IV

Look at the two adjacent figures.
One of them is contained in each of
the drawings below.

In each of the following drawings, mark
that part which is the same as one of the
adjacent figures. Mark only one figure
in each drawing.

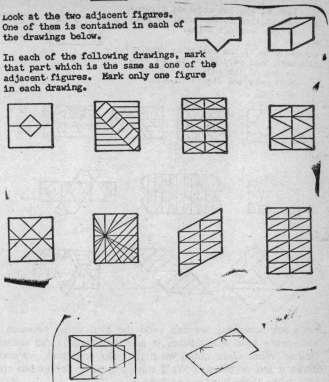

At first, Andy was simply angry. "Why don't you go
ahead?" he asked Bill. "Why do you break up the game? Do
you think it's nice to stop in this silly way?"

There was a pause. Andy glanced at Bill, and Bill just
looked sad. Then Andy said in a different tone of voice: "I'm
sorry."

There was another pause. Suddenly Andy said: "Look
here. Such playing *is* nonsense." He looked as if something
slowly began to dawn on him, and continued: "This sort of
game is funny. I'm not really unfriendly to you. . . ." And then
he mumbled something like "Must it . . . ?" His face lit up
and he said happily: "I have an idea—let's play this way:

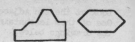

PART V

Look at the two adjacent figures.
One of them is contained in each
of the drawings below.

In each of the following drawings,
mark that part which is the same
as one of the adjacent figures.
Mark only one figure in each
drawing.

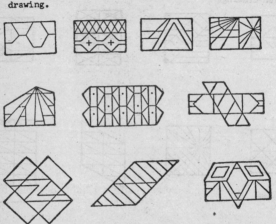

Let's see how long we can keep the bird going between us
and count how many times it goes back and forth without
falling. What score could we make? Do you think we could
make it ten or twenty? We'll start with easy serves but then
let's make them harder and harder . . ."

Bill agreed happily: "That's a good idea. Let's."

They started to play—not the competitive game of badminton, but a different, co-operative new game. Andy had
solved the problem.

There's a long analysis of this example in Dr. Wertheimer's book, and I wish I could quote it all. He points out that
Andy solved the problem by completely changing his mental
picture of the situation. Instead of looking at the game as
something that existed for his own enjoyment and at Bill as
someone to play against, he suddenly saw the game as
something to be enjoyed by both of them. "Often," Wertheimer writes, "one must first forget what he happens to wish
before he can become susceptible to what the situation itself
requires. . . . This transition is one of the great moments in

many genuine thought processes. . . . Real thinkers forget about themselves in thinking."

Not only that, real thinkers can detach their minds from habitual, established patterns of thought and apply far-removed, seemingly unrelated mental frameworks. Their minds don't move in narrow grooves but range over a wide area of possible patterns.

The newspapers, not long ago, carried a report of brain-wave studies on Albert Einstein and a couple of other mathematical geniuses. The theory behind the experiments was that a creative, original thinker has the ability to quickly "scan" one group of brain cells after another. It was found that Einstein's brain did this much better and faster than an ordinary brain.

All of which gives you a pretty clear picture of how you can get bright ideas. After studying a problem, do either or both of these things:

1. Look for a seemingly irrelevant key factor in the situation.

2. Look for a seemingly unsuitable pattern in your mind. This isn't very specific, but it's obviously more helpful than just sitting and waiting for an inspiration.

Let me wind up this chapter with a bright idea that made history. With Duncker's and Wertheimer's studies in mind, read how Franklin D. Roosevelt thought up the idea of Lend-Lease.

In December, 1940, Britain desperately needed material help against the Nazis. The United States, however, was not at war; Congress and the people were unwilling to give Britain a tremendous loan to buy war materials. How to help Britain without a loan was a seemingly insoluble problem.

On December 2, Roosevelt went on a two-weeks' Caribbean cruise. He spent those two weeks in thinking over the problem, searching for the key factor, the novel pattern.

After two weeks he returned. He had solved the "impossible" problem. He called a press conference and explained his simple plan to help Britain: "Now, what I am trying to do is eliminate the dollar sign. That is something brand-new in the thoughts of everybody in this room, I think—get rid of the silly, foolish old dollar sign. . . . Well, let me give you an illustration. Suppose my neighbor's home catches fire, and I have a length of garden hose . . ."

You see the two basic ingredients of a bright idea? Roosevelt had found the "detachable" key factor—the dollar sign; and he had found a totally new pattern no one had ever thought of in connection with a foreign loan—lending your neighbor a garden hose.

It was brilliantly simple. And it changed the course of history.

Chapter Twenty-Five

HOW TO SOLVE A PUZZLE

A good many years ago Mr. A. A. Milne—who gave our children the Winnie-the-Pooh books—wrote a column for a British magazine. He faithfully produced a charming little essay for every issue until he suddenly found himself stymied. As he explained to his readers the next time, someone had challenged him with a word game and he was unable to think of anything else until he had solved it. The word—whose rearranged letters spell an everyday English word—was

TERALBAY.

According to legend, Lord Melbourne gave this word to Queen Victoria once and it kept her awake all night.

Mr. Milne didn't tell his readers what the solution was. But he explained clearly his *method* of solution.

> The way to solve a problem of this sort is to waggle your eyes and see what you get. If you do this, words like *alterably* and *laboratory* emerge, which a little thought shows you to be wrong. You may then waggle your eyes again, look at it upside down or sideways, or stalk it carefully from the southwest and plunge upon it suddenly when it is not ready for you. . . . I have no doubt that after hours of immense labor you will triumphantly suggest *rateably*. I suggested that myself, but it is wrong. There is no such word in the dictionary. The same objection applies to *bat-early*—it ought to mean something, but it doesn't.

I don't mean to say that the Milne Method of solving word

games is bad. It's more or less what everybody does, and it's basically sound. But it can be improved upon.

The *teralbay* kind of puzzle—like every other kind—has a hidden clue somewhere. Once you've spotted it, the puzzle is solved. The difficulty lies in the fact that the situation before you is confused; you have to get rid of the confusion before you can even start working on the problem. After all, the point is not to read the word *teralbay* over and over to find a hidden meaning, but to form a new word from the letters *t, e, r, a, l, b, a,* and *y.*

So the thing to do is this: Try at random other patterns of arrangement, in the hope that the hidden clue will emerge in the process. You may arrange the letters alphabetically

A A B E L R T Y

or in reversed alphabetical order

Y T R L E B A A

or alphabetically with alternating consonants and vowels

B A L A R E T Y

or the same reversed

Y T E R A L A B

and so on. Or you may try arrangements ending in *able* or *ably* like

R A Y T A B L E

or

T E A R A B L Y.

(This last one you'll find in small type in *Webster's Unabridged,* but it obviously won't do.)

If you do this—systematically run through various random arrangements—you'll have a better chance than if you just waggle your eyes. At least, I used that method and finally did solve the puzzle, after hours of work. When I got to the *able* words, I happened upon

TRAYABLE.

I liked that word very much, but in the end I had to admit that there wasn't any such word. However, the *tray* in it turned out to be the hidden clue: suddenly I had the solution. Of course! What Lord Melbourne meant was— (You may want to play with this, so I put the solution on page 245, along with solutions to the other puzzles in this chapter.)

In other words, the first step in getting rid of confusion is rearrangement. Any kind of rearrangement is better than staring at the confusing arrangement before you. For example, there's the sign a GI saw on a post in Italy during World War II:

TOTI
EMUL
ESTO

String the letters out in one line instead of three, and you'll have no trouble.

Often, however, rearrangement is not enough. You have to do some sort of translation; you have to look at the elements in the puzzle in some other form. Eugenio Rignano, in his *Psychology of Reasoning*, has a fine example of this. He was surprised and puzzled, he writes, when he heard for the first time this sentence: "Since more people live in London than anyone has hairs on his head, there must be at least two people there with the same number of hairs." Yet he immediately realized that this was so when he began mentally to line up the inhabitants of London, starting with a totally bald man, followed by a man with one hair, a man with two hairs, and so on. Naturally, since the population of London is larger than the maximum number of hairs on people's heads, he had lots of leftover people whose hair-count matched that of people in the lineup. Visualized in this way, the puzzle was no puzzle any more.

Another kind of translation is the use of mathematical symbols. It's the best technique, for instance, if you want to solve the following type of puzzle:

> The ages of a man and his wife are together 98. He is twice as old as she was when he was the age she is today. What are their ages?

This is easy to solve if you know enough algebra to set up a couple of equations, calling, say, the husband's age x and the wife's age y.

Maybe you have the feeling that the puzzles I have given you so far are particularly mean. You are right. They are problems plus: puzzles with an extra element of confusion added. Let's now look at some problems that are presented straight.

Here's a nice example. Read the following sentence and count how many f's there are:

> Finished files are the results of years of scientific study combined with the experiences of years.

(Now do it again slowly and see if you were right the first time.)

Then there are two neat problems that I gave dozens of my friends and students last year.

1. Find the smallest number that can be divided evenly by 7 but leaves a remainder of 1 when divided by 2, 3, 4, 5, or 6.
2. Smith, Brown, Jones, and Robinson played three rubbers of bridge at 1¢ a point. No one had the same partner twice. Playing against Jones, Brown won a rubber of 900 points. Smith won a 600-point rubber, the smallest of the evening, when he played against Robinson. Jones lost $10 altogether. How did Robinson fare?

I ought to warn you that it may take you quite a while to solve these two problems. My friends and students took anywhere from five minutes to an hour for each. (There was an interesting difference in their way of going about it; I'll come to that in Chapter 29.) But—since I want to make a point here—I'll give you a break: the key to the solution in both cases is the seemingly irrelevant word *smallest*. In the first puzzle you have to find the *smallest* number, in the second you are told that the 600-point rubber was the *smallest* of the evening. Among my human guinea pigs 24 per cent overlooked that clue in the first puzzle and 32 per cent in the second.

These figures may seem incredible. Why should a bunch of intelligent adults have trouble spotting these simple clues? Why should one-fourth or one-third of them overlook these clues, with all the time in the world to solve the problem?

Once you know it, the word *smallest* in both puzzles seems to stick out like a sore thumb. How is it possible not to see it?

This is the sort of question you ask yourself after you have finished a good mystery story. "Why, of course!" you say to yourself. "X was the murderer; I ought to have guessed that long ago. The clues were all there, right in front of my eyes. How did I manage to miss them?"

The basic principle, then, of most puzzles or mystery stories is the "hidden" clue—the thing that you don't see because it seems utterly irrelevant. The question is: Is this only a feature of made-up puzzles and mysteries or does the principle operate in real-life problems too?

It so happens that the two most famous authors of mystery stories provided an answer to this question—Edgar Allan Poe and Sir Arthur Conan Doyle. Both ventured into the detection of actual crimes; both were highly successful. Let's see how the methods of C. Auguste Dupin and Sherlock Holmes apply to real-life mysteries.

Poe turned detective when he cleared up the case of Mary Cecilia Rogers, who was murdered near New York City in 1842. He chose to publish his solution, thinly disguised as fiction, in the story "The Mystery of Marie Roget." It is a matter of history that Poe's solution was essentially right and that of the police was wrong.

Mary Rogers lived with her mother on Nassau Street and was employed in a cigar store downtown. One Sunday morning in June she left home (supposedly to visit an aunt) and disappeared. Four days later her body was found in the Hudson near Weehawken. The official theory was that she had been the victim of a gang of hoodlums.

Poe knew nothing about the case except what he had read in the papers. But by analyzing the published facts he disproved the theory that the murder was the work of a gang and showed who the real murderer was.

We don't need to go into all the details here, since Poe's main point was very simple. Mary Rogers had disappeared once before, about three-and-a-half years before her death; at that time she had turned up again after a week, behaving as if nothing had happened. Obviously she had spent that week with a lover. Neither the police nor the newspapers connected that earlier disappearance with her tragic death three years later; they didn't see any parallel between an old amorous adventure and a kidnaping by a gang. Poe focused on that seemingly irrelevant clue; once he had done so, everything fell into place and it was clear that Mary Rogers was murdered by her lover.

Conan Doyle's performance as a real-life detective didn't deal with a murder, but the case was even more spectacular than that of Mary Rogers. There had been a flagrant miscarriage of justice.

In December, 1906, the creator of Sherlock Holmes received a letter and a batch of newspaper clippings from a man named George Edalji. Mr. Edalji had just been released from prison after having served three years for a crime of which he had been convicted. He was unable to continue his career as a lawyer and asked Conan Doyle to help him prove his innocence.

Conan Doyle—like Poe sixty-five years earlier—studied the newspaper clippings. He learned that Edalji had been declared guilty of killing animals near the village of Great Wyrley in 1903. The killings had obviously been the work of a maniac who roamed the countryside by night; they had been accompanied and announced by mad anonymous letters sent to the local police. The letters—together with other circumstantial evidence—convinced the police, and later the court, that Edalji was the killer. Their most damning feature was their similarity to a group of anonymous letters written seven years before. Those earlier letters had been directed against George Edalji's father and the police had always considered George their author.

Conan Doyle—again like Poe sixty-five years earlier— found the clue in the previous event. He too focused on a seemingly irrelevant point. These are his words:

> At the beginning, one point is so obvious that I wonder it has escaped notice. This is the extraordinary long gap between the two sets of letters. Letters, childish hoaxes, abound up to late December of '95. Then, for nearly seven years, *nobody* gets an abusive letter. To me this did not suggest that the culprit had changed his whole character and habits overnight, reverting to them with equal malice in 1903. It suggested absence; that someone had been away during that time.

After this, the solution of the mystery was easy. All that was necessary was to find someone in the community who had spent those seven years abroad or at sea and fitted the description of a mad letter-writer and animal-killer. The man was found and, after a long struggle, George Edalji was publicly vindicated and readmitted to the bar.

Do these two cases prove my point? I think so. But, after all, you may say, Edgar Allan Poe and Sir Arthur Conan Doyle were amateur detectives. Do professional detectives work the same way in solving a puzzling case?

In 1949 the newspapers carried a story that shows the essence of professional detective work. I mean the story of Mr. Goetz' Van Gogh.

Mr. William Goetz, a Hollywood movie executive, bought a picture by Vincent Van Gogh called "Study by Candlelight." He paid over $50,000 for it. After some time Van Gogh's nephew, Mr. Vincent W. Van Gogh, declared publicly that the picture was a fake. Mr. Goetz didn't take this lying down and submitted the picture to a jury of experts appointed by the Metropolitan Museum in New York.

"Study by Candlelight" is a self-portrait of Van Gogh, resembling his many other self-portraits. It bears his signature, has a title in his handwriting, and includes a small study of a Japanese head and some Japanese inscriptions. The jury studied all this, together with the material, the colors, the brushwork and so on, and declared the painting as doubtful at best. "Any one of the unfavorable factors might be accounted for in reason," they concluded, "but the accumulation was too great to be counterbalanced; furthermore, the favorable factors were broad and intangible."

Mr. Goetz naturally wasn't happy with this verdict. He hit upon an ingenious plan. He shipped the picture back to Europe and then brought it back to the United States. There the expected thing happened: the Treasury Department asked for a $5,000 customs duty, since the picture was a fake and not a duty-free original work of art. Mr. Goetz refused to pay a penny since in *his* opinion it was a genuine Van Gogh. And so the case was thrown into the lap of professional Treasury Department detectives.

The detectives analyzed ... the jury of experts had analyzed before. But ... used on one thing the four art experts had paid ... tion to whatever: the meaning of the Japanese ... Three Japanese experts were called in and ... und some typical mistakes a European ... wn. at's more, they found those same mistakes in ... se inscriptions by Van Gogh whose authenticity Whereupon the Treasury Department decided that Mr. Goetz was the owner of a genuine Van Gogh.

Of course, it is still possible that the museum experts were right and the detectives were wrong. That's not my point. My point is that the professional detectives—just like those two illustrious amateurs, Poe and Conan Doyle—solved the case by focusing on a seemingly irrelevant detail. They found a "hidden" fact that had been in plain view all the time.

Probably this phrase will remind you of another of Edgar Allan Poe's classic tales—"The Purloined Letter." In that story, the police know that a certain blackmailer is in possession of a stolen letter; they repeatedly search him and his apartment but can't find it. Poe's detective genius, C. Auguste Dupin, figures that the clever criminal must have hidden the letter by putting it right under the noses of the police. So he pays a visit to the blackmailer in his room and immediately spots a half-torn, soiled, crumpled envelope in a "card-rack of pasteboard that hung dangling by a dirty blue ribbon from a little brass knob just beneath the middle of the mantelpiece."

Dupin explains the principle of his solution like this:

There is a game of puzzles which is played upon a map. One party playing requires another to find a given word—the name of town, river, state, or empire—any word, in short, upon the motley and perplexed surface of the chart. A novice in the game generally seeks to embarrass his opponents by giving them the most minutely lettered names; but the adept selects such words as stretch, in large characters, from the end of the chart to the other. These, like the over-largely lettered signs and placards of the street, escape observation by dint of being excessively obvious; and here the physical oversight is precisely analogous with the moral inapprehension by which the intellect suffers to pass unnoticed those considerations which are too obtrusively and too palpably self-evident.

"The Purloined Letter" is not the first of Poe's classic detective stories but the third in a sense all mystery stories are variations upon its theme. There is good reason for that: A mystery writer who observes the established rules of the game must do two things: (a) he must show the detective-hero's ingenuity in solving the puzzle and give him (b) he must play fair with the reader and show the important clues at the same time. He must therefore hide and mention them casually in the course of the story as. The only way to do solve were irrelevant. In other words, they must be hidden in plain view like "The Purloined Letter."

Recently a well-known mystery writer, giving away some of his trade secrets, made this point very clear:

> How does your detective find out who did it? He may no longer, as he could in Sherlock's time, pick up significant clues and pocket them, with neither by your leave nor explanation to the reader. He may not—at least not too obviously—rely on intuition. . . . And if he relies on the method of slow accumulation the reader will grow bored. . . . The modern answer, by and large, is the gimmick—the single, or perhaps double, revealing clue, *which the reader might also notice were he bright enough.*

So, if you want to train yourself in clear thinking and problem-solving, you might do worse than read whodunits—those perennial variations upon Poe's "The Purloined Letter" or, for that matter, upon Dr. Duncker's box problem. Mind you, you'll have to avoid the corpse-cluttered, hard-boiled pseudo-mysteries, and you'll have to match your wits actively with the detective rather than passively wait for the solution. But if you read standard-formula whodunits in the proper spirit, they may well help you tackle your everyday problems.

Most of those problems, too, are solved by looking sharply at something that's been staring you in the face all the time.

ANSWERS TO PUZZLES

1. *Teralbay.* The solution is: *betrayal.*
2. *Husband's and wife's ages.* They are 56 and 42.
3. *Smallest number.* 301
4. *How did Robinson fare?* He lost $8.

Chapter Twenty-Six

ANIMAL, VEGETABLE, OR MINERAL

The birth of ideas has often been described. Poets talk of divine inspiration, ordinary people talk of hunches, psychologists talk of combinations, incubations, intimations, and illuminations, Professor Wertheimer talks of recentering and restructuring, Professor Spearman talks of the educing of correlates, and the patent law talks of the flash of genius. Everybody seems to agree that ideas are born suddenly and mysteriously.

Well and good. Luckily we all have those hunches and flashes of insight and get our fair share of ideas after a good night's sleep, or while we are shaving, or during a hot bath.

But what if we don't? What if there is a problem to be solved and we have no clue, no routine to fall back on, and no happy inspiration? Is there a method by which we can hunt for ideas systematically, prosaically, in broad daylight?

There *is* such a method. As far as I know, it is the only one. Thomas Hobbes, in 1651, described it this way:

> Regulated thought is a seeking. Sometimes a man seeks what he has lost. . . . Sometimes a man knows a place determinate, within the compass whereof he is to seek; and then his thoughts run over all the parts thereof, in the same manner as one would sweep a room to find a jewel; or as a spaniel ranges the field, till he find a scent; or as a man should run over the alphabet, to start a rhyme.

A twentieth-century chemist, Dr. Wilder D. Bancroft, said the same thing in more modern terms:

> . . . One must eventually present something construc-

tive. The answer is to be found in the game of Twenty
Questions. When I was a small boy, it was a very popular
game to try to find, by asking a series of questions, what
the others had selected. The first question was always:
animal, vegetable, or mineral? After that the questions
must be ones that could be answered by yes or no. . . .
The trick was to frame the questions so as to eliminate
a large portion of the possible field each time and to
reach the goal by successive eliminations. . . . The method might be called the either-or method, or the Socratic
method. The latter sounds more impressive. That simple
little game exemplifies the principles of scientific research and it would be a good thing if our graduate
students would play it regularly as part of their research
training.

Dr. Bancroft was quite right in comparing idea-hunting to
the game of Twenty Questions. If you're interested in producing ideas, the game of Twenty Questions is the ideal model. It
is well worth close study.

Let's spend a few minutes eavesdropping on twenty ques-
tions as it was played every week for some years on the air.
Our master of ceremonies is Bill Slater; the regulars are Fred
Vandeventer, newscaster, Florence Rinard, his wife, Herb
Polesie, movie producer, and young Johnny McPhee; the
guest this particular evening is Miss Nina Foch, the actress.
Here is one game:

BILL SLATER: This one's vegetable.

MYSTERY VOICE: Here we go back to the days when
knights were bold indeed. Bill is asking them to identify
King Arthur's Round Table.

BILL SLATER: Mystery Voice has told our friends at
home. This is going to take a bit of a battle, I think.

FRED VANDEVENTER: Is it wood or a wood product?

BILL SLATER: Yes.

FRED VANDEVENTER: Is it wood?

BILL SLATER: It's wood.

JOHNNY MCPHEE: Does this thing exist?

BILL SLATER: No.

FLORENCE RINARD: If it did exist, would it be manufactured?

BILL SLATER: Yes, if this did exist it would be manufactured.

HERB POLESIE: Is it connected with one professional person?

BILL SLATER: Yes.

FLORENCE RINARD: Was it large enough for people to be inside of it?

BILL SLATER: No. What were you thinking of?

FLORENCE RINARD: A wooden horse.

BILL SLATER: Yes, that's what you were thinking of—the Trojan Horse.

FLORENCE RINARD: Is this in American fiction?

BILL SLATER: No.

FRED VANDEVENTER: Is it in British fiction?

BILL SLATER: Yes, partly there.

FRED VANDEVENTER: Is it in prose fiction?

BILL SLATER: It has been in that form, yes.

FRED VANDEVENTER: Is it small enough to be carried about?

BILL SLATER: No.

FLORENCE RINARD: Is it a building?

BILL SLATER: No, it's not a building.

FRED VANDEVENTER: Is it a means of transportation?

BILL SLATER: No.

FRED VANDEVENTER: Is there any other—I'll ask this a different way: When this is manufactured, is it put together with something else?

BILL SLATER: Well, usually yes.

FRED VANDEVENTER: I mean such as nails and screws and—

BILL SLATER: Yes. The sort of thing you're after is usually put together with things like that.

FLORENCE RINARD: Is this a piece of furniture?

BILL SLATER: Yes.

FLORENCE RINARD: Is it a chair?

BILL SLATER: No.

JOHNNY MCPHEE: A round table?

BILL SLATER: It's a table!

JOHNNY MCPHEE: A round table?

BILL SLATER: Yes.

JOHNNY MCPHEE: King Arthur's Round Table?

BILL SLATER: Right!

Another game:

BILL SLATER: The subject's vegetable.

MYSTERY VOICE: The state of Vermont is famous for a

number of things. But when your sweet tooth is watering, you think of The Maple Trees of Vermont.

FRED VANDEVENTER: Is this wood or a wood product?

BILL SLATER: Is it wood or a wood product? I have to say yes to that.

JOHNNY MCPHEE: Is it manufactured?

BILL SLATER: No.

JOHNNY MCPHEE: Are we after a tree or part of a tree?

BILL SLATER: Partly.

JOHNNY MCPHEE: A group of trees?

BILL SLATER: A group of trees.

JOHNNY MCPHEE: Are they fictional?

BILL SLATER: No, they're real.

FLORENCE RINARD: Do they exist?

BILL SLATER: They exist.

FLORENCE RINARD: Are they in Europe?

BILL SLATER: No, they're not in Europe.

FRED VANDEVENTER: Are they in the United States?

BILL SLATER: They are in the United States.

HERB POLESIE: Are they in California?

BILL SLATER: They are not in California. You're thinking of the redwood trees.

HERB POLESIE: Indeed, and beautiful they are.

JOHNNY MCPHEE: Are they east of the Mississippi?

BILL SLATER: They are.

JOHNNY MCPHEE: And south of the Mason-Dixon line?

BILL SLATER: No.

FRED VANDEVENTER: Are they—If you were approaching them from the south, would you cross the Hudson River to get to them?

BILL SLATER: Yes, you would.

FRED VANDEVENTER: Are they in New England?

BILL SLATER: Yes.

FLORENCE RINARD: Are they one particular kind of trees?

BILL SLATER: They are.

FLORENCE RINARD: Maple?

BILL SLATER: Yes.

FLORENCE RINARD: Are they the trees they get maple syrup from?

BILL SLATER: Yes.

JOHNNY MCPHEE: Any particular state?

BILL SLATER: Yes.

JOHNNY MCPHEE: The maple sugar trees of Vermont?

BILL SLATER: Right!

A third game:

BILL SLATER: This subject is animal.

MYSTERY VOICE: The subject this time is that fabled Face on the Barroom Floor.

JOHNNY MCPHEE: Is this a whole animal?

BILL SLATER: No, this is not.

FLORENCE RINARD: Is this a living animal?

BILL SLATER: No, this is not a living animal.

FRED VANDEVENTER: Is it part of a human being?

BILL SLATER: It's part of a human being you're after, yes.

HERB POLESIE: Does my mother-in-law look like this in any way?

BILL SLATER: I doubt it, Herb.

JOHNNY MCPHEE: Is this human being fictional?

BILL SLATER: Yes, the human being involved is fictional.

FRED VANDEVENTER: Is this part of a man?

BILL SLATER: No, it's not part of a man.

FLORENCE RINARD: Is this in American fiction?

BILL SLATER: Yes, I think you'd call it American fiction.

FRED VANDEVENTER: Is it in prose fiction?

BILL SLATER: No.

JOHNNY MCPHEE: Could it be from a song?

BILL SLATER: No, it's not from a song.

NINA FOCH: Is it—I'm afraid this has been asked—a poem?

BILL SLATER: Yes, it's involved in a poem.

NINA FOCH: Is it the innkeeper's daughter? With the long hair? By Noyes, you know?

BILL SLATER: No. An interesting girl, the innkeeper's daughter with the long hair. But that's not who it was that we're concerned with.

FLORENCE RINARD: Is this hair?

BILL SLATER: No, it's not hair you're after.

FRED VANDEVENTER: Is this in a poem by a—a rather famous author?

BILL SLATER: No.

FRED VANDEVENTER: In other words, we know it because of the poem and not because of the author?

BILL SLATER: I think that's correct, Van.

FLORENCE RINARD: This wouldn't be The Face on the Barroom Floor?

BILL SLATER: Florence Rinard!!

Isn't this fun to read? It's even more fun to listen to or play yourself. If you've never played Twenty Questions, you'd better start right now and find out what you have missed. You can be sure it'll be a long time until you're as expert as the Vandeventers, Herb Polesie, or Johnny McPhee.

But, of course, my purpose here is more serious. Twenty questions, as I said, is *the* model of productive thinking. How did these experts play the game?

Well, if we analyze those three games, we find three basic rules of Twenty Questions strategy. They are:

1. Don't waste time with wild stabs.

2. Ask questions that have an even chance of being answered yes or no.

3. Vary your approach.

That wild stabs are bad is rather obvious, of course. Anyone can see that those questions about the Trojan Horse, the California Redwoods and the innkeeper's daughter in *The Highwayman* were sheer waste.

The even-chance principle isn't quite as obvious. Let me explain. Twice, when the subject was vegetable, the radio experts asked first: "Is it wood or a wood product?" Why did they do this? Because they had found by experience that the question "Is it wood?" did not divide the field evenly. If the answer was no, they had to go on and ask "Is it a wood product?" So they developed the combined question "Wood or wood product?" which they knew went just about down the middle of the range of possibilities. Similarly, to narrow down the whole of the United States, they asked first "East or west of the Mississippi?" and then "North or south of the Mason-Dixon line?" To start with the question "East or west of the Hudson River?" would have been poor strategy.

Finally: Vary your approach. It took the panel seven geographical questions to locate those trees in New England; with six more of these questions they could have pinned them down to one particular state. But they were smarter than that. They shifted to the question "What kind of trees?" and went from there directly to the solution.

And now let's see how we can apply the Twenty Questions technique to thinking in general. In everyday life, of course, we have no M.C. who supplies the yeses and noes; we have to ask *ourselves* each question and answer it as best we can.

If we don't know whether the answer is yes or no, we may be able to say "Probably yes" or "Probably no"; if we don't know that either, we may be able to find out. And, of course, we don't have to stick to twenty questions; we may get the solution after only ten, or we may have to ask thirty or forty.

For example, a friend of mine is an engineer who used to work abroad. Some years ago his company transferred him to their New York City headquarters and he had to find a place to live for himself, his wife and their two boys. This is the kind of problem where you start from scratch, without any kind of lead or clue.

Using the twenty questions method, my friend began to ask himself questions: Do I want a house or an apartment? (A house.) One or two stories? (Two will be all right.) Am I prepared to pay more than $20,000? (No.) More than $15,000? (Rather not.) Will I commute midtown or downtown? (Downtown.) Am I willing to commute more than twenty miles? (Yes.) More than thirty miles? (Yes.) Will an older house be satisfactory? (No.) Does it have to have a dining room? (Not necessarily.) Do I want a large yard? (Rather.)

After he had asked himself many more questions about locations, communities, neighborhoods, schools, churches, taxes, shopping centers, parks, beaches, and so on, my friend was as close to a solution as he could be while sitting in an armchair and thinking. The rest was easy. He and his family now live happily in a house that's just right for them.

A problem of this sort is not essentially different from a business or industrial problem. For instance, I looked up the section on plant location in an engineering handbook. I found that the engineer has to check, one by one, the following questions: (1) raw materials; (2) fuels and purchased power; (3) labor supply; (4) geographic factors; (5) water resources; (6) transportation facilities and rates; (7) markets; (8) laws and established public practices; (9) special company and industrial policies; and (10) other possible tangible or intangible considerations.

Scientific or industrial research offers some excellent examples of the twenty questions technique. For example, Dr. Flanders Dunbar, in her book *Mind and Body,* tells about a company that operated a large fleet of trucks and became alarmed at a terrific increase in accidents. The management looked into one question after another. They tested everything from the weather to the reaction time of the employees. No success. They tried intensive safety training for the drivers.

It didn't help. They tried penalties for those who had accidents and survived. Still the accident rate went on rising.

Finally, the company executives asked themselves whether the accident rate had anything to do with the drivers themselves. So they shifted drivers who had had accidents to work inside the plant. That did it. The problem was solved and the accident rate went down to normal. (The former drivers kept on having accidents in the plant, but that's another story —and a fascinating one too.)

Running through a list of questions or classifications is in fact a characteristic feature of all professional work. Engineers, for instance, use the so-called "search for power" technique and try mentally whether a given problem can be solved electrically, hydraulically, chemically, mechanically, or electronically. Doctors making diagnoses run through lists of diseases with similar symptoms. Lawyers drafting contracts or wills weigh various possibilities of corporate or estate structure. Accountants do the same with different types of accounts, and librarians, of course, with different book classifications.

A few years ago, a book was published that offers a nonprofessional person the sort of helpful check list that every professional carries in his head. It is called *Your Creative Power* and was written by Mr. Alex F. Osborn of the New York advertising firm Batten, Barton, Durstine & Osborn. Mr. Osborn devotes almost one hundred pages to a detailed discussion of his check list of problem-solving questions; you'll learn a lot if you get the book and study those hundred pages carefully. All I can give you here is a brief list of Mr. Osborn's main questions:

To what other uses can this be put?
Is there something similar I could partially copy?
What if this were somewhat changed?
What about making it bigger?
What if this were smaller?
What can I substitute?
How else can this be arranged?
What if this were reversed?
What could I combine this with?

This is an idea-provoking list if there ever was one, but I think it's too much of an advertising man's list to be generally useful. If you follow Mr. Osborn's method of producing ideas, you may wind up with Mr. Osborn's kind of ideas, and they may not always be the right solutions for your problems. He is fond, for instance, of "the Lucky Strike auctioneer, the penguin yodeling 'Kooool' cigarettes, the choo-choo train puffing 'Bromo Seltzer,' the Rinso-white whistle, and the Lifebuoy foghorn," and he is enthusiastic about "a new soapbook, with the story lithographed on the inside cover, and the characters portrayed by illustrations molded on cakes of soap."

Adapting the Osborn list to non-advertising purposes, I have drawn up a little list of my own—the kind of questions that may come in handy in solving such ordinary-life problems as buying a family home. Here it is:

What am I trying to accomplish?
Have I done this sort of thing before? How?
Could I do this some other way?
How did other people tackle this?
What kind of person or persons am I dealing with?
How can this situation be changed to fit me?
How can I adapt myself to this situation?
How about using more? Less? All of it? Only a portion? One only? Two? Several?
How about using something else? Something older? Something newer? Something more expensive? Something cheaper?
How near? How far? In what direction?
How soon? How often? Since when? For how long?
Could I do this in combination? With whom? With what?
How about doing the opposite?
What would happen if I did nothing?

Of course, this list is very general. But you can easily see that it may help in solving everyday problems. In fact, these are the kind of questions everybody asks himself more or less at random; it's useful to have them down in black and white.

However, for an expert twenty questions player a list like this is not enough. It's handy for the opening moves of the game, for the animal-vegetable-mineral or wood-or-woodproduct stage. Beyond that, the more unusual the category, the more searching and fruitful the question. To approach The Face on the Barroom Floor, Mr. Vandeventer had to think up a brand-new division of the field: "Little-known poem by famous author or famous poem by little-known author?"

In the same way, the genius problem-solver raises questions

that are way beyond the standard repertory. He arrives at a solution by asking himself whether badminton can be played as a noncompetitive game or whether foreign loans can be given in goods rather than money.

Such original classifications are rare, of course. They are hard to think of at the spur of the moment. That's why novel, unusual classifications are always valuable; watch out for them and add them to your mental repertory as you go along.

Collecting unusual classifications is a sort of hobby of mine. Here are some of my more interesting specimens:

E. M. Forster quotes a literary scholar who classified the weather in novels as "decorative, utilitarian, illustrative, planned in preestablished harmony, in emotional contrast, determinative of action, a controlling influence, itself a hero, and non-existent."

Professor Folsom of Vassar College classified love as "sexual, dermal, cardiac-respiratory, and unclassifiable."

Mr. Russell Lynes of *Harper's Magazine* classified people as "highbrows, middlebrows, and lowbrows" and as "intellectual snobs, regional snobs, moral snobs, sensual snobs, emotional snobs, taste snobs, occupational snobs, political snobs, and reverse or anti-snob snobs."

Professor W. Lloyd Warner of the University of Chicago classified people socially as "upper-upper-class, lower-upper-class, upper-middle-class, lower-middle-class, upper-lower-class, and lower-lower-class."

Professor Paul F. Lazarsfeld of Columbia University classified people as "opinion leaders and opinion followers."

The German psychiatrist Kretschmer classified people by body types as "pyknic" (round), "asthenic" (thin), and "athletic" (muscular); later Professor William H. Sheldon of Columbia University renamed these types "endomorphs" (fat), "mesomorphs" (strong), and "ectomorphs" (skinny) and called the corresponding temperament types "viscerotonic" (easy-going), "somatotonic" (active), and "cerebrotonic" (nervous).

William James classified people as "tough-minded and tender-minded," C. G. Jung classified them as "introverts and extroverts," and Friedrich Nietzsche classified them as "Dionysian and Apollonian."

And the late Yale geographer Ellsworth Huntington classified people according to what month they were born in, maintaining that most geniuses are conceived in early spring.

The significance of all this for clear thinking and problem-solving isn't always immediately obvious, but it may make quite a difference whether you are dealing with an asthenic, lower-upper-class, middlebrow housewife who was born in April and is a tough-minded opinion leader, or with a viscerotonic, upper-middle-class executive who is an occupational snob and was born an extrovert in November.

Seriously, though, it is true that new classifications will often completely change our attitudes and our thinking.

In the field of nutrition, for instance, the chemical classification of foods has made a vast difference in everybody's eating habits.

In politics, our outlook has changed since the old classification of right *vs.* left has given way to the new one of totalitarian *vs.* democratic.

And history looks different to us since Spengler and Toynbee wrote of the rise and fall of civilizations rather than nations.

All of which may seem pretty far afield from the good old game of twenty questions. But I think the connection is clear. Twenty questions offers a simple strategy for solving everyday problems, but it can also be used to attack and solve the most important problems of our age. As I said, it is the model of modern scientific research technique. Quite possibly, the logic of twenty questions is now the heir to the throne vacated by formal logic.

Future students of twenty questions logic will conceivably start their analysis with a simple mathematical fact: Twenty questions asked by a perfect player cover a range of 1,048,576 possible solutions. In other words, if you know how, you can use twenty questions to pick the one idea in a million.

Now do you believe that twenty questions is a powerful tool of thinking?

Chapter Twenty-Seven

THE MORE OR LESS SCIENTIFIC METHOD

Perhaps the most famous incident in the history of science occurred in the third century B.C. in Syracuse, Sicily. The mathematician Archimedes was taking a bath. His mind was busy with a scientific problem. King Hiero of Syracuse had ordered a golden crown and suspected the goldsmith of having cheated him by using some silver instead of the gold he'd been supplied with. The king had asked Archimedes to prove it.

Suddenly Archimedes noticed that his body caused some water to spill over. In a flash he realized the solution of the problem: he'd take the crown's weight in pure gold, dip it into water, and see whether the overflow was the same as that of the crown. Whereupon he jumped out of the tub, ran home naked as he was, and shouted to everyone he met: "Eureka! Eureka! . . . I've found it! I've found it!"

Perhaps the *least* famous incident in the history of science occurred in the twentieth century A.D. in the United States. The chemist J. E. Teeple was taking a bath. His mind was busy with a scientific problem. He stepped out of his bath, reached for a towel, dried himself, shaved, took another bath, stepped out of it, reached for a towel and discovered that the towel was wet. Thinking about his scientific problem, he had taken two baths. He had *not* found the solution to his problem.

The first of these incidents has been retold a million times; the second is trivial. Nevertheless, the second is the one that gives the truer picture of the scientific method.

In the first place, the story about Archimedes puts the spotlight on the happy discovery, giving the impression that this sort of thing is typical of a scientist's life. Actually, "Eureka!" moments are few and far between. Einstein once said: "I think and think, for months, for years, ninety-nine times the conclusion is false. The hundredth time I am right." And that's Einstein, the greatest scientific genius of our time. I leave it to you to estimate the percentage of correct solutions in an ordinary scientist's work. Most of their lives are spent like Mr. Teeple's half-hour in the bathroom, thinking and thinking and getting nowhere.

But there's a more important reason why Archimedes crying "Eureka!" isn't a good picture of a scientist. Today no scientist, dressed or undressed, would dream of telling people "I've found it!" as soon as he has hit upon a bright idea. Even less would he do the modern equivalent—announce his discovery immediately to the press. Just the contrary. He would take care not to breathe a word about it to anyone, but quietly go to his laboratory and run some tests—and more tests—and more tests.

A scientist today doesn't consider a bright idea as a revelation of the truth; he considers it as something to be disproved. Not just proved, mind you; it's his obligation as a scientist to think of all conceivable means and ways to *dis*prove it. This habit is so ingrained in him that he doesn't even realize it any more; he automatically thinks of a theory as something to find flaws in. So he does experiments and hunts for every error he can possibly think of; and when he is through with his own experiments, he publishes his findings not in a newspaper but in a scientific journal, inviting other scientists to do some other experiments and prove him wrong.

And when the hunt for errors has subsided and a theory gets established and accepted—do scientists think they've got hold of a new truth? No. To them, all scientific findings are only *tentative* truth, "good until further notice," to be immediately discarded when someone comes along with another theory that explains a few more facts. Absolute truth doesn't even interest them; they get along very happily, thank you, with a set of working hypotheses that are good only at certain times and for certain purposes. The most famous example of this today is the theory of light. There is a wave theory that fits certain investigations, and a particle theory that fits certain others. Years ago physicists stopped trying to find out which is true and which is false. The Danish Nobel prize winner, Niels Bohr, has called this the principle of complementarity, saying that after all "waves" and "particles" are only handy metaphors in dealing with certain facts; so why not use whichever is more practical at the moment? Never mind what light is "really"; let's get on with the job of finding out what it *does*. Or, as one physicist said, "Let's use the particle theory on Mondays, Wednesdays, and Fridays, and the wave theory on Tuesdays, Thursdays, and Saturdays."

For the layman, the most important thing about science is this: that it isn't a search for truth but a search for error. The scientist lives in a world where truth is unattainable, but where it's always possible to find errors in the long-settled or the obvious. You want to know whether some theory is really scientific? Try this simple test: If the thing is shot through with *perhapses* and *maybes* and hemming and hawing, it's probably science; if it's supposed to be *the* final answer, it is not.

So-called "scientific" books that are supposed to contain final answers are never scientific. Science is forever self-correcting and changing; what is put forth as gospel truth cannot be science.

But what does *science* mean? If someone asked you for a definition, you'd probably be on the spot. If pressed, you might come up with something like the definition in Webster's: "A branch of study . . . concerned with the observation and classification of facts, esp. with the establishment . . . of verifiable general laws . . ."

That's a pretty good description of what the word means to the average person. Does it mean the same thing to scientists? It does not. In 1951 Dr. James B. Conant, who was trained as a chemist, published *his* definition of science: "An interconnected series of concepts and conceptual schemes that have developed as a result of experimentation and observation and are fruitful of further experimentation and observation." As you see, the two definitions are almost exact opposites. *You* think science deals with facts; a scientist thinks it deals with concepts. *You* think science tries to establish laws; a scientist thinks it aims at more and more experiments.

And what is the scientific method? Your answer is apt to be: "The classification of facts." Dr. Conant's answer is again different. Look up *Scientific method* in the index of his book, *Science and Common Sense*, and you'll find this: "Scientific method. *See* Alleged scientific method." In other words, Dr. Conant thinks there *isn't any* scientific method.

That surely is extreme. Even if there is no clearly definable scientific method, there's a way in which scientists work, and it's certainly worth knowing about. Let's look at a careful description by Dr. W. I. B. Beveridge, a British biologist:

The following is a common sequence in an investigation of a medical or biological problem:

(*a*) The relevant literature is critically reviewed.

(*b*) A thorough collection of field data or equivalent observational enquiry is conducted, and is supplemented if necessary by laboratory examination of specimens.

(*c*) The information obtained is marshalled and correlated and the problem is defined and broken down into specific questions.

(*d*) Intelligent guesses are made to answer the questions, as many hypotheses as possible being considered.

(*e*) Experiments are devised to test first the likeliest hypotheses bearing on the most crucial questions.

The key word here is *guesses* in (*d*). In the popular view the emphasis is on (*b*), the collection of data. But not among scientists. They like to distinguish between "accumulators" and "guessers," and they're pretty much agreed that it's the guessers that are important. In more fancy terms, you could say that the modern emphasis is on deduction rather than induction, or that the Aristotelian method is now more esteemed than the Baconian. What it comes down to is simply this: Our top scientists say we need more ideas rather than more facts; they want more Einsteins who just sit and think rather than Edisons who have a genius for tinkering in the laboratory. After all, Edison, as one of them has said, "was not a scientist and was not even interested in science."

Meanwhile, our research relies far more on accumulating than on guessing. General Electric, with its training courses in "Creative Engineering," is the exception; the American Cancer Society, which is openly resigned to "whittling away at this mass of mystery," is typical of the general rule.

Which is why Dr. Sinnott, when he was director of the Sheffield School of Science at Yale, said:

It must be ruefully admitted that we have not produced our share of great new germinative ideas in recent years. In atomic research, for example, most of the fundamental theoretical progress was made either by European scientists or men who had received their training abroad. We are strong in application, in development and engineering, but much less so in the fundamental contributions of the theory on which all these are based. . . . We are in danger of being overwhelmed by a mass of undigested results.

And what is the method used by those hard-to-find "guessers"? If we try to analyze it, we come right back to Duncker's description of problem-solving, to his "solutions from below" and "solutions from above." Scientific problems are solved either by finding a seemingly irrelevant key factor or by applying a seemingly unsuitable thought pattern. Which means that scientific discoveries are made in one of two ways: by accident or by hunch.

Take any history of science, and you'll find that it is a history of accidents and hunches. Both types of discoveries are equally fascinating.

If you're interested in accidents, for instance, scientific history looks like this:

In 1786, Luigi Galvani noticed the accidental twitching of a frog's leg and discovered the principle of the electric battery.

In 1822, the Danish physicist Oersted, at the end of a lecture, happened to put a wire conducting an electric current near a magnet, which led to Faraday's invention of the electric dynamo.

In 1858, a seventeen-year-old boy named William Henry Perkin, trying to make artificial quinine, cooked up a black-looking mass, which led to his discovery of aniline dye.

In 1889, Professors von Mering and Minkowski operated on a dog. A laboratory assistant noticed that the dog's urine attracted swarms of flies. He called this to the attention of Minkowski, who found that the urine contained sugar. This was the first step in the control of diabetes.

In 1895, Roentgen noticed that cathode rays penetrated black paper and discovered X-rays.

In 1929, Sir Alexander Fleming noticed that a culture of bacteria had been accidentally contaminated by a mold. He said to himself: "My, that's a funny thing." He had discovered penicillin.

Of course, all these accidents would have been meaningless if they hadn't happened to Galvani, Perkin, Roentgen, and so on. As Pasteur has said, "Chance favors the prepared mind." What is necessary is an accidental event plus an observer with *serendipity*—"the gift of finding valuable or agreeable things not sought for." (Horace Walpole coined that beautiful word.)

On the other hand, if you're interested in hunches, scientific history looks like this, for example:

Harvey describes his discovery of the circulation of the blood:

I frequently and seriously bethought me, and long revolved in my mind, what might be the quantity of blood which was transmitted, in how short a time its passage might be effected and the like. . . . I began to think whether there might not be a motion, as it were, in a circle.

James Watt invents the steam engine:

On a fine Sabbath afternoon I took a walk. . . . I had entered the green and had passed the old washing house. I was thinking of the engine at the time. I had gone as far as the herd's house when the idea came into my mind that as steam was an elastic body it would rush into a vacuum, and if a connection were made between the cylinder and an exhausting vessel it would rush into it and might then be condensed without cooling the cylinder. . . . I had not walked further than the golf house when the whole thing was arranged in my mind.

Darwin writes about his theory of evolution:

I can remember the very spot in the road, whilst in my carriage, when to my joy the solution occurred to me.

Kekule tells how he discovered the benzene ring on top of a London bus:

I sank into a reverie. The atoms flitted about before my eyes. . . . I saw how two small ones often joined into a little pair; how a larger took hold of two smaller, and a still larger clasped three or even four of the small ones, and how all spun around in a whirling round-dance. . . . The cry of the conductor, "Clapham Road," woke me up.

Walter B. Cannon discovers the significance of bodily changes in fear and rage:

These changes—the more rapid pulse, the deeper breathing, the increase of sugar in the blood, the secretion from the adrenal glands—were very diverse and seemed unrelated. Then, one wakeful night, after a considerable collection of these changes had been disclosed, the idea flashed through my mind that they could be nicely integrated if conceived as bodily preparations for supreme effort in flight or in fighting.

Does all this mean that some scientists are good at hunches and some others blessed with serendipity? Not at all. The accidental clue needs a receptive mind; the hunch has to grow from a study of facts. The good guesser works both ways, depending on what he has to go on. Here's one more example that shows a combination of both methods. It is typical of modern scientific research in many ways.

During World War II, a team of psychologists studied the propaganda effect of orientation films. Among other things, they tried to find out whether films changed the opinions and attitudes of soldiers who saw them, and whether and how these changes lasted. They had a hunch that the effect of the films would gradually wear off and that after some time, soldiers would forget the factual details and revert to their original opinion.

This idea may seem rather obvious to you. It seemed obvious to the psychologists too—but, being scientists, they decided to test it anyway. So they gave the soldiers a test after one week and another test after nine weeks.

As expected, the soldiers had forgotten most of the facts in the film during those eight weeks. But, "clearly contrary to the initial expectation," the general propaganda effect of the film—the opinion change—had considerably *increased* between the first and the second test. There was not the slightest doubt about it: the soldiers had forgotten the details of the film, but its message had sunk in deeper.

The research team cheerfully accepted this unexpected fact and immediately proceeded to account for it by a hypothesis. They found that it could be explained through a theory by the British psychologist, Bartlett, published in 1932. Bartlett had written that "after learning, that which is recalled tends to be modified with lapse of time in the direction of omission of all but general content and introduction of new material in line with the individual's attitudes." In other words, as time passes, we're apt to forget details but *reinforce* what we remember of the general idea.

Well, what have we here? Doubtless the research team made a valuable discovery. Yet the whole story is as unlike that of Archimedes in his bath as can be. For one thing, there is no single scientist, but a team of thirteen men and two women. Second, the discovery is exactly the opposite from what the scientists expected to find. Third, it is immediately connected up with an idea thought up by another scientist in another country, twenty years before.

And finally, there is no "Eureka!", no shouting from the housetops, no happy announcement to the world. Instead, after reporting their discovery and stating their hypothesis, the researchers add casually: "These highly speculative suggestions indicate some very interesting areas for future research."

Chapter Twenty-Eight

THE HARNESSING OF CHANCE

The wildly improbable happens every day.

Not long ago there was a picture in *Life* that showed a group of deer including three albinos. Photographer Staber Reese took it in northern Wisconsin, where there are 850,000 white-tailed deer, twenty of which are albinos. Reese figured that the mathematical odds against a picture with three albino deer in it were 79 billion to one.

Or consider the odd coincidences that happen in everyone's life. For example, on page 197 of this book I listed some of the Chukchee names for reindeer. I had found these names referred to (but not given) in a book by Franz Boas, and went to the New York Public Library to copy them from Boas' source—the tattered, fifty-year-old seventh volume of the report on the Jesup North Pacific Expedition by Waldemar Bogoras. When I came home that evening, I found the latest copy of *The New Yorker*. The first thing I read in it was a "footloose correspondent" report on Lapland, listing the various names for reindeer used by the Lapps.

Or here is something a little more exotic. In 1923 the poet and literary scholar Leonard Bacon went to the University of California library and took out a twenty-year-old book published in Vienna. On the train to Monterey, he opened the book and began to read the introduction. When he got to the acknowledgments, he came upon the arresting name Lord Talbot de Malahide. (This was long before the Boswell papers were found at Malahide Castle.) At this point Mr. Bacon got bored with his book and turned to the San Francisco *Chronicle*. There he found a social note that Lord and Lady Talbot de Malahide were staying at the St. Francis Hotel.

Too trivial for you? Then consider the following case. In 1908 the Rev. James Smith, pastor of a small Negro congre-

gation at Reid's Ferry, Virginia, mysteriously disappeared.
Soon afterward the corpse of a large Negro was found in
the Nansemond River near the church. There was evidence of
a blow on the head with a blunt instrument. The body was
unrecognizable, but its clothes were identified as similar to
those worn by Smith. Also, a woman friend of Smith who
had not seen the body told the authorities that if it was
Smith, they'd find a ring with a purple setting on the little
finger of the left hand. They did.

The most likely suspect of the murder was Smith's rival
and successor, the Rev. Ernest Lyons. He was tried, convicted
of second-degree murder, and sentenced to eighteen years in
prison.

Three years later Smith was found alive in North Carolina,
where he had absconded with church funds. He wore a ring
with a purple setting on the little finger of his left hand. The
fateful ring on the corpse in the river had been sheer coinci-
dence. Lyons had served three years in prison for "murder-
ing" a man who was still alive.

There is no complete defense against the sea of improba-
bilities that surrounds us. But there are weapons. Armed with
probability theory and statistics, it is possible to face calmly
this world of coincidences and seemingly miraculous events.

Above all, the statistical approach is an antidote against
the shudder and the helplessness we feel in the face of the
extraordinary. Mr. Reese figured that the chances against his
getting that deer picture were 79 billion to one. He may have
been wrong, of course; but even if he was right, the oddest of
chances is a more comfortable thing to contemplate than
something that cannot possibly happen but does. At the
Monte Carlo roulette table, red once came up thirty-two
times in a row. This must have been an uncanny thing to
watch for those who were there, but they too had the comfort of knowing that it wasn't a miracle. It was just something that happens once in four billion times.

The other way round, the statistical approach is also helpful
because it teaches you that you can't always expect the average. Don't believe it if people tell you that statisticians reduce
everything to averages. It just isn't so: they know better than
anyone else that an average is just one point on a curve.

In short, the statistical view gives you a pretty realistic
picture of what the world is like. We are all apt to assume that
the good, the bad, and the medium are fairly evenly distributed; but the statisticians can prove that this is wrong. Their
bell-shaped, so-called "normal" curve shows that ordinarily

there are more medium cases than either good or bad ones, and there are always some that are *very* good or *very* bad. Suppose you are interested in girls and classify them as "good-looking," "so-so," and "plain." Do you expect to find about one-third of each? A statistician will tell you that you mustn't overlook the exceptional cases at either end of the scale and that you must be prepared to see more of the average. His "normal" distribution will look like this:

Beautiful	7 per cent
Good-looking	24 per cent
So-so	38 per cent
Plain	24 per cent
Ugly	7 per cent

Look around you, and you'll find that statisticians know a thing or two.

Most important, statistics teaches you not to rely on a single instance, or even a few. You need lots of cases to establish a fact—not as true, mind you, but as highly probable. One case is nothing; ten cases are nothing. A thousand cases? Maybe they show a trend.

But then, of course, it's not always possible to assemble a thousand cases, and even if you do, you're apt to run into errors and mistakes. The larger the figures, the larger the sources of error. In July, 1950, Dr. Roy V. Peel, national director of the Census Bureau, revealed that even with the best scientific methods census figures "should be within about one per cent of the truth." In September, 1949, the U.S. Bureau of Labor Statistics discovered it had underrated the number of unemployed by one million.

So, since complete surveys aren't practical and are far from foolproof, statisticians are usually content to take samples. In theory, a small random sample tells almost as much as a full survey. But there is a joker in this statement: it's the word *random*.

If you draw slips with names from a drum, it's supposedly random. But even in that case statisticians will tell you that certain elements may influence your choice. What you think is random—like closing your eyes and dropping a pencil on a page—isn't random to a statistician at all. They use printed tables of random numbers, and even with those they're always afraid of some bias creeping in somewhere.

For instance, statisticians have discovered that three-fourths of the population are apt to call "heads" rather than "tails" in coin tossing. Why, nobody knows. They have found that if you arrange five test questions so that the correct answers are "yes," "no," "yes," "no," "yes," people will unconsciously shy away from that pattern. Looks too symmetrical to be right. They have found that if you pick a sample of people whose name begins with a certain letter, the sample will be biased. Names are connected with nationality, and therefore with income and social status.

In social surveys and public opinion polls, random sampling seems to be particularly impossible. True, there is a new system—"area sampling"—that excludes the interviewer's bias and forces him to question certain people whether he wants to or not; but even that method is far from foolproof. The older system—"quota sampling"—leaves it to the interviewer to make up his quota of interviewees. This is the method of the Gallup poll and most other public opinion polls. It *never* produces a random sample. When you stop to think about it, that's quite obvious, since interviewers are just like other people and dislike dirt, noise, smells, sickness, stair-climbing, unfriendliness, language difficulties and all the other embarrassments and troubles that make up a truly random sample. No wonder there are about 15 per cent more well-educated, native-born, one-family-house dwellers in most quota samples than there are in the American population.

All of this, however, is comparatively simple. Statistics gets really complicated when we get into the business of two-way statistics—in other words, correlations. This is where we get into the statistical solution of problems.

To understand what correlation is all about, let's go back for a moment to that nineteenth-century genius, John Stuart Mill—the man whose I.Q. was estimated the highest of all time; the man who learned ancient Greek at the age of three. Having read Aristotle's logic in the original when he was twelve, Mill thought that something ought to be done about it. After some twenty-five years, he did: in 1843 he published his own *Logic* as a substitute.

Mill started with an analysis of the methods used in scientific research. So, instead of the old rules of the syllogism, he came up with four methods of experimental inquiry. These, he proudly announced, were the only possible ones—"at least, I know not, nor am I able to imagine, any others. . . . They compose the available resources of the human mind for ascertaining the laws of the succession of phenomena."

Now what are Mill's "methods"? Basically, there are two: the "method of agreement" and the "method of difference"

—which may be combined into the "joint method of agreement *and* difference." There are also two more specialized methods: the "method of residues" and the "method of concomitant variations." Mill explains all these with great complexity and Early Victorian detail, but fortunately we don't have to bother with all that. By the time John Dewey got around to writing his book on *How We Think* in 1910, Mill's rules were just good enough for a brief footnote, stating casually that only the "joint method of agreement and difference" was of any use. Well, the "joint method of agreement and difference" consists simply in varying one factor while keeping all others constant. Long ago it was phrased unsurpassably by Professor C. F. Chandler of Columbia University: "Vary one thing at a time, and make a note of all you do."

The effect of this—of varying one thing at a time—can be measured by the statistical technique of correlation. You take a large number of cases, measure the variable you are interested in, measure another variable for comparison, and work out the relationship between the two. Basically, it's nothing but a refinement of the kind of thing you do naturally to find the cause of any effect. If you sit under a lamp and the light goes out, you fetch another bulb and screw it in: you vary one factor, keeping everything else constant. If the new bulb works, you're satisfied you've found the cause of the light going out. If it doesn't, you vary other factors, one at a time: you try another plug, you change a fuse, and so on. Each step is a scientific experiment in miniature.

So far, so good. But often you do the same thing *without* experimenting. You see that a change in one factor is accompanied by a certain effect, and you think you've discovered the cause. This is Mill's method of "concomitant variations." It may work—sometimes; or it may not. Since you didn't set up the experiment, you can't control anything; and the effect may have been produced by a million reasons you don't know of.

For example, there is the classic case of the village of Polykastron in Greece. Early in 1950 the United Nations International Children's Emergency Fund distributed powdered milk to expectant mothers there. Shortly afterward, the first two women who used it gave birth to twins on the same day—the first twins born in the village in ten years. The women of Polykastron drew the obvious conclusion; they decided they'd rather *not* use UN powdered milk.

Why, these were poor Greek peasant women, you say:

educated people are not apt to make such mistakes. But they do. Conspicuous correlations fool everybody, including scientists. For instance, in 1927 Dr. Manfred Sakel discovered that schizophrenia can be treated by administering overdoses of insulin. Overdoses of insulin often produce a convulsive shock. So hundreds of psychiatrists, just like the Greek women, drew the obvious conclusion and began to treat schizophrenia and other mental diseases by simply giving their patients electric shocks and leaving out the insulin. At a 1950 psychiatric convention, Dr. Sakel sadly explained that electric shocks are actually harmful and that the insulin cure is really based on restoring a patient's balance of hormones. For over twenty years, he said, the standard procedure had been based on a misconception.

This is the sort of thing to keep in mind before putting too much faith in correlations. Statisticians have even more impressive examples. One of them discovered a correlation of .90 between the number of storks' nests in Stockholm and the number of babies born there over a period of years. Another (this was a favorite example of the late Professor Morris Cohen) found, over a certain period, a correlation of .87 between the membership of the International Machinists' Union and the death rate of the state of Hyderabad.

You want to know the meaning of these figures? They look like percentages but they are not: they are correlation coefficients. Let's spend a minute or two on getting the hang of the basic principle.

Correlation coefficients come in assorted sizes between plus one and minus one. Plus one means perfect correlation: if x happens, y always happens too. Minus one means perfect *negative* correlation: if x happens, y never happens. Zero means no correlation whatever: if x happens, y may or may not happen, you can't tell.

For example, let's take some fictitious correlation coefficients between *age* and *value:*

+.90: Value regularly increases with age (e.g. wine)
+.45: Value often increases with age (e.g. paintings)
.00: Value has nothing to do with age (e.g. diamonds)
—.45: Value often decreases with age (e.g. houses)
—.90: Value regularly decreases with age (e.g. news)

I didn't give examples of plus one or minus one, because perfect correlations virtually don't exist. Statisticians consider a correlation of .90 (like that between Stockholm storks' nests and babies) as practically perfect.

And now that I have given you proper warning against

putting blind faith in correlations, let me show you what they are good for.

Take, for instance, an analysis of certain intelligence tests for boys who wanted to qualify for the Army or Navy college training program during World War II. Researchers figured the averages of the scores for each of the forty-eight states and correlated those averages with other statistics. Here are some of their findings:

+.83: Intelligence test scores increased with number of telephones per thousand.

+.69: Intelligence test scores increased with number of foreign-born per thousand.

+.67: Intelligence test scores increased with number of residents per 100,000 in *Who's Who*.

—.01: Intelligence test scores had nothing to do with number of persons killed in auto accidents per 100,000.

—.53: Intelligence test scores decreased with percentage of population without library service.

—.53: Intelligence test scores decreased with number of lynchings (1882-1944) per 100,000.

—.66: Intelligence test scores decreased with number of rural homes without privies per 1,000.

"Without much facetiousness," the researchers summed up, "we interpret these results to mean that the probabilities of reaching a high educational achievement are much greater if one comes from a high income state which is highly urban, which is not in the South, and which has such advantages as library service available to most of its population, has a high proportion of foreign-born citizens, a large number of residents in *Who's Who*, and many telephones."

Or take a statistical study by Dr. Sheldon Glueck of Harvard University and his wife, Dr. Eleanor Glueck. They tried to find the causes of juvenile delinquency. More scientifically speaking, they tried to isolate certain factors that distinguish delinquent boys from those who are not.

Dr. and Mrs. Glueck devoted ten years to their study. Being scientists, they began their study by making certain guesses. Being scientists, they then proceeded to test these guesses. They assembled mountains of data on five hundred delinquent and five hundred non-delinquent boys. When they had collected all the statistics on the factors they were interested in, they looked for differences in the degree of correlation.

They found, among other things, that the parents of delinquent boys were often more erratic than those of other boys; that between-children are more likely to become delinquent than either first or last children; that delinquent boys were usually more muscular than others and scored higher in certain parts of intelligence tests. On the whole, they found that delinquency is connected with a boy's home life, with his temperament and character, and with his ability to get along with people. In fact, Dr. and Mrs. Glueck drew up a "prediction table" by which six-year-olds can be spotted as future delinquents if a long list of factors is known. But, of course, they didn't say that this prediction was infallible or that they had found once and for all the causes of juvenile delinquency. They just reported what they gingerly called a "tentative causal formula or law."

Now this is exactly the kind of thing people are apt to explain by "fate" or "bad blood" or "slum conditions" or whatever other pet explanation they are fond of. The Glueck study is a beautiful example of the scientific approach. The Gluecks didn't look for a single cause; in fact, they didn't look for "a cause" at all. They looked for certain factors that were to a certain degree connected with delinquency. And they concluded, *not* that juvenile delinquency was due to this or that, but that if a combination of certain factors was present to a certain degree, the result would probably be a tendency to delinquency.

Of course I don't mean to say that in everyday life you shouldn't decide anything before you have made a ten-year statistical study. But you can use the scientific approach as a model. Instead of the black-and-white, single-track, everyone-knows-that-this-is-due-to-that approach, get used to the idea that this is a world of multiple causes, imperfect correlations, and sheer, unpredictable chance.

It is true that the scientists, with their statistics and their probabilities, have made a stab at the harnessing of chance. But they know very well that certainty is unattainable. A high degree of probability is the best we can ever get.

Chapter Twenty-Nine

HOW NOT TO RACK YOUR BRAIN

It's time to sum up.

Have we gotten any closer to clear thinking after our excursions into law, psychology, science, and statistics? Have we arrived at any rules?

Well, if you've learned anything from this book, you'll know that there can't *be* any rules. Or rather, that the first rule of clear thinking is not to go by rules.

However, let's at least draw up a list of reminders. Here it is:

1. Try to remember that everybody, including yourself, has only his own experience to think with.

2. Try to detach your ideas from your words.

3. Translate the abstract and general into the concrete and specific.

4. Don't apply general rules blindly to specific problems.

5. To solve a puzzling problem, look for a seemingly irrelevant key factor in the situation and for a seemingly unsuitable pattern in your mind.

6. Narrow the field of solutions by asking "twenty questions."

7. Remember that bright ideas are often wrong and must be tested.

8. Don't underrate the influence of chance.

If you are the kind of person who likes advice highly concentrated and neatly packaged, this is about the best I can do for you.

Except for one thing. The art of thinking, like every other art, has also an element of sheer routine about it—the basic mechanics of the thing—when to do precisely what in what way. The art of writing, for instance, includes, at a lower level, penmanship or typing; the art of painting, a knowledge

273

of brushes and paints. In the same way, the art of thinking includes a certain amount of mechanics: when to think; where to find ideas; how to use thinking tools. So, while it is impossible to draw up a list of thinking rules, it is quite possible to give you some definite, practical thinking *tips*.

To begin with, there are what is known as "stages of thought." There is a typical, known sequence to the production of ideas—a sequence that is the same whether the product is a symphony, a mathematical theorem, a treaty, or an advertisement. The literature on this fascinating subject reads like nothing else on earth; it's a branch of psychology, but it was written by chemists, novelists, mathematicians, biologists, poets, and a very few psychologists. It is studded with case histories of artistic and intellectual creation, from Descartes and Mozart to Einstein and Thomas Wolfe. It has two great classics: Professor John Livingston Lowes' monumental study of how Coleridge created his poem *Kubla Khan*, and Henri Poincaré's famous lecture on how he arrived at the theory of Fuchsian functions.

Among other things, this literature contains at least a dozen descriptions of "stages of thought," all somewhat similar. Here are four of them:

First, the four stages listed in *The Art of Thought* by Graham Wallas, a political scientist:

1. Preparation—the stage during which the problem is investigated.

2. Incubation—the stage during which you are not consciously thinking about the problem.

3. Illumination—the appearance of the "happy idea."

4. Verification.

Next, the five stages of Mr. James Webb Young, an advertising man who wrote a little book, *A Technique for Producing Ideas:*

1. The gathering of raw materials—both the materials of your immediate problem and the materials which come from a constant enrichment of your store of general knowledge.

2. The working over of these materials in your mind.

3. The incubating stage—where you let something beside the conscious mind do the work of synthesis.

4. The actual birth of the Idea—the "Eureka! I have it!" stage.

5. The final shaping and developing of the idea to practical usefulness.

Third, the four stages of Mr. J. F. Young, of the General

Electric Company, who was interested in "Developing Creative Engineers":

1. Definition of the problem.
2. Manipulation of elements bearing on solution.
3. Period resulting in the intuitive idea.
4. The idea is shaped to practical usefulness.

Fourth, the stages listed by a psychologist, Dr. Eliot Dole Hutchinson:

1. Preparation or orientation.
2. Frustration, renunciation or recession, in which for a time the problem is given up.
3. The period or moment of insight.
4. Verification, elaboration or evaluation.

On the whole, however, psychologists aren't too fond of this sort of approach. Take for instance the 1950 president of the American Psychological Association, Dr. J. P. Guilford of the University of Southern California. In his presidential address he said, with an air of marked distaste:

> In the writings of those who have attempted to give a generalized picture of creative behavior, there is considerable agreement that the complete creative act involves four important steps. . . . The creator begins with a period of preparation, devoted to an inspection of his problem and a collection of information or material. There follows a period of incubation during which there seems to be little progress in the direction of fulfillment. But, we are told, there is activity, only it is mostly unconscious. There eventually comes the big moment of inspiration, with a final, or semi-final solution, often accompanied by strong emotions. There usually follows a period of evaluation or verification, in which the creator tests the solution or examines the product for its fitness or value. Little or much touching up may be done to the product.

Dr. Guilford adds:

> Such an analysis is very superficial from the psychological point of view. It is more dramatic than it is suggestive of testable hypotheses. It tells us almost nothing about the mental operations that actually occur. The concepts do not lead directly to test ideas . . .

Well, that puts Messrs. Lowes, Poincaré, Wallas, J. W.

Young, J. F. Young, Hutchinson, et al., in their places, but it also gives us an excellent summary of the "considerable agreement" on the stages of thought. Dr. Guilford may not like it, but the body of evidence for the four stages of thought is there, for all to see.

And now that we have a good composite picture of the thinking process, let's see how we can practically improve the mechanics of each stage.

Let's start with Mr. J. F. Young's first step, the definition of the problem. For this I can give you four practical tips:

1. *Write the problem down.* The most important tools for a problem-solver are pencil and paper. If you want evidence for this obvious proposition, take my friends and students who were exposed to the two little problems on page 240. Among the solutions done on paper, 80 per cent were right; among those done in the head, 88 per cent were wrong.

2. *Translate the problem into simple language.* All translation helps; translation into concrete, plain language helps most. J. B. S. Haldane, the famous biologist, claimed that he made many of his discoveries while writing popular-science articles for factory workers.

3. *If the problem can be stated mathematically, state it mathematically.* Mathematics is a treasure house of problem-solving formulas. If you can use it, by all means do so. If you don't know enough mathematics, pass the problem on to someone who does.

4. *If the problem can be stated graphically, state it graphically.* A graph often helps you understand something that looks unintelligible in words or figures. Louis Bean, the only man who has been consistently right in predicting election results, says he performs this magic trick with charts and graphs. Again, if you are not up on this technique, pass the problem on to someone who is.

Next, let's proceed to the preparation stage. The first practical tip here is simple but basic: *Don't rely on your memory.*

Everyone's memory is unreliable. And as if this wasn't enough trouble, we usually remember the trivial and forget the essential.

Of course you know what silly little things we remember. W. W. Sawyer, an English mathematician, sums it up nicely:

> There are hundreds of things—odd remarks, pointless little stories, tricks with matches, stray pieces of information—which seem to have no use in life, but which

stay in your memory for years. At school we read a history book. . . . No one remembers the history. . . . But there were certain footnotes in it; one about a curate who grew crops in the churchyard and said it would be turnips next year; a lady who blacked out a picture and said "She is blacker within"; a verse about someone longing to be at 'em and waiting for the Earl of Chatham —everyone knew these years after they left school.

These are the things we remember. And what are the things we forget? At school you learned how to find a square root. Can you do it now? I can't. I bet you can't either.

For your comfort, let me quote the great mathematician Henri Poincaré: "I am absolutely incapable of adding without mistakes." And the famous writer Somerset Maugham: "I often think how much easier life would have been for me and how much time I should have saved if I had known the alphabet. I can never tell where I and J stands without saying G, H to myself first. I don't know whether P comes before R or after, and where T comes in has to this day remained something that I have never been able to get into my head.

Alekhine, the late world chess champion, once played fifteen blind games simultaneously. After some time he asked an umpire for a cigarette. "How absent-minded of me!" he said. "I left my cigarette case at home again!"

So this is the main instrument we have for thinking. Here's a fair example of how it works in an actual case. Miss May Lamberton Becker, who for many years wrote the column "The Reader's Guide" in the New York *Herald Tribune*, once got the following inquiry from a reader:

> Many years ago I read a novel which I should like to read again. I do not remember the title or the author. . . . It was an English novel and the chief character was a man. I believe he had a title, but I'm not sure about that. He was perfectly formed from the waist up but his legs were abnormally short.

Miss Becker described the process by which she arrived at the answer:

> There's no use making a strong effort at recall. It is like sitting beside a small, dark pool, keeping your eye fixed on it and expecting something to come up. What had come up immediately, like a bubble to the surface, was a sense of repulsion, something remembered as mon-

strous. Then . . . I knew I'd read it years ago, early in
the century. Then . . . it was written by somebody using
a pseudonym—a short one—foreign-sounding . . . a
man's but the writer was a woman. Then . . . the word
Sir began to emerge from the submerged title; the sense
of getting warmer was so strong I went to Keller's
Reader's Digest of Books and found in no time that it
was *The History of Sir Richard Calmady* by Lucas Malet,
the daughter of Charles Kingsley, Mrs. Harrison. The
whole jerky process went so rapidly that the book was
recovered in less than eight minutes.

The moral is clear: *Don't rely on your memory but use
written or printed sources.* Half the secret of good thinking
is the intelligent use of sources.

Luckily for you, the use of source materials is easier today
than ever before. In the last fifty years there has been a sort
of revolution; it is a thousand times easier for you today to
use source materials than it was for Aristotle, Bacon, Descartes, Newton, Goethe or any other great thinker of the past.

This sounds exaggerated but it is true. Up to some fifty
years ago, bibliography—the hunting of sources—was something every thinker had to do for himself. If he was lucky,
he found what he needed; if not, he missed it. Gregor Mendel's
experiments in heredity were published in 1866; in 1900
they had to be rediscovered by Correns, de Vries and
Tschermak-Seysenegg.

Today such a thing couldn't happen. Every branch of
science is covered bibliographically, and every scientist automatically follows the bibliography of his field. And this is
not all. You, the layman, can now prepare your thoughts
exactly like a scientist. The results of scientific thinking are
regularly transmitted to you. Scientists rarely bother to tell
laymen about their findings; but scores of popularizers now
study scientific bibliographies and pass on to the layman
everything he ought to know.

There's no excuse any more for by-passing published information; the sum of the world's recorded knowledge is as
near as the nearest library. If you can't get to a library, you
can write or phone; if the material you want isn't there, you
can get it through interlibrary loan.

Of course, reading books, magazines, and newspapers is
only half the job. The other half is using all this material in
place of that wretched memory of yours. This means note-taking and filing. How you do it is up to you; pick your own

system. But note-taking and filing there has to be; practically all the world's ideas have come out of notes and files.

The book you are reading now came out of a file drawer with thirty-five folders—one for each chapter. Something like this file drawer is behind almost every book in existence—including even humor books. (The late Will Cuppy amassed and filed hundreds of three-by-five index cards before writing each of his charming essays on topics like the minnow or the dodo.)

But don't get the impression that the first stage of thinking is always a solitary game of shuffling index cards. There's a more sociable way of drawing on other people's thoughts: the discussion method.

Discussion method, of course, is only a fancy name for conversation. To shape your thoughts, exchange ideas with others. Have a group of people sit around and talk, and you'll find that together they'll have more ideas than each of them separately. This is a clear case of the whole being more than its parts. Conversation is the greatest idea generator known to man.

It is impossible to overrate the idea-producing power of conversation. Some of the best education is "Mark Hopkins on one end of the log and James Garfield on the other"; some of the shrewdest business deals are those arranged over the luncheon table; some of the greatest scientific discoveries have come out of informal chats at annual meetings.

Are there any rules for idea-producing conversation? Well, a few are obvious: keep the talk on the subject; let everyone contribute something; take notes of what has been said. A few are not so obvious: don't forget to sum up once in a while; don't be afraid of pauses. The most important rule of all is this: when you're not talking, listen. Don't sit there, unhearing, rehearsing what you're going to say next.

How many people should there be in the group? The minimum, of course, is two; but what is the maximum? There is no answer, except that everyone should have a chance to say something. Put a dozen people in a room, and you'll find that four or five hardly open their mouths.

What's the best composition of the group? Again, there's no answer. But try to get as many viewpoints as possible. Get the young and the old together, executives and wage earners, farmers and professors, men and women.

Now suppose you have done your library work, assembled your notes, talked with others. Are you through with the preparation stage? Not quite. There are a few more things you can do to help your ideas to the surface.

First, remember the twenty questions technique. Practically, this means: Use a check list. Just a few days ago I made out my income tax return. When I went over the check list of deductions, I came upon *Thefts and Losses* and remembered that last summer my camera had been stolen. Result: About $12 saved. See?

Don't stick to a set list of classifications, though. Add new ones. Shuffle your index cards around; redistribute the material in your folders. If you find a promising new category, add it to the list; it'll come in handy some time. Once, *The New Yorker* ran an item of "Incidental Intelligence": An executive, going through his secretary's files after hours, found in the H drawer a fat folder marked HAPPEN, POSSIBLY SOMETHING WILL. That secretary wasn't as dumb as you may think.

Next, "turn the problem around." Often a problem can be solved by looking at it upside down. A mathematician, Karl Jacobi, said that this is *the* basic formula for mathematical discoveries. I am not sure that's true; but it's certainly a technique worth trying. Are you dealing with a general rule, a proverbial truth, a basic principle? Remember what George Santayana said: "Almost every wise saying has an opposite one, no less wise, to balance it." Here's a pet example of mine. You know the saying, "Never strike a child in anger"? Well, Bernard Shaw once wrote this: "If you strike a child, take care that you strike it in anger. . . . A blow in cold blood neither can nor should be forgiven."

Third, don't be afraid of the ridiculous. Alfred North Whitehead wrote: "Almost all really new ideas have a certain aspect of foolishness when they are first produced." There's a good reason for that. As you have seen, problems are often solved by looking at things in a seemingly unsuitable pattern. There's something funny about such a sudden shift of focus; in fact, surprise twists are the basic element of humor. It's downright ridiculous to compare a loan to Britain to lending a neighbor a garden hose; but that ridiculous idea solved the problem.

End of preparation stage. What follows next? Dr. Hutchinson said it best: Frustration. Remember that. When you are through with the preparation stage and frustration sets in, don't worry: it's natural. Relax and give your unconscious a chance.

To put your unconscious to work, the first rule is to give it time. As long as you're working frantically to find the solution, your unconscious doesn't have a chance. Relax; do something else; go to the movies; get some sleep.

If you have to solve a problem, turn away from it for a time and attend to some other routine matter. Above all, be sure you have time to think. Don't clutter your day with a lot of details. Spend some time by yourself—and I mean by yourself: don't be a slave to the telephone.

And don't think that problems are solved between nine and five only. The unconscious picks its own times and places. Some time ago a group of research chemists were asked when and how they got their scientific ideas. Here are some of their answers:

"While dodging automobiles across Park Row and Broadway, New York."

"Sunday in church as the preacher was announcing the text."

"At three o'clock in the morning."

"In the evening when alone in the study room."

"In the morning when shaving."

"In the early morning while in bed."

"Just before and just after an attack of gout."

"Late at night after working intensively for some hours."

"Invariably at night after retiring for sleep."

"In the plant one Sunday morning about 9 A.M. when no one was around."

"While riding in a very early train to another city."

"While resting and loafing on the beach."

"While sitting at my desk doing nothing, and thinking about other matters."

"After a month's vacation, as I was dressing after a bath in the sea."

The classic statement on the matter was made in 1891 by the German physicist Helmholtz at a banquet on his seventieth birthday:

> After investigating a problem in all directions, happy ideas come unexpectedly, without effort, like an inspiration. So far as I am concerned, they have never come to me when my mind was fatigued, or when I was at my working table. . . . They came particularly readily during the slow ascent of wooded hills on a sunny day.

A charming picture—but wooded hills on sunny days are hard to come by in modern life. Sleep at night, on the other hand, is available to us all. And there we run into a question. Some of those chemists got their ideas in the evening, some others in the morning. Which is the better time for producing ideas?

A surprising answer to this question comes from Dr. Nathaniel Kleitman of the University of Chicago. Dr. Kleitman found that everybody runs through a daily cycle of rising and falling temperature; the mind is creative when our temperature curve is up and sluggish when it is down. People, Dr. Kleitman says, fall in three groups: the morning types who hit their mental stride in the morning, the evening types who are at their best late in the afternoon, and the lucky morning-and-evening types, who have a level high temperature "plateau" from morning till evening. If you hate to get up in the morning, chances are your mind will sparkle in the evening; if you are a washout at a late bridge game, you may be a champion problem-solver at 6 A.M.

Even if you know what type you are, you can't always arrange your life and work accordingly. But you can do certain things. If you are a morning type, don't spend the first half of your day with dull routine and try to be creative in the afternoon; if you are an evening type, defer productive work till the end of the day.

Professional writers often furnish good examples of thinker's schedules. Here are a few:

Ernest Hemingway: "The earliest part of the morning is the best for me. I wake always at first light and get up and start working."

John O'Hara: "My working time is late at night. Evenings I'd go and sit around drinking coffee and talking to people until about midnight, then go back to my room and write. . . . Usually I kept going until about seven o'clock."

Helen MacInnes: "After dark I start some music I like, sit on the living room couch with a pad and pencil and write a chapter."

Katharine Brush: "I start at eight each morning and work through lunch until two-thirty or so. Then I knock off for the afternoon and often work again in the evening. If I'm not going to work in the evening, I keep at it longer in the afternoon."

Arnold Toynbee, the British historian: "I write every morning, whether I am in the mood or not. I sit down to write straightaway after breakfast, before dealing with my correspondence or any other business, and I do this writing at home. Then I go for lunch to the Royal Institute of International Affairs, and, in my office there, from after lunch till 6:45, dictate my letters, see people, do my work in editing the Institute's political history of the war, and do my writing for this history as well. In fact, I give half my day to one job and half to another, and find refreshment in switching my mind to and fro in this way."

Claude G. Bowers, the biographer-diplomat: "I prefer the smallest room I can find for my work and artificial light, finding this shuts out the present and makes for concentration. . . . *Jefferson and Hamilton, The Tragic Era,* and the Beveridge were written at night while writing editorials for *The Evening World* by day. Dinner at 5:30 and from 6 to 11 I shut myself in my cubbyhole. . . . During seventeen years as Ambassador in Spain and Chile I have found time to write by avoiding bridge and golf."

With these writers, we have passed through the preparation, frustration, and relaxation stages, and have arrived at the stage of creation. Once the idea is born, tips are unnecessary—except one: *write it down.* The best idea is useless if it is lost and forgotten. Catch your ideas alive. Keep a notebook handy; if you don't have a notebook, find a pad; if you can't find a pad, use an old envelope. But don't let the idea get away. It may never come back.

I started this chapter with a list of reminders. I'll end it with a list of tips:

1. Write the problem down.

2. Translate the problem into plain English.

3. If possible, translate the problem into figures, mathematical symbols, or graphs.

4. Don't rely on your memory but use written or printed sources.

5. Know how to use a library.

6. Take notes and keep files.

7. Discuss the problem with others.

8. Use a check list of categories, adding new ones from time to time.

9. Try turning the problem upside down.

10. Don't be afraid of the ridiculous.

11. If you feel frustrated, don't worry. Relax; turn to other work; rest; sleep.

12. Take time to be by yourself. Free yourself of trivial work. Shut out interruptions.

13. Know the time of day when your mind works best and arrange your schedule accordingly.

14. When you get an idea, write it down.

Chapter Thirty

FREEDOM FROM ERROR?

There are few things in the word that are as popular as error.

Some errors have been corrected and exposed for centuries but are as popular as ever; some others fly in the face of everyday experience but are widely believed in as gospel.

Popular errors have been listed and classified in many books; the New York Public Library has over twenty-five of them. The oldest is Sir Thomas Browne's *Vulgar Errors,* published in 1646; one of the latest was *The Natural History of Nonsense* by Bergen Evans, published in 1946. Quite a few of the errors dealt with by Sir Thomas Browne were still popular when Mr. Evans wrote his book three hundred years later. For example, both books discuss the misconception "that man's heart is to the left."

I have no ambition to add to the shelf of popular-error books, but you may be interested in a brief list of misconceptions I ran across myself. I'll set them down here in the time-honored style:

1. That Galileo climbed the Tower of Pisa and dropped two cannon balls of different weight to disprove Aristotle's theory that heavier bodies fall faster. (He didn't.)

2. That Voltaire said: "I don't agree with what you say, but I will defend to the death your right to say it." (He never said so. The quotation comes from a book *about* Voltaire, written in 1907.)

3. That, in our legal system, the defendant is presumed to be innocent until he is proved guilty, while on the European continent he is presumed to be guilty until he is proved innocent. (Wrong. European law has the presumption of innocence too; in fact, it's in the French Constitution but not in ours.)

4. That Abraham Lincoln jotted down the Gettysburg

Address on the back of an old envelope while he was going to Gettysburg on the train. (On the contrary: he worked on it for weeks and made corrections in it even *after* it had been delivered.)

5. That in a game of heads or tails, the chances of the next toss depend on the previous ones. (No. The odds are always fifty-fifty; "a coin has no memory.")

6. That Mark Twain said: "Everybody talks about the weather, but nobody does anything about it." (He didn't; supposedly Charles Dudley Warner wrote it in an editorial for the Hartford *Courant* about 1890.)

7. That in World War II the Army Air Force used color-blind men because they could detect camouflage better than others. (Untrue; in fact, experiments showed that men with normal vision did better.)

8. That Adolf Hitler's real name was Schicklgruber. (It wasn't. Schicklgruber was the maiden name of his grandmother; his father was born out of wedlock, but legitimized as Hitler.)

I rather expect most or all of these popular errors to be part of your mental equipment; it would be surprising if they weren't. Practically everybody believes these things. More than that: people take special pride in their misinformation. *Life* magazine once ran a little test entitled "Are You Educated?" and included familiarity with that old story about Galileo as part of the test. A New York newspaper used that pseudo-Voltaire quotation as the motto on its editorial page. A book on law for laymen solemnly expounded that myth about "our" presumption of innocence. The book *Mark Twain at Your Fingertips* listed the remark about the weather as a genuine saying by Mark Twain.

Why is error so popular? Even my brief list shows clearly some of the reasons.

In the first place, error is often more attractive than truth. Real life is apt to be a drab, humdrum, unglamorous business; but things-that-aren't-so are usually spectacularly exciting and fill us with a tingling sense of wonder and awe. Galileo disproving Aristotle on the Tower of Pisa—Lincoln writing his speech on the train to Gettysburg: Why, can these things have actually happened? we ask—and then believe them even more strongly just *because* they seem unbelievable. Not so long ago, Mr. Immanuel Velikovsky wrote a book in which he "proved scientifically" that the sun stood still at Jericho and that scores of other Biblical miracles actually happened.

Scientists enjoyed a hearty laugh, but the general public made the book a leading best-seller of 1950.

Another thing that makes error popular is that we like life to be nice and simple. Of course, life isn't like that; it's complex, irregular, hard to understand, and generally a messy thing to deal with. But error has a wonderful neatness. The laws of probability are hard to grasp, but anybody can understand that the chances of tails coming up next are better when heads have come up ten times. This is utterly wrong, to be sure; but isn't it wonderful how it simplifies things?

A third reason for our wrong beliefs goes deeper. We believe what is *comfortable* to believe. If problems are troublesome, there *must* be an easy solution; if we are worried, there *must* be something that will make us feel good. This, I think, is at the bottom of the last two on my little list of errors. To be color-blind makes you feel inferior; so there *must* be some situation where it turns out to be a good thing after all. Adolf Hitler was painful to live with on the same planet; so people derived whatever comfort there was from pinning on him the ridiculous label Schicklgruber.

The search for comfort in our worries and troubles produced the second great best-seller of 1950: *Dianetics* by L. Ron Hubbard. Like *Worlds in Collision* by Velikovsky, *Dianetics* was denounced by all scientists. But since it promised an easy cure for all our mental ills, thousands and thousands of people ate it up.

Dianetics, in fact, was only one in a long line of "comfort" books—the literature on how to relax and not to worry about anything. These books are commonly classified as nonfiction books, but that doesn't mean they are factual. People read them regardless of whether they contain information or misinformation, or how much of either; they take them as sedatives.

Some years ago, Miss Lee R. Steiner wrote a disturbing book about all this, called *Where Do People Take Their Troubles?* It presented a fantastic gallery of phony advisers people go to. Rather than think through their own problems, millions of Americans consult astrologers, graphologists, advice-to-the-lovelorn columnists, spiritualists, radio counselors, numerologists, palmists, New Thought practitioners, and yoga teachers.

In other words, error is popular because people are afraid to grow up. Clear thinking means facing the fact that life is full of difficult problems, that we cannot escape from pain, discomfort and uncertainty, that we cannot attain happiness by turning away from reality. As Sigmund Freud said, we need "education to reality." Once we have had it, we "will be in the same position as the child who has left the home where he was so warm and comfortable. But, after all, is it not the destiny of childishness to be overcome? Man cannot remain a child forever; he must venture at last into the hostile world."

Even if we are willing to face reality and tackle our problems by thinking, we're up against the plain fact that thinking is hard. Sydney Smith said: "I never could find any man who could think for two minutes together." And Sir Joshua Reynolds wrote: "There is no expedient to which a man will not resort to avoid the real labor of thinking." Thomas A. Edison was so fond of this last quotation that he put up signs with it all over his plant.

Yes, thinking is hard work, and that's why the greatest enemy of thinking is sheer inertia. Some time ago, I ran across a story in the *New York Times* that dealt with a UN report on economic help to Bolivia.

> The reasons for the lack of economic progress [the *Times* reported] lie mainly not in the lack of knowledge of what is needed, or even technical know-how in a restricted sense, but in the unwillingness or inability of governments to do what is needed. . . . The U.N. mission found that studies and recommendations on Bolivia's needs, going back forty years, were piled high in government archives. All studies recommended more or less the same thing, and little or nothing had ever been done about any of them. Knowledge of what to do was obviously not the problem.

In a sense, we are all in the same situation as the government of Bolivia. We know what to do about most of our problems, but we don't use that knowledge. We could improve our personal finances by budgeting, but we don't budget; we could improve our health by dieting, but we don't diet; we could improve our careers by studying, but we don't study. Information is piled high in our lives' archives, but we don't use it. Thinking is too hard.

Of course, we don't like to put it so bluntly. Instead, we rationalize. Thinking isn't too hard, we say, but it's impractical, unrealistic, long-hair stuff, it won't work. The practical thing is to go ahead without thinking, leaving things the way they have always been, doing what everybody else has always done. Never mind the rational approach; the irrational way is familiar and so much nicer and easier.

Whenever scientists come up with new rational solutions to seemingly irrational problems, our first reaction is to resist their ideas. Our second reaction is to get rid of them as something thought up by cranks. We don't want anyone to encroach upon the province of the irrational; we like to have a large slice of life where we don't have to do any thinking. Nature, art, life and death, chance—let's simply accept them; the human mind shouldn't meddle with these things.

Meanwhile, in spite of all this hostility, scientists persist in the analytical and mathematical study of the irrational. We may shrug it off, but there is dynamic symmetry (the mathematical analysis of art design from the Parthenon to Le Corbusier's houses), there is the Schillinger system of musical composition on a mathematical basis, and there are statistical studies of patterns in people's conversations, of cycles in our emotional ups and downs, of the law that governs the degree of repetition in the programs of the Boston Symphony Orchestra, and of the relationship between the number of marriages and the number of city blocks between boys and girls in Philadelphia. There is the mathematical approach to the strategy of bluffing in poker, the study of mathematical biophysics, the factor analysis of human abilities and temperament, and Professor D'Arcy Thompson's classic book *On Growth and Form,* which deals with the mathematics of such things as splashes and bubbles, bee's cells, the shapes of eggs, blood corpuscles, chromosomes, falling drops, spirals, streamlines, corals, snow crystals, elephants' teeth, and the horns of sheep and goats.

This is the sort of thing that makes us feel uneasy; although it's all fascinating, we'd much rather the mathematicians would leave these matters alone. When it comes to practical applications, we're apt to be stubborn and resentful. It is this distrust of the rational approach that accounts, in part, for our sales resistance to all forms of insurance and for our general resistance to such things as health insurance, business cycle theory, city planning, and proportional representation.

Of course, we all pride ourselves on having an open mind. But what do we mean by that? More often than not, an open mind means that we stick to our opinions and let other people have theirs. This fills us with a pleasant sense of tolerance and lack of bias—*but it isn't good enough.* What we need is not so much an open mind—readiness to accept new ideas—but an attitude of distrust toward *our own* ideas. This, as I said before, is the scientific habit of thought: as soon as you have an idea, try to disprove it. "To have doubted one's own first principles," Justice Oliver Wendell Holmes once wrote, "is the mark of a civilized man."

To do that is the hardest thing of all. Our first principles, our basic ideas, are those most intimately tied up with our personality, with the emotional make-up we have inherited or acquired. Detached, impersonal thinking is almost impossible; it hardly ever actually happens. In 1940 a team of social scientists studied the thinking of voters in Sandusky, Ohio, to find out why they voted the way they did. The scientists found that people voted according to their income, religion, age, occupation, and so on, following the pattern of their relatives, neighbors, and friends. They did *not* vote on the basis of a detached, impartial weighing of the issues. "Dispassionate, rational voters," the survey concluded, "exist mainly in textbooks on civics, in the movies, and in the minds of some political idealists. In real life, they are few."

Yes, clear thinking is rare. To approach it, we need above all that indispensable quality of the scientific spirit—humility. Like good scientists, we must be ready to sacrifice some of our personality and habits of thought as we face each new problem. For life's problems are always new, and defy all ready-made solutions.

That's what makes life so interesting.

PART 2

Hints and Devices

Chapter Thirty-One

HOW TO WRITE FOR BUSY READERS

Until some fifty years ago, nobody doubted that practical writing must be brief. To be sure, old-style business English sounds horrible by present standards ("Yrs. of the 20th inst. rec'd and contents noted"), but at least our grandfathers knew the virtue of brevity. Today's executive wouldn't feel right if he put a simple thought in only eight words. Before he knows it, he has dictated thirty-two: "Your letter of May 20, 1960, addressed to the Executive Director of this organization, has been referred to me for reply. I greatly appreciate having the information contained in the above communication." Maybe that's better public relations or human relations or what not, but it does waste an awful lot of the reader's time.

Can the trend be reversed? I think it can. All that's necessary is to apply newspaper and news-magazine techniques to letters and reports. American journalism has learned how to write for busy readers; let's copy the formula for government and industry.

How do journalists save their readers time? In two ways: *first*, they make it easy to skip; *second*, they make it easy to read fast.

It's simple to show readers what to read and what to skip. Newspapers do it by starting most stories with summary leads, by putting summary headlines on top of those leads and by using the front page as a quick summary of the paper itself. The reader gets the gist of each story and of the day's news at a glance; if he needs just the bare information, he can skip the rest. Nobody would buy a paper if he had to read it all through to find out what's going on.

The same can be done with letters, memos, and reports. They should start with summary lead sentences and paragraphs; they should have headlines and sub-headlines; if they're long, their leads, heads and subheads should be summarized on the front page. Leads should give readers the main point and nothing *but* the main point; heads and subheads should summarize the leads. They should not be titles—like *Sales Department*—but real headlines—like *Sales Up 64% Last Week*. (Here's a tip: Reading experts say headlines shouldn't be all caps, but caps and lower case. Don't use the shift lock but the underliner on the 6 key.)

To learn how to save words and letters, let's look at *Time* and other news magazines. They've developed a sort of formula: I'll summarize it for you in ten points.

1. *Use few articles, prepositions, and conjunctions.* Research shows that twenty-five little words account for *one-third* of all English writing: *the, and, a, too, of, I, in, was, that, it, he, you, for, had, is, with, she, has, on, at, have, but, me, my, not.* The alone accounts for 5 per cent; *and* for 3 per cent. Cutting all unnecessary *the's, and's, that's, of's,* etc. will save enormous amounts of time and paper. As to *the,* "evidence we have" is just as good English as "the evidence we have"; the plural "consumers" says the same as "the consumer." *And* can often be replaced by a comma or semicolon. *That* can be left out half the time: "he said he agreed" is better than "he said that he agreed." *Of* can be saved by using adjective nouns like "the policy anniversary date" instead of "the anniversary date of the policy."

2. *Use pronouns rather than repeating nouns.* Once a business or government writer has written "The Inter-Allied Doodle Manufacturing Company, Inc.," he'll happily repeat "The Inter-Allied Doodle Manufacturing Company, Inc." dozens of times. "It" will do just as well. Or, better still and more informal, "they."

3. *Learn to "factor" expressions.* "Factoring," in mathematics, means writing $a (b + c)$ instead of $ab + ac$. Use the same principle in writing. Instead of "operating revenue and operating costs" write "operating revenue and costs."

4. *Use the active rather than the passive voice.* This is old, old advice. But the typical business letter still has "Your assistance is needed" instead of "Please help us." A model letter in a recent textbook begins: "There is being forwarded to your office under separate cover a full report . . ." Why

not "I am sending you . . ."? What's wrong with the first-person pronoun?

5. *Use verbs rather than nouns.* More old advice, badly needed. In most business writing, "we know" becomes "we have information" and "they do" appears as "they carry on activities."

6. *Use contractions.* English permits you to contract *do not* to *don't* and make one word out of two. Why not do it in writing? What's so dignified about memos and reports? You *speak* contractions, don't you? There's no law that says you can't write them.

7. *Use short names.* Once is enough for mentioning full long names. After you've written "American Society for Scientific Methods of Squaring the Circle" or "President Adolphus U. K. Popwhiffle," relax and call them the Circle Squarers and Popwhiffle.

8. *Use figures, symbols, abbreviations.* As long as your reader understands, use the shortest possible symbol. In '60, most people over 16 have the I.Q. to tell a memo from a phone call or the NAM from the FTC.

9. *Use punctuation to save words.* Commas, colons, parentheses are often more expressive than words. The colon, for instance, seems to be the favorite space-saving device of *Time* magazine. As they would say, *"Time's* favorite: the colon."

10. *Cut all needless words.* My last rule is a catch-all reminder that every single word eats paper and reading time. If you've written "prior to," replace it by "before"; if you've written "factual information," strike it out and say "facts." My pet example is this bit from a business English textbook: "The informal report is usually short in length." Maybe—but this sort of writing is just *too long in length*.

These ten rules have nothing to do with good English, "correct" grammar, or even easy readability. If you follow them, you may come up with deathless prose or jerky, ungrammatical nonsense. But you *will* save your reader time— as I said, up to 50 per cent. Figure reading time at about 200 words a minute for an average executive or professional salary, and you'll be amazed at the amount in dollars and cents my ten little rules add up to.

It all sounds very simple and easy. And yet it isn't. Somehow it seems hard to break away from this sort of thing: "According to our agreement your company is to furnish services periodically on alternate days of the week in amounts to be specified at irregular intervals. Due to circumstances beyond our control, we herewith ask you to interrupt your services for one period only, effective Monday, May 30, 1960. Please note that services are to be resumed as of Wednesday, June 1, 1960, in the same amount and manner as heretofore."

Which is typical 1960 business English applied to a note to the milkman. The original reads: "Please skip Monday."

Chapter Thirty-Two

HOW TO SAY IT WITH STATISTICS

Sooner or later everyone who writes about facts has to write about statistics, too. But how do you present statistics to the average reader—the man or woman who can't add a row of figures and hates the mere thought of long division?

Dozens of books deal with the preparation of tables and graphs, but I haven't found a single one on the useful art of making statistics painless. I don't say this short chapter will fill the gap. But I think my twelve points may help you.

Naturally, I'll have to use a set of statistical data for an example. Here's a neat one from a recent survey of *Time* readers. They were asked, "How much cash do you carry?" They answered like this:

Men Repliers		*Women Repliers*	
	% of men		% of women
Less than $5	9.9	Less than $5	14.6
$ 5 to $12	31.0	$ 5 to $ 7	26.4
$ 13 to $24	21.4	$ 8 to $12	25.7
$ 25 to $49	19.8	$13 to $24	18.0
$ 50 to $99	10.2	$25 to $49	9.6
$100 and over	5.2	$50 and over	2.9
Not stated	2.5	Not stated	2.8
Average	*$30.70*	*Average*	*$14.37*

Now here are my twelve points on how to make statistics readable:

1. *Help your reader spot trends*. Experiments have shown that most people are poor trend-spotters. Don't expect tables or graphs to tell the story by themselves: they won't. It's you who'll have to point out the thing that jumps to the eye—that is, that jumps to *your* eye but not his or hers.

In my example, you'd have to say in so many words: Among *Time* readers, men carry about twice as much cash as women.

2. *Pick the right average.* There are three statistical averages: the mean (the sum total divided by the number of cases); the median (the mid-point between the upper and the lower half); and the mode (the case that is most common).

Most writers pick the mean as *the* average. *Time* magazine did in my little example. But the mean isn't always the best average to use. Quite often the median or the mode will give the reader a clearer picture. Why? Because the three averages refer to three different ideas.

The mean is the *socialistic* average. It shows what things would be like if everybody got an equal share. Reality isn't like that, and so the mean usually gives a distorted picture. In my example, the mean is $30.70 for men and $14.37 for women. That's an accurate figure, but it isn't realistic. If you think that the mean is a good average to use, I'd like to point out that you, as an average American, have four defective teeth and $3 worth of gold in your mouth and consume each year 100 bottles of soft drinks, 16 lollipops and two ounces of snuff.

The median is the *middle-of-the-road* average. It shows the case that's smack in the middle between the extremes. Usually that gives a better picture to the reader than the mean. In my example, the median is $13—$24 for men and $8—$12 for women. As you see, it tells a different story than the mean. If your data don't show the median, work it out yourself. It's usually worth it.

The mode is the *fashionable* average—the pattern that is followed most often, the case you're most likely to come across. For data like "How much cash do people carry?" it's the most revealing of all the averages. If you met *Time* readers in the street, how much money would they be apt to have on them? Answer: he, $5—$12; she, $5—$7.

3. *Point out the range.* Averages tell only half the story; the other half is the range or spread. Statisticians use standard deviations and such to describe the spread; unfortunately, these measures don't mean a thing to the ordinary reader. So the best you can do is to give a rough idea of the range. Say something like "Women readers of *Time* carry between $1 and $50 in their purses." As a rule, don't talk about the average without giving the range too.

4. *Point out the exceptions.* Statisticians have little interest in the exceptions and fringe cases; readers love them. Never

waste the opportunity of throwing in a sentence like this: "Among men who read *Time*, quite a few have more than $100 in their wallet.".

5. *Don't bury figures in text.* Readers like figures least when they are sprinkled all over a paragraph. Spare them this sort of thing:

"Among women repliers, 14.6% carried less than $5; 26.4% carried $5—$7; 25.7%, $8—$12; 18.0%, $13—$24; 9.6%, $25—$49; and 2.9%, $50 and over."

6. *Beware of tables.* Spare your reader tables if you can. Tables are often needed for reference, of course; but you can't expect people to read them. So, if possible, cut your tables to a minimum.

But then, you'll ask, what can you do with your figures aside from putting them in your text or in tables? Answer:

7. *Use spot tables.* There doesn't seem to be a word for the thing I'm talking about, so I had to coin one. A *spot table* highlights a few significant figures by centering them on the page. It has two or three columns of two to four items and usually no heading.

For example, here is a spot table about what money *Time* readers (female) carry in their purses:

84.7%	Up to $25
12.5%	Over $25
2.8%	Don't say

8. *Make your figures round.* Long figures are hard to read; long figures with decimals are *very* hard to read. So use round figures. Round them to the nearest whole number, or ten or hundred or thousand or million or billion—whichever is the unit that tells your story best. If you're writing about money in people's pockets don't say $30.70; say $31. If you're writing about the federal budget, don't say $3,070,549,637.81; say $3 billion.

Besides, more often than not a long trail of digits isn't accurate to begin with.

9. *Make your figures small.* Short, round figures are good; small figures are even better. And I mean small: say, the figures under 13 that are usually spelled out by the printers. Try it with percentage figures: Instead of 84.7%, say "five out of six." Instead of 12.5%, say "one in eight."

My last three points deal with graphic presentation. To begin with, most readers are just as poor at chart-and-graph reading as they are at table-reading and trend-spotting. So, if you want to help them visually, stay off charts and graphs. Use pictorial statistics; that's what they were invented for. But if you do, keep these three points in mind:

10. *Keep pictorial statistics simple.* The little symbolic pictures are devices to convey ideas. If you fancy them up, you'll defeat your purpose. If you want a symbol of a male *Time* reader, simply show a man who reads *Time*. Don't picture a man who reads *Time*, sitting on his front porch, smoking his pipe, surrounded by his wife and children. It isn't fair to the *Time* reader who is a bachelor, lives in a city apartment and doesn't smoke.

11. *Explain your symbols.* No symbol or picture explains itself. A man who reads *Time* is clear enough as the symbol of a male *Time* reader, but it cannot tell exactly what is meant. Does the symbol stand for a subscriber? Or does it take in newsstand buyers? And what about the fellow who borrows a copy from a friend or reads one in a library?

So don't rely on your symbols to tell all. Use them, but use words too to explain what the symbols mean.

12. *Don't try to use pictorial statistics for two things at once.* Even with little pictures, there's a limit to what readers can take. To understand a relationship by matching shorter and longer rows of little men is one thing; to trace complex ratios by shuttling back and forth between uneven arrays of various symbols is another. My *Time* example would tempt a pictorial statistician to show rows of little men at right and rows of folding money at left. Most readers will skip such a table. People don't like to interrupt their reading for complicated parlor games.

And that ends my twelve points. I hope you'll find them helpful.

Chapter Thirty-Three

HOW TO TEST READABILITY

Readable, according to most dictionaries, means "easy or interesting to read." So the readability test in this book has two parts. One part gives you a score of "reading ease"—an estimate of the ease with which a reader is going to read and understand what you have written. The other part of the test gives you a score of "human interest"—an estimate of the human interest that your presentation (rather than your subject) will have for the reader. Together, the two scores give you an estimate of both aspects of readability.

Full test or sampling?

If your piece of writing is reasonably short, or if you want to be as exact as possible in your readability estimate, apply the readability test to all the material. Otherwise it is more practical to take samples.

How to pick samples

If you take samples, be sure to take enough for a fair test. Ordinarily, three to five samples of an article and twenty-five to thirty of a book will do.

Don't try to pick "good" or "typical" samples; take them at random. It is best to go by a strictly numerical scheme. For instance, take every third paragraph of a short article or every other page of a longer piece. But don't use the introductory paragraphs of your piece as samples; usually they are not typical of the style of the whole piece. If you want to test the readability of the introduction, test it separately.

Take samples of 100 words each. Start each sample at the beginning of a paragraph.

How to count words

Count each word in your piece of writing. If you are using samples, take each sample and count each word in it up to 100. After the 100th word, put a pencil mark. (In the examples in this book, 100 words are marked by $_{100}$.)

Count as a word all letters, numbers, or symbols, or groups of letters, numbers, or symbols, that are surrounded by white space. Count contractions and hyphenated words as one word. For example, count each of the following as one word: *1948, $19,892, e.g., C.O.D., wouldn't, week-end.*

How to figure the average sentence length

As your next step, figure the average number of words in your sentences. If you test a whole piece of writing, this means that you count all the sentences and then divide the number of words by the number of sentences, rounding off the result. For example, if you have 183 words and 9 sentences, the average sentence length is 20.

If you are using samples, count the number of sentences in each sample; then add the number of sentences in all samples and divide the number of words in all samples by the total number of sentences.

In a 100-word sample, the 100-word mark will usually fall in the middle of a sentence. Count such a sentence as one of those in your sample, if the 100-word mark falls after more than half of the words in it; otherwise disregard it. For example, the sentence *"This was not the case"* should be counted in if the 100-word mark falls after the word *not,* but disregarded if the 100-word mark falls before it.

If you had three 100-word samples, containing 3, 9, and 7 sentences, your average sentence length would be 300 divided by 19, or 16 words.

In counting sentences, count as a sentence each unit of thought that is grammatically independent of another sentence or clause, if its end is marked by a period, question mark, exclamation point, semicolon, or colon. Incomplete sentences or sentence fragments are also to be counted as sentences. For example, count as two sentences: *What did the minister talk about? Sin.* Count as two sentences: *The Lord is my shepherd; I shall not want.* Count as three sentences: *There are two arguments against this plan: 1. It is too expensive. 2. It is impractical.* Count as two sentences: *Result: Nobody came.* But count as one sentence only: *He registered, but he did not vote.* (Two independent clauses, combined into a compound sentence with only a comma.) Count as one sentence: *There were three people present: Mary, Robert, and John.* (The words after the colon are not a separate unit of thought.) Count as one sentence: *This project is supposed to: (a) provide training; (b) stimulate suggestions.* (No part of this is an independent clause. Count such material as one sentence even if it is paragraphed.)

In dialogue, count the words *he said* or other speech tags as part of the quoted sentence to which they are attached. For example, count as one sentence: *He said: "I have to go."* Count also as one sentence: *"That's all very well," he replied, showing clearly that he didn't believe a word of what we said.*

For more examples of how to count sentences, study the separation of sentences shown in the Examples. They are marked in this book by /.

How to figure the average word length

As your next step, figure the average word length in syllables. To do that, count all syllables and divide the total number of syllables by the number of words. In the formula, this measure is expressed as the number of syllables per hundred words; therefore, multiply your result by 100.

If you use 100-word samples, count the total number of syllables in all your samples and divide by the number of samples.

Both ways you will get the number of syllables per hundred words.

Count syllables the way you pronounce the word; e.g., *asked* has one syllable, *George's* two, *determined* three, and *pronunciation* five. Count the number of syllables in symbols and figures according to the way they are normally read aloud, e.g., two for *$* ("dollars"), three for *R.F.D.* ("are-eff-dee"), and four for *1916* ("nineteen sixteen"). However, if a passage contains lengthy figures or more than a few, your estimate will be more accurate if you leave these figures out of your syllable count; in a 100-word sample, be sure to add instead a corresponding number of words after the 100-word mark.

How Easy?

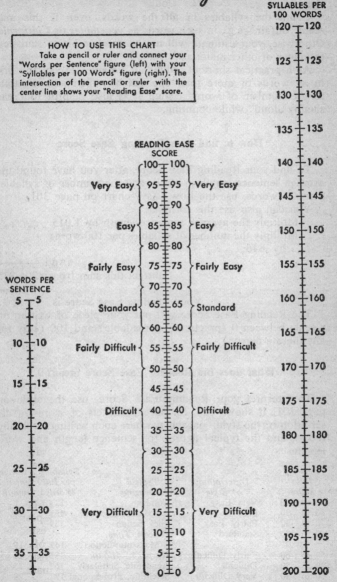

SYLLABLES PER
100 WORDS

120 — 120
125 — 125
130 — 130
135 — 135
140 — 140
145 — 145
150 — 150
155 — 155
160 — 160
165 — 165
170 — 170
175 — 175
180 — 180
185 — 185
190 — 190
195 — 195
200 — 200

HOW TO USE THIS CHART
Take a pencil or ruler and connect your
"Words per Sentence" figure (left) with your
"Syllables per 100 Words" figure (right). The
intersection of the pencil or ruler with the
center line shows your "Reading Ease" score.

READING EASE
SCORE

100 — 100
Very Easy { 95 — 95 } Very Easy
90 — 90
Easy { 85 — 85 } Easy
80 — 80
Fairly Easy { 75 — 75 } Fairly Easy
70 — 70
Standard { 65 — 65 } Standard
60 — 60
Fairly Difficult { 55 — 55 } Fairly Difficult
50 — 50
45 — 45
Difficult { 40 — 40 } Difficult
35 — 35
30 — 30
25 — 25
20 — 20
Very Difficult { 15 — 15 } Very Difficult
10 — 10
5 — 5
0 — 0

WORDS PER
SENTENCE

5 — 5
10 — 10
15 — 15
20 — 20
25 — 25
30 — 30
35 — 35

If in doubt about syllabication rules, use any good dictionary.

Count the syllables in all the words, even if this may seem "unfair," e.g., in such words as *vegetables* or *California*. Otherwise, your estimate will not be comparable to statistical estimates of other materials.

As a practical shortcut, count all syllables except the first in all words of more than one syllable; then add the total to the number of words tested. It is also helpful to "read silently aloud" while counting.

How to find your Reading Ease Score

To find your Reading Ease Score, after you have found the average sentence length in words and the number of syllables per 100 words, use the HOW EASY? chart on page 301.

You can also use this formula:

Multiply the average sentence length by 1.015 . . . . . .
Multiply the number of syllables per 100 words
  by .846   . . . . . .
                                              Add ———
                      Subtract this sum from 206.835
                                              ———

                      Your Reading Ease Score is . . . . . .

The Reading Ease Score will put your piece of writing on a scale between 0 (practically unreadable) and 100 (easy for any literate person).

What does the Reading Ease Score mean?

To interpret your Reading Ease Score, use the table on page 301. It shows you, for seven brackets of scores, a description of the style, magazines where such writing is usually found, and the typical figures for sentence length and word length.

Reading Ease Score	Description of Style	Typical Magazine	Syllables per 100 Words	Average Sentence Length
90 to 100	Very Easy	Comics	123	8
80 to 90	Easy	Pulp fiction	131	11
70 to 80	Fairly Easy	Slick fiction	139	14
60 to 70	Standard	Digests, *Time*, Mass non-fiction	147	17
50 to 60	Fairly Difficult	*Harper's, Atlantic*	155	21
30 to 50	Difficult	Academic, Scholarly	167	25
0 to 30	Very Difficult	Scientific, Professional	192	29

How to count "personal words"

To find your Human Interest Score, first count the number of "personal words" per 100 words. If you are testing a whole piece of writing, divide the total number of "personal words" by the total number of words and multiply by 100. If you use 100-word samples, count the "personal words" in each sample and divide the total number of "personal words" in all samples by the number of samples.

"Personal words" are:

(1) All first-, second-, and third-person pronouns except the neuter pronouns *it, its, itself,* and the pronouns *they, them, their, theirs, themselves* if referring to things rather than people. For example, count the word *them* in the sentence *When I saw her parents, I hardly recognized them,* but not in the sentence *I looked for the books but couldn't find them.*

However, count *he, him, his* and *she, her, hers* always, even where these words refer to animals or inanimate objects.

(2) All words that have masculine or feminine natural gender, e.g., *John Jones, Mary, father, sister, iceman, actress.* Do not count common-gender words like *teacher, doctor, employee, assistant, spouse,* even though the gender may be clear from the context. Count singular and plural forms.

Count a phrase like *President Harry S. Truman* as one "personal word" only. (Only the word *Harry* has natural masculine gender.) *Mr. Smith* contains one "personal word" with natural gender, namely *Mr.; Miss Mary B. Jones* contains two, namely *Miss* and *Mary.*

(3) The group words *people* (with the plural verb) and *folks.*

In the examples at the end of the chapter, "personal words" are printed in bold-face type.

How to count "personal sentences"

As your next step, count the number of "personal sentences" per 100 sentences.

If you are testing a whole piece of writing, divide the total number of "personal sentences" by the total number of sentences and multiply by 100. If you use samples, divide the number of "personal sentences" in all your samples by the number of sentences in all your samples and multiply by 100.

"Personal sentences" are:

(1) Spoken sentences, marked by quotation marks or otherwise, often including speech tags like "he said," set off by colons or commas. For example: *"I doubt it." We told him, "You can take it or leave it." "Don't you realize the implications?" he asked, in spite of the fact that he obviously didn't himself.*

But don't count as "personal sentences" those that include quoted phrases, like *The Senator accused the Administration of doing an "about face."* Don't count indirect quotations, like *The name was misspelled, he explained.*

Count all the sentences included in long quotations, as in Example 2.

(2) Questions, commands, requests, and other sentences directly addressed to the reader. For example: *Does this sound impossible? Imagine what this means. Do this three times. You shouldn't overrate these results. This is a point you must remember. It means a lot to people like you and me.* But don't count sentences that are only indirectly or vaguely addressed to the reader, like *This is typical of our national character* or *You never can tell.*

(3) Exclamations. For example: *It's unbelievable!*

(4) Grammatically incomplete sentences, or sentence fragments, whose full meaning has to be inferred from the context. Examples: *Doesn't know a word of English. Handsome, though. Well, he wasn't. The minute you walked out. No. Not so. No doubt about that. I was going to.*

If a sentence fits two or more of these definitions, count it only once.

In the examples, "personal sentences" are italicized.

How to find your Human Interest Score

To find your Human Interest Score, after you have counted "personal words" and "personal sentences," use the HOW INTERESTING? chart on page 306.

You can also use this formula:

Multiply the number of "personal words" per 100 words by 3.635 . . . . . .

Multiply the number of "personal sentences" per 100 sentences by .314 . . . . . .

The total is your Human Interest Score . . . . . .

The Human Interest Score will put your piece of writing on a scale between 0 (no human interest) and 100 (full of human interest).

What does the Human Interest Score mean?

To interpret your Human Interest Score, use this table. It shows you, for five brackets of scores, a description of the style, magazines where such writing is usually found, and the typical figures for "personal" words and sentences.

Human Interest Score	Description of Style	Typical Magazine	Per Cent "Personal Words"	Per Cent "Personal Sentences"
60 to 100	Dramatic	Fiction	17	58
40 to 60	Highly Interesting	New Yorker	10	43
20 to 40	Interesting	Digests, Time	7	15
10 to 20	Mildly Interesting	Trade	4	5
0 to 10	Dull	Scientific, Professional	2	0

This may help you

In applying the twin formulas, remember that the Reading Ease formula measures *length* (the longer the words and sentences, the harder to read) and the Human Interest formula measures *percentages* (the more "personal" words and sentences, the more human interest).

If you do much testing, you may find it practical to mark every ten words with little penciled numbers, 1, 2, 3, etc. Or you may find it worthwhile to use a mechanical counter.

After you've had a little practice, it shouldn't take you more than 2½ minutes to test one sample—that is, count 100 words and find both the Reading Ease and Human Interest scores.

How Interesting?

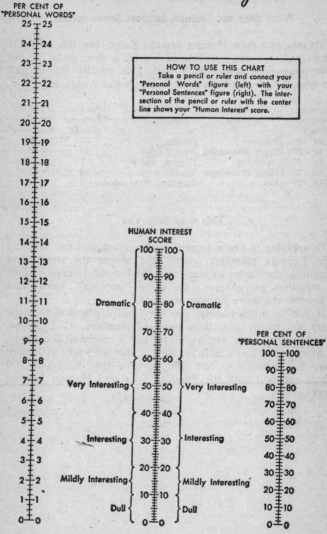

PER CENT OF "PERSONAL WORDS"

25 — 25
24 — 24
23 — 23
22 — 22
21 — 21
20 — 20
19 — 19
18 — 18
17 — 17
16 — 16
15 — 15
14 — 14
13 — 13
12 — 12
11 — 11
10 — 10
9 — 9
8 — 8
7 — 7
6 — 6
5 — 5
4 — 4
3 — 3
2 — 2
1 — 1
0 — 0

HOW TO USE THIS CHART
Take a pencil or ruler and connect your "Personal Words" figure (left) with your "Personal Sentences" figure (right). The intersection of the pencil or ruler with the center line shows your "Human Interest" score.

HUMAN INTEREST SCORE

100 — 100
90 — 90
Dramatic   80 — 80   Dramatic
70 — 70
60 — 60
Very Interesting   50 — 50   Very Interesting
40 — 40
Interesting   30 — 30   Interesting
20 — 20
Mildly Interesting   10 — 10   Mildly Interesting
Dull   0 — 0   Dull

PER CENT OF "PERSONAL SENTENCES"

100 — 100
90 — 90
80 — 80
70 — 70
60 — 60
50 — 50
40 — 40
30 — 30
20 — 20
10 — 10
0 — 0

EXAMPLE 1

From the Bible (Matthew 6:25-29):

"Therefore I say unto you, Take no thought for your life, what ye shall eat, or what ye shall drink; nor yet for your body, what ye shall put on. / Is not the life more than meat, and the body than raiment? /

"Behold the fowls of the air: / for they sow not, neither do they reap, nor gather into barns; / yet your heavenly Father feedeth them. / Are ye not much better than they? /

"Which of you by taking thought can add one cubit unto his stature?/

"And why take ye thought for raiment? / Consider the lilies of the field, how$_{100}$ they grow; / they toil not, neither do they spin. /

"And yet I say unto you, that even Solomon in all his glory was not arrayed like one of these." /

129 words	12 words per sentence	13% "personal" words
11 sentences	122 syllables per 100 words	100% "personal" sentences
17 "personal" words		
11 "personal" sentences	Reading Ease Score: 91	Human Interest Score: 79

NOTE: Many parts of the Bible have extremely high Reading Ease Scores. Since this selection is part of the Sermon on the Mount, all sentences were considered quoted, "personal" sentences. The words *they* and *them* were not considered "personal," where they referred to birds and lilies rather than people. The independent clauses beginning with *for* and *yet* were counted as separate sentences.

EXAMPLE 2

From *The Life of Johnson* by James Boswell (July 21, 1763):

Sir, I love the acquaintance of young people; because, in the first place, I don't think myself growing old. / In the next place, young acquaintances must last longest, if they do last; / and then, Sir, young men have more virtue than old men; / they have more generous sentiment in every respect. / I love the young dogs of this age: / they have more wit and humour and knowledge of life than we had; / but then the dogs are not so good scholars. / Sir, in my early years I read very hard. / It is a sad reflection, but a true$_{100}$ one, that I knew almost as much at eighteen as I do now. / My judgment, to be sure, was not so good; / but I had all the facts. / I remember very well, when I was at Oxford, an old gentleman said to me, 'Young man, ply your book diligently now, and acquire a stock of knowledge; / for when years come upon you, you will find that poring upon books will be but an irksome task.' " /

---

175 words	13 words per sentence	16% "personal" words
13 sentences	124 syllables per 100 words	100% "personal" sentences
28 "personal" words		
13 "personal" sentences	Reading Ease Score: 89	Human Interest Score: 89

NOTE: Again, an example of 100% direct quotation. Note the variety of punctuation between the independent sentences. Note also that in the first sentence the dependent clause beginning with the subordinating conjunction *because* was not counted as a separate sentence in spite of the semicolon.

EXAMPLE 3

From *The Adventures of Huckleberry Finn* by Mark Twain:

If Emmeline Grangerford could make poetry like that before she was fourteen, there ain't no telling what she could 'a' done by and by. / Buck said she could rattle off poetry like nothing. / She didn't ever have to stop to think. / He said she would slap down a line, and if she couldn't find anything to rhyme with it would just scratch it out and slap down another one, and go ahead. / She wasn't particular; / she could write about anything you choose to give her to write about just so it was sadful. / Every time a man died, or a$_{100}$ woman died, or a child died, she would be on hand with her "tribute" before he was cold. / She called them tributes. / The neighbors said it was the doctor first, then Emmeline, then the undertaker— / the undertaker never got in ahead of Emmeline but once, and then she hung fire on a rhyme for the dead person's name, which was Whistler. / She warn't ever the same after that; / she never complained, but she kinder pined away and did not live long. /

---

181 words	15 words per sentence	14% "personal" words
12 sentences	131 syllables per 100 words	0% "personal" sentences
25 "personal" words		
0 "personal" sentences	Reading Ease Score: 81	
		Human Interest Score: 51

NOTE: *Huckleberry Finn* is written as if the story were told by Huck to the reader. This quality escapes the formula; the percentage of "personal" sentences is 0. Therefore the Human Interest Score is comparatively low. The dialect words are counted just as if they were standard English, e.g., *ain't* is counted as a one-syllable word. The word *Whistler* is not counted as a "personal" word since it refers here to the name itself rather than the person.

EXAMPLE 4

From *Gulliver's Travels* by Jonathan Swift:

I had three hundred cooks to dress my victuals, in little convenient huts built about my house, where they and their families lived, and prepared me two dishes apiece. / I took up twenty waiters in my hand, and placed them on the table: / an hundred more attended below on the ground, some with dishes of meat, and some with barrels of wine, and other liquors, slung on their shoulders; / all which the waiters above drew up as I wanted, in a very ingenious manner, by certain cords, as we draw the bucket up a well in Europe. / A dish of$_{100}$ their meat was a good mouthful, and a barrel of their liquor a reasonable draught. / Their mutton yields to ours but their beef is excellent. / I have had a sirloin so large, that I have been forced to make three bits of it; / but this is rare. / My servants were astonished to see me eat bones and all, as in our country we do the leg of a lark. / Their geese and turkeys I usually eat at a mouthful, and I must confess they far exceed ours. / Of their smaller fowl I could take up twenty or thirty at the$_{200}$ end of my knife. /

---

204 words	19 words per sentence	15% "personal" words
11 sentences	127 syllables per 100 words	0% "personal" sentences
30 "personal" words		
0 "personal" sentences	Reading Ease Score: 80	Human Interest Score: 55

NOTE: This is a fairly typical example of old English prose. The sentences are longer than they would be in corresponding modern writing, and since most of them are compound rather than complex, the Reading Ease Score underrates the actual readability of such material. On the other hand, the words are considerably shorter than those in current writing. Note, by the way, that the words *convenient* and *ingenious* are both counted as three-syllable words, following the syllabication given in the *American College Dictionary* and *Webster's*.

EXAMPLE 5

From *Bleak House* by Charles Dickens:

I took care that the necessary preparations were made for Mr. Boythorn's reception, and we looked forward to his arrival with some curiosity. / The afternoon wore away, however, and he did not appear. / The dinner-hour arrived, and still he did not appear. / The dinner was put back an hour, and we were sitting round the fire with no light but the blaze, when the hall-door suddenly burst open, and the hall resounded with these words, uttered with the greatest vehemence and in a stentorian tone: /

"We have been misdirected, Jarndyce, by a most abandoned ruffian, who told us to take$_{100}$ the turning to the right instead of to the left. / He is the most intolerable scoundrel on the face of the earth. / His father must have been a most consummate villain, ever to have such a son. / I would have had that fellow shot without the least remorse!" /

"Did he do it on purpose?" Mr. Jarndyce inquired. /

"I have not the slightest doubt that the scoundrel has passed his whole existence in misdirecting travellers!" returned the other. / *"By my soul, I thought him the worst-looking dog I had ever beheld, when he was telling me to take the turning to$_{200}$ the right. / And yet I stood before that fellow face to face, and didn't knock his brains out!"* /

---

218 words	18 words per sentence	13% "personal" words
12 sentences	141 syllables per 100 words	67% "personal" sentences
29 "personal" words		
8 "personal" sentences	Reading Ease Score: 69	Human Interest Score: 68

NOTE: In counting the words here, the rules were followed strictly, in spite of the fact that today such expressions as *dinner-hour* and *hall-door* are usually printed without hyphens.

EXAMPLE 6

From *Man Stands Alone* by Julian S. Huxley:

Psychologically, one of the most interesting things about bird courtship is the frequency with which in display the birds will carry in their beaks a piece of the material of which their nest is built. / This holds good even for the Adelie penguins, charmingly described by Dr. Levick. / Here the nest is nothing but a rim of stones round a depression; / and accordingly the male presents stones to his mate as part of his courtship. / Interestingly enough, this action sometimes becomes diverted to serve other instincts and emotions, such as wonder— / the birds will present stones to dogs and to$_{100}$ men / *and Dr. Levick confesses to having felt quite embarrassed the first time he was the recipient!* / Still another tale hangs by these stones. / The sitting birds are all the time stealing stones from each other's nests. / Levick painted a number of stones different colours, and placed them at one margin of the nesting area. / After this he could mark the rate of their progress (all by theft!) across the colony; and found that the red stones travelled much quicker than the rest. / This is of great theoretical interest, for red is a colour which is to all intents and$_{200}$ purposes absent in the penguin's environment— / and yet they prefer it above all others. / If a male penguin could grow a red patch he would probably be very quick to gain a mate. /

---

233 words	17 words per sentence	4% "personal" words
14 sentences	144 syllables per 100 words	7% "personal" sentences
10 "personal" words		
1 "personal" sentence	Reading Ease Score: 68	Human Interest Score: 16

note: This is a good example of popularized scientific writing. It is addressed to the general reader and the Reading Ease Score of 68 puts it in the "standard" bracket. Note that the abbreviation *Dr.* is counted as a two-syllable word since it is pronounced "doctor." The word *male* is counted as a "personal" word where it is used as a noun with masculine gender; it is not counted where it is used as an adjective. The independent clause following the dash after the word *wonder* and the clause following the dash after the word *environment* are both counted as separate sentences since they are separate units of thought. The sentence ending with an exclamation point is considered a "personal" sentence because it is an exclamation. The other exclamation point (inside a sentence) is disregarded.

EXAMPLE 7

From *The American Scholar* by Ralph Waldo Emerson:

If it were only for a vocabulary, the scholar would be covetous of action. / Life is our dictionary. / Years are well spent in country labors; in town; in the insight into trades and manufactures; in frank intercourse with many men and women; in science; in art; to the one end of mastering in all their facts a language by which to illustrate and embody our perceptions. / I learn immediately from any speaker how much he has already lived, through the poverty or the splendor of his speech. / Life lies behind us as the quarry from whence we get titles and$_{100}$ copestones for the masonry of today. / This is the way to learn grammar. / Colleges and books only copy the language which the field and work-yard made. /

---

127 words	18 words per sentence	7% "personal" words
7 sentences	145 syllables per 100 words	0% "personal" sentences
9 "personal" words		
0 "personal" sentences	Reading Ease Score: 66	Human Interest Score: 26

NOTE: Emerson's style with its epigrammatic sentences and abundance of metaphors is probably more difficult to read than a Reading Ease Score of 66 would show. Note that the words from *Years* to *perceptions* are all counted as one sentence and one thought unit in spite of the six semicolons.

EXAMPLE 8

From *Psychology* by William James:

There is an everlasting struggle in every mind between the tendency to keep unchanged, and the tendency to renovate, its ideas. / Our education is a ceaseless compromise between the conservative and the progressive factors. / Every new experience must be disposed of under *some* old head. / The great point is to find the head which has to be least altered to take it in. / Certain Polynesian natives, seeing horses for the first time, called them pigs, that being the nearest head. / My child of two played for a week with the first orange that was given him, calling it a "ball."$_{100}$ / He called the first whole eggs he saw "potatoes," having been accustomed to see his "eggs" broken into a glass, and his potatoes without the skin. / A folding pocket-corkscrew he unhesitantly called "bad-scissors." / Hardly any one of us can make new heads easily when fresh experiences come. / Most of us grow more and more enslaved to the stock conceptions with which we have once become familiar, and less and less capable of assimilating impressions in any but the old ways. / Old-fogyism, in short, is the inevitable terminus to which life sweeps us on. /

---

193 words	18 words per sentence	6% "personal" words
11 sentences	152 syllables per 100 words	0% "personal" sentences
12 "personal" words		
0 "personal" sentences	Reading Ease Score: 60	Human Interest Score: 22

NOTE: William James was famous for his interesting and easy style. This passage, according to the scoring, is "standard" and "interesting"—a rare exception among textbooks. Notice the technique of easy explanation: The abstract theme of the passage is expressed in the first four sentences. Then follow four sentences giving several concrete examples of two kinds. The abstract generalization is then repeated and summarized in two more sentences. Finally, it is rephrased and pointed up with a colloquial touch as "old-fogyism."

EXAMPLE 9

From *The Theory of the Leisure Class* by Thorstein Veblen: *

The case of the fast horse is much like that of the dog. / He is on the whole expensive, or wasteful and useless—for the industrial purpose. / What productive use he may possess, in the way of enhancing the well-being of the community or making the way of life easier for men, takes the form of exhibitions of force and facility of motion that gratify the popular aesthetic sense. / This is of course a substantial serviceability. / The horse is not endowed with the spiritual aptitude for servile dependence in the same measure as the dog; / but he ministers effectually to$_{100}$ his master's impulse to convert the "animate" forces of the environment to his own uses and discretion and so express his own dominating individuality through them. / The fast horse is at least potentially a racehorse, of high or low degree; / and it is as such that he is peculiarly serviceable to his owner. / The utility of the fast horse lies largely in his efficiency as a means of emulation; / it gratifies the owner's sense of aggression and dominance to have his own horse outstrip his neighbour's. / This use being not lucrative, but on the whole pretty consistently wasteful, and quite$_{200}$ conspicuously so, it is honorific, and therefore gives the fast horse a strong presumptive position of reputability. / Beyond this, the race horse proper has also a similarly non-industrial but honorific use as a gambling instrument. /

---

235 words	20 words per sentence	6% "personal" words
12 sentences	164 syllables per 100 words	0% "personal" sentences
13 "personal" words		
0 "personal" sentences	Reading Ease Score: 48	Human Interest Score: 22

NOTE: Veblen was notorious for his cumbersome style. This passage was chosen for its high human interest; however, Veblen's use of words like *substantial serviceability* and *presumptive position of reputability* drags down the Reading Ease Score.

EXAMPLE 10

From *The Ambassadors* by Henry James:

This assault of images became for a moment, in the address of the distinguished sculptor, almost formidable: / Gloriani showed him in such perfect confidence, on Chad's introduction of him, a fine, worn handsome face, a face that was like an open letter in a foreign tongue. / With his genius in his eyes, his manners on his lips, his long career behind him and his honors and rewards all round, the great artist, in the course of a single sustained look and a few words of delight at receiving him, affected our friend as a dazzling prodigy of type. / Strether had$_{100}$ seen in museums—in the Luxembourg as well as, more reverently, in other days, in the New York of the billionaires—the work of his hand; knowing too that, after an earlier time in his native Rome, he had migrated, in mid-career, to Paris, where, with a personal lustre almost violent, he shone in a constellation: / all of which was more than enough to crown him, for his guest, with the light, with the romance, of glory. / Strether, in contact with that element as he had never yet so intimately been, had the consciousness of opening to it, for the$_{200}$ happy instant, all the windows of his mind, of letting this rather gray interior drink in, for once, the sun of a clime not marked in his old geography. /

---

229 words	38 words per sentence	10% "personal" words
6 sentences	143 syllables per 100 words	0% "personal" sentences
24 "personal" words		
0 "personal" sentences	Reading Ease Score: 47	Human Interest Score: 36

NOTE: Henry James' style is extreme in the complexity of its long sentences. The Reading Ease Score of 47 probably underrates the actual difficulty of this passage for a modern reader; however, the high human interest may carry him through. Note that the clause after the colon, beginning with the words *all of which,* was considered an independent clause and counted as a separate sentence, but the participial phrase beginning with the words *knowing too that* was not.

EXAMPLE 11

From *Reconstruction in Philosophy* by John Dewey: *

The increasing acknowledgment that goods exist and endure only through being communicated and that association is the means of conjoint sharing lies back of the modern sense of humanity and democracy. / It is the saving salt in altruism and philanthropy, which without this factor degenerate into moral condescension and moral interference, taking the form of trying to regulate the affairs of others under the guise of doing them good or of conferring upon them some right as if it were a gift of charity. / It follows that organization is never an end in itself. / It is a means of promoting *association,* of multiplying effective points of contact between persons, directing their intercourse into the modes of greatest fruitfulness.

---

118 words	30 words per sentence	3% "personal" words
4 sentences	175 syllables per	0% "personal"
	100 words	sentences
3 "personal" words		
0 "personal" sentences	Reading Ease Score: 29	Human Interest
		Score: 11

NOTE: An example of highly abstract, very difficult writing. The importance of the idea expressed here is almost wholly obscured by the style.

Chapter Thirty-Four

HOW TO RAISE READABILITY

Testing readability is not an end in itself. Often you will want to go on from there; if your score turns out to be too low, you'll want to know how to raise it. This section shows briefly how to do that.

Focus on your reader

There's no point in controlling readability if you don't know who you are writing for. Find out as much as you can about your readers' education, reading habits, age, sex, occupational background, and so on. Even a clear conception of the characteristics of "the general reader" is better than writing in a vacuum.

Focus on your purpose

What are you writing for? What do you expect your readers to do? Read your piece casually? Study it? Use it for reference? Read it for entertainment during leisure hours? Be sure of what you are trying to do and write accordingly.

Design your writing functionally

Once you know your audience and your purpose, you can design your piece of writing to fit. Ordinarily this means that you start raising your readability score by raising the count of "personal words." For easy and interesting reading, a story design is usually best—either sustained narrative or anecdotes, illustrative examples, and practical applications, sandwiched between straight exposition. For instructions, the best design is the direct "you" approach, or cookbook style. (See Example 14b.)

In other words, you can raise the "personal words" count by using the first and second persons for yourself and your reader, and by explaining your ideas through the experiences of people. (See Examples 6, 8, 13, and 15.) Use actual people if you can; if you use fictitious characters, be sure the reader knows they are fictitious.

After the "personal words" count, raise the count of "personal sentences." In today's professional writing the proportion of dialogue to narrative is rising steadily. To make narrative fully readable, direct quotations at key points are essential. (See Example 15.)

Even without quoted dialogue the conversational approach to the reader will increase readability. (See Example 3.)

Break up sentences and paragraphs

Next, shorten the length of the average sentence. To do this, look for the joints in complex sentences and change dependent clauses to independent clauses. (See Example 12.)

There is a natural relation between the length of sentences and the length of paragraphs. After you have shortened your sentences, break up your paragraphs to fit the changed rhythm.

Find simpler words

Finally, shorten the average length of your words. Some of the long, complex words may be technical terms that shouldn't be changed. As for the rest, remember that complexity rather than length makes for reading difficulty. Many complex words are abstract nouns. Change these nouns into verbs, particularly simple verbs with adverbs. For example, instead of *condescension* use *look down on*. It is usually better to recast sentences than simply replace one word by another.

Help your reader read

You will raise your readability scores indirectly if you try to help your reader in the job of reading. Point out to him what is specially significant, tell him to remember what he should remember, prepare him for what he is going to read, and summarize for him what he has read.

Learn to cut

The most common fault of writing is wordiness; the most important editorial job is cutting. Cutting unessentials will make essentials stand out better and save the reader time.

If your piece of writing is too long, some readers may skip it altogether. Often you have to design a piece of writing to attract readers by sheer brevity.

Rearrange for emphasis

Readers remember best what they read last. Rearrange your writing with that in mind. Do this with words, sentences, and larger units. Prepare your reader's mind for your ideas, and then build them up for greatest impact.

Punctuate for readability

Current punctuation practice gives you much leeway. Use punctuation to speed up reading and to clarify the meaning of words and sentences. If you use short sentences, use semicolons and colons to show their connection. Underlining (italics) and parentheses will help convey conversational emphasis or casualness.

As a rule, design your writing for being read aloud.

Don't write down to your reader

While you are working on words, sentences, paragraphs, and punctuation, don't lose sight of the first and most important point: remember your readers. Don't overrate their reading habits and skills, but don't underrate them as human beings. Otherwise you'll defeat your purpose.

EXAMPLE 12a

From The Constitution of the United States (Article I, Section 10):

No State shall enter into any treaty, alliance, or confederation, grant letters of marque and reprisal, coin money, emit bills of credit, make any thing but gold or silver coin a tender in payment of debts, pass any bill of attainder, ex post facto law, or law impairing the obligation of contracts, or grant any title of nobility. /

No State shall, without the consent of the Congress, lay any imposts or duties on imports or exports, except what may be absolutely necessary for executing its inspection laws, and the net produce of all duties and imposts, laid by any State$_{100}$ on imports or exports, shall be for the use of the Treasury of the United States; / and all such laws shall be subject to the revision and control of the Congress. /

No State shall, without the consent of the Congress, lay any duty of tonnage, keep troops or ships of war in time of peace, enter into any agreement or compact with another State, or with a foreign power, or engage in war, unless actually invaded, or in such imminent danger as will not admit of delay. /

---

187 words	47 words per sentence	0% "personal" words
4 sentences	152 syllables per 100 words	0% "personal" sentences
0 "personal" words		
0 "personal" sentences	Reading Ease Score: 31	Human Interest Score: 0

NOTE: The Constitution is, of course, written in eighteenth-century legal English. The words are shorter and simpler than those of today, but the sentences are far longer than those a modern reader is used to.

EXAMPLE 12b

From *Our Constitution and What It Means* by William Kottmeyer: *

Article I, Section 10
What the States May Not Do

No State shall make a treaty or tie itself up with another country. / No State may give people the right to fight or work against other countries. / No State may stamp its own coins or print its own money. /

No State may use anything but gold and silver for money. / No State may take away a man's property. / No State may punish a man for something not wrong when he did it. / No State may make a law to wipe out written agreements made in the right way. /

No State may give a man a noble title (prince, duke, etc.). / 100

Unless Congress agrees, no State may put taxes on goods coming in or going out of a State, except to keep its inspection laws working. / This tax money shall go to the National Government. / Congress may change any such State tax law. /

No State may tax ships. / No State may keep an army (except State militia). / No State may make agreements with another State or with a foreign country unless Congress agrees. / No State may go to war unless it is attacked and cannot delay fighting. /

---

186 words	12 words per sentence	4% "personal" words
15 sentences	133 syllables per 100 words	0% "personal" sentences
6 "personal" words		
0 "personal" sentences	Reading Ease Score: 82	Human Interest Score: 14

NOTE: Mr. Kottmeyer's book is an explanation of the Constitution in simple words for use in adult education classes. The simplification is carried out mainly by shortening the sentences from an average of 47 words to an average of 12.

EXAMPLE 13a

From *Better Life Insurance Letters* by Mildred F. Stone:*

We are in receipt of your letter requesting a change of beneficiary. / You failed to inform us as to the final payee in case the said beneficiary predeceased the insured. / Kindly advise and will contact the home office. /

---

38 words	13 words per sentence	11% "personal" words
3 sentences	158 syllables per	100% "personal"
4 "personal" words	100 words	sentences
3 "personal" sentences		

Reading Ease Score: 60   Human Interest
Score: 71

NOTE: Maybe an exaggerated example of the gruff, old-style business letter. Both readability scores seem to overrate the readability of this letter. The Reading Ease Score is comparatively high because of the short sentences, disregarding their abruptness. The Human Interest Score is relatively high because of the general personal approach in all letters.

* Copyright 1950 by National Underwriter Co., Cincinnati, Ohio. Used by permission.

EXAMPLE 13b

From *Better Life Insurance Letters* by Mildred F. Stone:*

Your change of beneficiary request will be sent to the Company promptly as soon as we can give them all necessary information. /

In case you should outlive Mrs. Evans, whom do you want to receive the life insurance money? / Probably you would want it then to go to your estate. / If so, please sign the enclosed form. / If you have other plans please write us in detail and we shall be glad to help you further. /

When you return this beneficiary change request send us your policy also so that we can mail them together to the Home Office. / The changed policy will be returned to you promptly. /

---

108 words	15 words per sentence	16% "personal" words
7 sentences	141 syllables per	100% "personal"
17 "personal" words	100 words	sentences

| | | |
| 7 "personal" sentences | Reading Ease Score: 72 | Human Interest Score: 89 |

NOTE: Miss Stone's rewrite aims at making the letter more pleasant and friendly rather than more readable. Nevertheless, both the Reading Ease Score and the Human Interest Score were raised considerably in the process. Note particularly how the impersonal word *beneficiary* was changed to *Mrs. Evans;* note also the colloquial usage of referring to the company as "them."

* Copyright 1950 by National Underwriter Co., Cincinnati, Ohio. Used by permission.

EXAMPLE 14a

From *Gobble-de-gook or Plain Talk?* (Air Matériel Command Manual No. 11-1, 1950):

(1) An employee who has a grievance or his representative will normally present the grievance, in the first instance, orally to the immediate supervisor. / The supervisor will consider it promptly and impartially, collecting the necessary facts and reaching a decision. / If the employee is not satisfied with the solution of the problem, he will be advised that he may discuss the problem with the next higher supervisor. /

(2) If the employee feels that an interview with the immediate supervisor would be unsatisfactory, he or his representative may, in the first instance, present his grievance to the next supervisor in line. / Where an$_{100}$ employee feels an interview with the second supervisor would likewise be unsatisfactory, he may seek counsel from the civilian personnel officer or his employee relations counselor, whose role will be to advise and aid him in facilitating the employee's approach to a supervisory level determined appropriate by the facts in the particular case. /

---

153 words	31 words per sentence	6% "personal" words
5 sentences	182 syllables per 100 words	0% "personal" sentences
9 "personal" words		
0 "personal" sentences	Reading Ease Score: 22	Human Interest Score: 22

NOTE: A fair example of the style used in most government documents. The sentences are long and complex, the words long and impersonal. Note the many common-gender nouns like *employee, representative,* or *supervisor.* Paragraph numbers were disregarded in counting words.

EXAMPLE 14b

From *Gobble-de-gook or Plain Talk?* (Air Matériel Command Manual No. 11-1, 1950):

Is something about your job bothering you? /
Here are the steps you can take to solve your problem. / *In most cases it will be solved at the first step.* / *If not, you have the right to keep going on up to the top.* / *You may present your own case or have someone do it for you.* /
Talk with your superior. / He has been told to give a prompt and fair answer to all problems. / Usually, a short friendly talk with him will fix things up. / *Be honest and sincere when you talk with him.* /
If you feel that your supervisor$_{100}$ will not handle your case fairly, you may go directly to his supervisor. / *Or, if you have gone to your supervisor and he didn't handle your problem to suit you, you may still go to his supervisor.* /
If you feel your case has not yet been, or will not be, handled fairly by either of them, go to your personnel technician. / *He can't give you a final answer, but he can tell you how to get it.* /

---

177 words
13 sentences
33 "personal" words
10 "personal" sentences

14 words per sentence
127 syllables per 100 words
Reading Ease Score: 85

19% "personal" words
77% "personal" sentences
Human Interest Score: 93

NOTE: This rewrite was done as a demonstration of the readability formula described in this book. The most important change is the use of the second person and the direct approach. Note the colloquial touches that make reading easier, such as contractions like *didn't* and *can't,* idioms like *fix things up,* and conversational emphases like "*his* supervisor."

EXAMPLE 15a

From "Ferrier Lecture. Some observations on the cerebral cortex of man," by Wilder Penfield (*Proceedings of the Royal Society,* B, v. 134, 1947, pp. 329-347):

This report is based largely on the accumulated experience of the neurosurgical operating room. / The cerebral cortex was stimulated in well over 300 operations under local anesthesia. / The purpose of these operations was usually to relieve symptomatic epilepsy by local excision of what may be called an epileptogenic focus in the grey matter of the brain. /

Success in long procedures like these depends on mutual understanding and trust between surgeon and patient. / During all operations included in this series, the result of each positive response to stimulation was marked by a numbered or lettered ticket laid on the cortex, and$_{100}$ the result was dictated through a microphone hanging over the operating table. / Photographs were taken of the operative field through a mirror above the operator's head by means of a camera placed outside a window in the wall of the operating room. / The positions of stimulation tickets were also drawn in on a standard brain chart which was sterilized so that the surgeon might make **his** own record in every case without break of aseptic technique. /

---

176 words	25 words per sentence	1% "personal" words
7 sentences	176 syllables per 100 words	0% "personal" sentences
1 "personal" word		
0 "personal" sentences	Reading Ease Score: 33	Human Interest Score: 3

NOTE: These are the two introductory paragraphs of a scientific paper that was used as a source for Mr. Silverman's article (see Example 15b). The style is typical of scientific writing; the technical terms used are, of course, easy for scientifically trained readers but difficult for laymen. Note the absence of "personal" words and the consistent use of the passive voice—both customary in scientific papers.

EXAMPLE 15b

From "Now They're Exploring the Brain" by Milton Silverman (*Saturday Evening Post,* October 8, 1949, pp. 26-27, 80, 83-86): *

The patient had been a wise, cheerful, fatherly clergyman. / When they brought him into the hospital, he was bewildered and a little frightened. / His left arm was paralyzed. /

"I guess I'm through," he told the intern on arrival. / "My arm went weak like this last night. / Yesterday I had three convulsive attacks, one after the other. / Each time there was a funny dream, and then I fainted." /

"Have you been having these attacks for very long?" /

The clergyman nodded. / *"For a good many months. / The first one came on a Sunday, just as I was preparing to give my sermon.*[100] / *There was a dream before that one too. / The dream almost always comes first." /*

When the doctors went over his record, one of them said, "The trouble isn't in his arm. / It must be in his brain, probably on the right side. / Those dreams at the beginning of his attacks point to the temporal lobe. / There is something wrong there— / maybe a tumor." /

They examined him and carried out tests and made X-ray photographs. / If a tumor was present, it didn't show itself. / They tried a brain-wave study, but this showed only some vague disturbance in the right side of*[200]* his brain. /

The doctors explained the situation to him and said, "We'd like to operate. / We want to go in and see what we can find." /

"All right," agreed the clergyman. / "I put myself in your hands. / Do the best you can. / I want to get better. / You see, my people need me." /

So they operated under local anesthesia and exposed the right side of his brain. / While he was completely conscious, able to move and talk and describe his sensations, they made a map of his brain surface. /

* Used by permission of Mr. Silverman and the *Saturday Evening Post.*

289 words	10 words per sentence	15% "personal" words
30 sentences	135 syllables per 100 words	70% "personal" sentences
43 "personal" words		
21 "personal" sentences	Reading Ease Score: 82	Human Interest Score: 76

NOTE: This is the lead (opening incident) in a *Saturday Evening Post* article dealing mainly with Dr. Penfield's work (see Example 15a.). It is typical of the popularization technique used in mass-circulation magazines. Exposition is shot through with appealing and interesting narrative and the narrative is heightened in many places by dramatization and dialogue. The case of the clergyman is mentioned briefly in the body of Dr. Penfield's paper; however, the quoted dialogue has apparently been reconstructed or invented by Mr. Silverman—a device widely used in popular magazine articles. Of course, the two examples are not strictly comparable in substance; but they do show clearly the tremendous difference in readability between a scientific paper for fellow scientists and a popular article for lay readers dealing with the same subject.

Chapter Thirty-Five

A QUICK SELF-TEST

The readability test shown in the last chapter was first published in 1949. It is now widely used by journalists, advertising copy writers, and other professional writers.

To give you a still simpler tool for everyday practical purposes, I have greatly changed and simplified that test, so that you can go through your writing just once, count certain items, and come out with a single score.

To test your writing—or any piece of written English, for that matter—start by counting the words. Or, if you want to make your job a little easier, count off exactly 100 words as a sample. Naturally, for a longer piece of writing, you'll want to take several samples. For instance, if you want to test an article of 3,000 words, you might take five 100-word samples, picked at random. (It's *not* a good idea to start with the opening paragraph, since that is usually not representative of the piece as a whole. The same applies to the ending.)

You'll run into a few questions as to what is a word. As a rule of thumb, count everything as a word that has white space on either side. Therefore, count the article "a" as a word, and the letter "a" in enumerations, and all numbers, abbreviations, etc. (Examples: "1958," "G.O.P.," "½," "Ph.D.," "e.g.") If an abbreviation point falls in the middle of a word, count it as one word, not two. Also count as one word contractions and hyphenated words, for instance, "don't," "I've," "half-baked," "pseudo-science."

All right. You have counted the words. (I suggest you put a pencil check mark after every ten words, so that you won't make any mistakes. Then put a bigger check mark after the hundredth word.) Now you are ready for the test count. Start again at the beginning and count one point for each of the following items:

1. Any word with a capital letter in it.

2. Any word that is underlined or italicized.

3. All numbers (unless spelled out).

4. All punctuation marks *except* commas, hyphens, and abbreviation points. (Periods, colons, semicolons, question marks, exclamation points, quotation marks, parentheses, brackets, apostrophes, etc.)

5. All other symbols, such as #, $, ¢, %, &.

6. One extra point each for the beginning and ending of a paragraph.

If you have taken a 100-word sample, the sum total of your points is your score. If you have taken several 100-word samples, add up the points in all the samples and divide by the number of samples. The result is your average score for the whole piece of writing tested. If you counted the points in a whole piece of writing, containing more or less than an even 100 words, divide the total number of points by the total number of words and multiply by 100 to get your score.

Your score is likely to be a number somewhere between 10 and 50. Here is what it means:

Up to 20	Formal
21 to 25	Informal
26 to 30	Fairly Popular
31 to 35	Popular
Over 35	Very Popular

I did again what I did sixteen years ago and checked the styles of various magazines. This is what I found:

Up to 20	*Columbia University Forum*
21 to 25	*Harper's, The New Yorker*
26 to 30	*Time, Reader's Digest*
31 to 35	*Saturday Evening Post*
Over 35	*Ellery Queen's Mystery Magazine*

The application for this for your own purposes is clear. In your everyday writing, you can't afford to stick to the formal, academic style of the *Columbia University Forum*, the *Yale Review*, and other learned journals and books. You must learn to break through to the informal style now used in all magazines and books addressed to the general public. Which means, in terms of this test, that you must learn how to score over 20.

To show you what can be done with a rather unpromising subject, I have selected an article from the *Saturday Evening*

Post, entitled "So You're All Tensed Up," by Harry J. Johnson, M.D., as told to Steve M. Spencer (March 15, 1958). I ran my test on a large number of samples from that article and found that the over-all score was 24. (The *Post* average score is much higher than that, due to the fiction pieces.)

The article, I think, is particularly instructive because it was the leading article in that issue of the *Post* and was written with the help of Mr. Spencer, who is one of the *Post's* senior editors. It's a typical example of professional nonfiction writing for a mass audience.

Here are the opening paragraphs:

> A cynical observer of the American business scene has remarked that there are only two kinds of executive, those who get ulcers and those who give ulcers to others. As a physician who each year interviews about 1,000 men, I cannot agree with such a sweeping indictment. Most executives, in my opinion, are pleasant fellows who work at a reasonable tempo, treat their associates with understanding and consideration, and enjoy fairly good health.
>
> But there are unquestionably enough of them in the cynic's two categories to generate plenty of problems in the world of interoffice memos and commuting brief-cases—problems coming under the general heading of tension.
>
> In a survey of tensions, just completed by the Life Extension Foundation . . .

Here is a typical passage from the middle of the article:

> Just how demanding, then, are the job requirements of the average American executive? More than half said they worked a nine-to-five day, although 40 per cent arrived at the office at eight and a third worked until six. A shade under three quarters of them spend less than five hours a week on homework, and 20 per cent spend five to ten hours. Four per cent work ten to fifteen hours at home, 1 per cent fifteen to twenty hours, and a very busy 1 per cent said they spend more than twenty hours a week on homework. Of those who did take work home, 22 per cent said they liked it, 57 per cent were resigned to it, and 21 per cent "loathed" it.
>
> "How does your wife feel about your business homework?" we then asked. Sixty-nine per cent said their

wives were "understanding," 19 per cent said they were "indifferent," and 12 per cent said they were "resentful."

The final paragraph reads:

> If you are tense, it is you yourself who can do the most to reduce that tension. Change your perspective. When molehills become mountains, ask yourself how important the irritating situation will be tomorrow. Build up your self-confidence and make the most of what you have. Don't fret about what you don't have. Be tolerant. When someone rubs you the wrong way, ask yourself what wrong he has really done you. What reason have you to criticize him? Isn't it usually jealousy? Finally, the old reliable admonition, be moderate. When you become impatient and impetuous, stop and think. Who loses most by the constant rushing and restlessness? Why, you do, of course. So calm down. Take a walk around the block.

Now let's analyze these sample passages a little. The over-all score of the article, as I said, was 24. How did Mr. Spencer do it? Let's look closely at what he did with the words and sentences and paragraphs to get Dr. Johnson's ideas and experiences across to the American public.

To begin with, let's compare the scores of the three samples. That of the opening paragraphs is 15, that of the passage from the middle is 24 (exactly representative of the article as a whole), and that of the ending, 29. Mr. Spencer started a little slowly and stiffly, then ran the course at a pretty even pace, and finished up in highly dramatic and effective style.

This too is rather typical. The beginning of a magazine piece—what the pros call the lead—is often considerably less informal than the rest of the piece, whereas the ending is usually an attempt to leave the reader with some prose fireworks. In this case, the lead was a brief, not too exciting anecdote, after which came a simple statement of what the article was: a report on a survey of tensions made by the Life Extension Foundation. The ending is also a classic specimen of the windup of such an article: a succinct summary of what the reader ought to do as a result of having read the piece.

Following the now accepted magazine procedure, the article is written in the "I" style "by Harry J. Johnson, M.D., as told to Steven M. Spencer." Also, as you will notice, the closing paragraph is addressed directly to "you," the reader of the article.

The specimen passage from the body of the article is a nice example of how to handle statistics. Note how expertly Mr. Spencer tells you about "more than half," "a shade under three quarters," and "a very busy 1 per cent." Note also that the 21 per cent who disliked homework are quoted as having used a much more colorful expression about it: they "loathed" it.

How did Mr. Spencer get all the capital letters into the article that brought the score up to 24? Let's see. First of all, there is the frequent appearance of the word "I," which was possible because Dr. Johnson was the official author of the article. Secondly, there is the liberal use of names and places. (At one point in the article, there is a reference to a company which had to remain anonymous. Mr. Spencer did better than that. He referred to it as "a company I shall call Ulcers, Inc." Neat, isn't it?) Thirdly, there are all the short sentences, particularly toward the end of the article. Each word beginning a sentence, of course, adds to the count of capital letters.

Mr. Spencer doesn't do too well on italicized words, but of course he gives us a lot of numbers, since he is dealing with a statistical subject. He is lavish with the next item that adds to the score—punctuation. There are plenty of periods (the sentences are quite short, on the average), plenty of semicolons and colons, and as many quotation marks as anyone can reasonably provide. Next, there are apostrophes. Mr. Spencer contracts most of the words that can be contracted as a matter of course: he writes "wouldn't," "he's," "he'd," "isn't," "I'll," "didn't," "aren't," "weren't," and "I've."

Finally, there are Mr. Spencer's paragraphs, which are admirably short. I counted the sentences and found that most of his paragraphs run to three or four sentences. Many have only two.

Now let's apply what we have learned from this example and set down some simple rules on how to get your score over 20. (This, of course, will be a brief summary of what you have read in Part 1 about informal language, the first-person-singular style, how to be exact, and how to use dialogue.)

1. Use the first person singular wherever possible.
2. Mention names, dates, and places. Specify. Illustrate. Cite cases. If you can't use actual names, give fictional ones, like "Ulcers, Inc."

3. Keep your sentences short, so that you'll have many opening words with capitals. If your average sentence has over 20 words, you'll have four periods and four first words beginning with a capital within each 100 words of your text. This isn't good enough; it's only 8 basic points for your score. If your average sentence runs to 16 words, you'll have 6 periods and 6 beginning capitals to start with—12 basic points. With that it ought to be easy to collect a few more to get over 20.

4. Emphasize words by underlining them. (They'll be italicized in print.) A single underlined word may raise the effectiveness of a letter enormously. The other day I worked on such a letter with a class of students. Everybody agreed that underlining a single word—*only*—made all the difference in the world. So, if you want to emphasize something, *underline it*.

5. Use numbers. Tell about how much, when, at what address. Tell the reader at what hour the event happened, even at what minute. (Remember *Dragnet?* "10:14 A.M. We went uptown.") Identify people by their age. Identify things by their price. Identify events by their date.

6. Use, as I said before, at least six periods within a hundred words. (Commas are on the decline. Use as few as possible. It will speed up reading.)

7. Use as many question marks as you can. This means, if you deal with a question, formulate it as a direct question with a question mark. (On the other hand, exclamation points are practically extinct today. Avoid them.)

8. Use parentheses freely to play things down. (See the parentheses I used in points 4, 5, 6, and 7.)

9. Contract all words that you would naturally contract in speaking. If you'd *say* "you'd," *write* "you'd."

10. Use as much dialogue as you can. Quote what people said, what they wrote, what they *would* say, even what they *might* say. "But how do you expect me to do this?" you'll say. Like this.

11. Keep your paragraphs short. Don't put more than two, three, four of your sixteen-word sentences into one paragraph.

12. Use other symbols, such as $ or &. In other words, use as much as possible all typewriter keys other than the letters —the digits, the punctuation marks, the shift key, the space bar, etc. Get variety on your page. Make it interesting *visually*.

And now, to show you two extremes of prose writing that I discovered with my test, I'll quote one example of prose that tests 95 and another that tests 12. They are worlds apart —in letter and in spirit.

First, here is a passage from *The Case of the Baited Hook* by Erle Stanley Gardner:

"When did you get here?"

"About half an hour ago."

"You didn't have any reason to think you'd find a body?"

"No."

"You've seen him before?"

"No."

"Talked with him over the telephone?"

"I called his office yesterday, yes."

"What time?"

"I don't know. I would say it was shortly before eleven o'clock."

"What did he say?"

"I had a tentative appointment with him," Mason said. "I wanted to cancel it, and make one at a later date."

"Have any argument?"

"Not exactly."

"What was your business with him?"

Mason smiled and shook his head.

"Come on," Sergeant Holcomb said. "Kick through. If we're going to solve a murder, we've got to have motives. If we knew something about that business you wanted to discuss with him, we might have a swell motive."

"And again," Mason said, "you might not."

Sergeant Holcomb clamped his lips shut. "Okay," he said.

This is the ultimate extreme—a score of 95, about four or five times as high as you would ordinarily get on bread-and-butter English prose. And yet, this doesn't sound in any way abnormal. It's simply a record of a rapid exchange that quite conceivably could have taken place. If it had been done with a tape recorder instead of by way of Erle Stanley Gardner's fertile imagination, it would probably not have looked very different on paper.

Now let's switch to John Dewey's passage with the low, low score of 12. It's from his book *Experience and Nature*.

Ghosts, centaurs, tribal gods, Helen of Troy and

Ophelia of Denmark are as much the meanings of events as are flesh and blood, horses, Florence Nightingale and Madame Curie. This statement does not mark a discovery; it enunciates a tautology. It seems questionable only when its significance is altered; when it is taken to denote that, because they are all meanings of events, they all are the same kind of meaning with respect to validity of reference. Because perception of a ghost does not signify a subtle, intangible form, filling space as it moves about, it does not follow that it may not signify some other existential happenings like disordered nerves, a religious animistic tradition; or, as in the play of Hamlet, that it may not signify an enhancement of the meaning of a moving state of affairs. The existential events that form a drama have their own characteristic meanings, which are not the less meanings of those events because their import is dramatic, not authentically cognitive. So when men gather in secret to plot a conspiracy, their plans are not the less meanings of certain events because they have not been already carried out; and they remain meanings of events even if the conspiracy comes to naught.

I must confess that I love this piece of prose. It's so beautifully meaningless—and ironically it deals, of all things, with meaning. What did John Dewey mean by "meaning" here? And just what is an "existential happening" in contrast to any other kind of happening? Ah, those "existential events whose import is authentically cognitive"! And the "statement that enunciates a tautology"! And "meaning with respect to validity of reference"!

No, I don't expect that you'll commit anything like this to paper. (If you *are* the kind of person who is likely to do that, I must tell you that you're a pretty hopeless case.) I simply put this quotation here as a warning example. My test formula will put your writing on a scale between Erle Stanley Gardner and John Dewey. It's up to you to use it as a frequent checkup and to find out whether you are improving (in the direction of Erle Stanley Gardner) or backsliding (in the direction of John Dewey). If you're slipping, you'd better take steps. For the awful truth is that it's much easier to write like John Dewey than like Erle Stanley Gardner.

A SAMPLE TEST

To show in detail how to apply the test, I'll use the first part of the article "Wonders of Direct Distance Dialing" by Frank J. Taylor (*Reader's Digest,* October, 1955, p. 61):

William Freylinck, plant service supervisor of the ultramodern Englewood, N. J., telephone exchange, was showing me the amazing "brain center" installed there four years ago. It looked like a pile of diminutive metal books within great stacks of cases connected by a tangle of bright-colored wires. Pushing a dial phone across his desk, Freylinck asked, "Know any number out West you can call?"

"Sure, I know a good number near San Francisco," I replied.

"Dial it and see what happens," he said, pulling a stop watch from a desk drawer.

Starting with the figures 4-1-5, call prefix for the San Francisco area, I dialed my own home, a seven-digit number. Within 25 seconds, I could hear the phone ringing, 3000 miles away. My wife was incredulous when I told her I had dialed her as easily and quickly as if I were phoning from across the street.

But Freylinck was apologetic: the average time to complete a call from Englewood by DDD (Direct Distance Dialing) is 18 seconds. The direct circuits may have been busy, he explained, and the brain center had lost seven seconds setting up the connection, perhaps by way of Dallas or some other route possibly 5000 miles long.

DDD is no longer an engineer's dream. Ten thousand customers of the Englewood exchange have been using the revolutionary new service since November 1951. Up to a quarter million customers of a score of other suburban exchanges have been dialing long-distance calls for a shorter period. By the end of this year 56 communities will have DDD, and early in 1956 the first two large cities, South Bend, Ind., and Hartford, Conn., will switch over. After that, the remainder of the country will go DDD as rapidly as a modernization program costing billions of dollars can be completed; and ultimately all of us will be able to dial directly almost any of the 58 million phones in the United States and Canada.

The Bell Telephone System's DDD robots were first tested in Englewood and other suburban areas because these fast-growing sections already had the latest in equipment, and the change-over to DDD would not be unduly time-consuming or costly. "We were confident that the machines in these pilot exchanges would work," Freylinck says. "What we didn't know was how the customers would like the arrangement."

Bell's customers reacted so enthusiastically that the 21 associated operating companies in the American Telephone and Telegraph network (with 46 million phones), most of the independent U. S. companies (with eight million phones), plus the Canadian companies (four million phones), soon decided to go ahead with the distance-dialing revolution.

Engineer John Meszar of the Bell laboratories recalls that the system's technicians realized, as long as four decades ago, that they *had* to invent robots. At the rate that Americans and Canadians were talking, more telephone operators would eventually be required than could be found. Today, even with automatic dialing, the Bell System requires a quarter of a million operators to handle collect, person-to-person, information-please and other nonautomatic calls. Bell expects to employ more, rather than fewer, operators when DDD blankets the country.

To apply the test, do this:

First, count the number of words. There are altogether 519 words in this excerpt. (Here are some of the words that may raise questions in your mind about how to count them: "N. J." is counted as two words because there is white space between the two abbreviations. "4-1-5" makes one word: no white space inside. "DDD" is one word, but "Direct Distance Dialing" makes three. "South Bend" is two words. "Fast-growing" is one word; so is "change-over." "U. S." counts as two words, like "N. J.," because it is here printed with white space between "U." and "S." "Person-to-person" makes one word, and so does "information-please," since it is here hyphenated.)

The first 100 words end after the word "San" of "San Francisco area"; the second 100 words after the number "5000" in "5000 miles long"; the third 100 words after the words "can be completed"; the fourth 100 words after "the" and before "American Telephone and Telegraph"; and the fifth 100 words after "person-to-person."

Now count the points for your score like this (it is easiest to add them up as you go along):

Points Counted:	Cumulative Score:
Beginning of first paragraph	1
Capital W in *William*	2
Capital F in *Freylinck*	3
Capital E in *Englewood*	4
N.	5
J.	6
Quotation mark before *brain*	7
Quotation mark after *center*	8
Period after *ago*	9
Capital I in *It*	10
Period after *wires*	11
Capital P in *Pushing*	12
Capital F in *Freylinck*	13
Quotation mark before *Know*	14
Capital K in *Know*	15
Capital W in *West*	16
Question mark	17
Quotation mark after *call?*	18
End of paragraph	19
Beginning of second paragraph	20
Quotation mark	21
Capital S in *Sure*	22
I	23
Capital S in *San*	24
Capital F in *Francisco*	25
Quotation mark	26
I	27
Period after *replied*	28
End of second paragraph	29
Beginning of third paragraph	30
Quotation mark	31
Capital D in *Dial*	32
Quotation mark after *happens*	33
Period after *drawer*	34
End of third paragraph	35
Beginning of fourth paragraph	36
Capital S in *Starting*	37
4-1-5 (numbers)	38

Points Counted:	Cumulative Score:
Capital S in *San*	39

The score for the first 100 words is 39. Next, count the score for the second 100 words:

Capital F in *Francisco*	1
I	2
Period after *number*	3
Capital W in *Within*	4
25 (a number)	5
I	6
3000 (a number)	7
Period after *away*	8
Capital M in *My*	9
I (after *when*)	10
I (after *her*)	11
I (after *if*)	12
Period after *street*	13
End of fourth paragraph	14
Beginning of fifth paragraph	15
Capital B in *But*	16
Capital F in *Freylinck*	17
Colon after *apologetic*	18
Capital E in *Englewood*	19
DDD (three capitals)	20
Parenthesis before *Direct*	21
Capital D in *Direct*	22
Capital D in *Distance*	23
Capital D in *Dialing*	24
Parenthesis after *Dialing*	25
18 (a number)	26
Period after *seconds*	27
Capital T in *The*	28
Capital D in *Dallas*	29
5000 (a number)	30

The score for the second 100 words is 30. Next, count the score for the third 100 words:

Period after *long*	1
End of fifth paragraph	2
Beginning of sixth paragraph	3
Capitals in *DDD*	4

Points Counted:	Cumulative Score:
Apostrophe after *engineers*	5
Period after *dream*	6
Capital T in *Ten*	7
Capital E in *Englewood*	8
Capital N in *November*	9
1951 (a number)	10
Period after *1951*	11
Capital U in *Up*	12
Period after the word *period*	13
Capital B in *By*	14
56 (a number)	15
DDD (capitals)	16
1956 (a number)	17
Capital S in *South*	18
Capital B in *Bend*	19
Capital I in *Ind.*	20
Capital H in *Hartford*	21
Capital C in *Conn.*	22
Period after *over*	23
Capital A in *After*	24
DDD (capitals)	25
Semicolon after *completed*	26

The score for the third 100 words is 26. Next, count the score for the fourth 100 words:

58 (a number)	1
Capital U in *United*	2
Capital S in *States*	3
Capital C in *Canada*	4
Period after *Canada*	5
End of sixth paragraph	6
Beginning of seventh paragraph	7
Capital T in *The*	8
Capital B in *Bell*	9
Capital T in *Telephone*	10
Capital S in *System's*	11
Apostrophe in *System's*	12
DDD (capitals)	13
Capital E in *Englewood*	14
DDD (capitals)	15
Period after *costly*	16
Quotation mark before *We*	17
Capital W in *We*	18

Points Counted:	Cumulative Score:
Quotation mark after *work*	19
Capital F in *Freylinck*	20
Period after *says*	21
Quotation mark before *What*	22
Capital W in *What*	23
Apostrophe in *didn't*	24
Period after *arrangement*	25
Quotation mark	26
End of seventh paragraph	27
Beginning of eighth paragraph	28
Capital B in *Bell's*	29
Apostrophe in *Bell's*	30
21 (a number)	31

The score for the fourth 100 words is 31. Next test the fifth 100 words:

Capital A in *American*	1
Capital T in *Telephone*	2
Capital T in *Telegraph*	3
Parenthesis before *with*	4
46 (a number)	5
Parenthesis after *phones*	6
U.	7
S.	8
Parenthesis before *with*	9
Parenthesis after *phones*	10
Capital C in *Canadian*	11
Parenthesis before *four*	12
Parenthesis after *phones*	13
Period after *revolution*	14
End of eighth paragraph	15
Beginning of ninth paragraph	16
Capital E in *Engineer*	17
Capital J in *John*	18
Capital M in *Meszar*	19
Capital B in *Bell*	20
Apostrophe in *system's*	21
Italicized word *had*	22
Period after *robots*	23
Capital A in *At*	24
Capital A in *Americans*	25
Capital C in *Canadians*	26
Period after *found*	27

Points Counted:	*Cumulative Score:*
Capital T in *Today*	28
Capital B in *Bell*	29
Capital S in *System*	30

The score for the fifth 100 words is 30. Now count the score of the remaining 19 words of the sample test:

Period after *calls*	1
Capital B in *Bell*	2
DDD (capitals)	3
Period after *country*	4
End of ninth paragraph	5

The score of the 19 remaining words is 5. Now figure the score of the whole sample of 519 words:

Score of first 100 words	39
Score of second 100 words	30
Score of third 100 words	26
Score of fourth 100 words	31
Score of fifth 100 words	30
Score of remaining 19 words	5
Total	161

161 divided by 519 times 100 makes 31. The score of the whole sample text is therefore 31—one point above the typical *Reader's Digest* range of "Fairly Popular" writing.

You can also work out the average score of the text on the basis of the five 100-word samples. This will give you exactly the same score of 31 (39 plus 30 plus 26 plus 31 plus 30 makes 156, divided by 5 makes 31). Note, however, that the first paragraph (the "lead" of the article) has a higher score than the rest and is therefore not representative.

Index